TEEN VIOLENCE

TEEN VIOLENCE

A GLOBAL VIEW

Edited by Allan M. Hoffman
and Randal W. Summers

A World View of Social Issues
Andrew L. Cherry, Series Adviser

Greenwood Press
Westport, Connecticut • London

Library of Congress Cataloging-in-Publication Data

Teen violence : a global view / edited by Allan M. Hoffman and Randal W. Summers.
　　　　p.　cm.—(A world view of social issues, ISSN 1526–9442)
　　　Includes bibliographical references and index.
　　　ISBN 0–313–30854–3 (alk. paper)
　　　　1. Juvenile delinquency—Cross-cultural studies.　2. Violence—Cross-cultural studies.
　　I. Hoffman, Allan M. (Allan Michael)　II. Summers, Randal W., 1946–　III. Series.
　　HV9069.T373　2001
　　　364.36—dc21　　　00–021046

British Library Cataloguing in Publication Data is available.

Library of Congress Catalog Card Number: 00–021046
ISBN: 0–313–30854–3
ISSN: 1526–9442

First published in 2001

Greenwood Press, 88 Post Road West, Westport, CT 06881
An imprint of Greenwood Publishing Group, Inc.
www.greenwood.com

Printed in the United States of America

The paper used in this book complies with the
Permanent Paper Standard issued by the National
Information Standards Organization (Z39.48–1984).

10　9　8　7　6　5　4　3　2　1

To our families with love:

Randal's family: Tully, Vivian, Quinn, Joan, Jamie, Kim, Dawn, Alycia, and Michael

Allan's family: Andrew and Emily

CONTENTS

SERIES FOREWORD

Why are child abuse in the family and homelessness social conditions to be endured or at least tolerated in some countries while in other countries they are viewed as social problems that must be reduced or eliminated? What social institutions and other factors affect these behaviors? What historical, political, and social forces influence a society's response to a social condition? In many cases, individuals around the world have the same or similar hopes and problems. However, in most cases we deal with the same social conditions in very dissimilar ways.

The volumes in the Greenwood series A World View of Social Issues examine different social issues and problems that are being faced by individuals and societies around the world. These volumes examine problems of poverty and homelessness, drugs and alcohol addiction, HIV/AIDS, teen pregnancy, crime, women's rights, and a myriad of other issues that affect all of us in one way or another.

Each volume is devoted to one social issue or problem. All volumes follow the same general format. Each volume has up to fifteen chapters that describe how people in different countries perceive and try to cope with a given problem or social issue. The countries chosen represent as many world regions as possible, making it possible to explore how each issue has been recognized and what actions have been taken to alleviate it in a variety of settings.

Each chapter begins with a profile of the country being highlighted and an overview of the impact of the social issue or problem there. Basic policies, legislation, and demographic information related to the social issue are covered. A brief history of the problem helps the reader better understand the political and social responses. Political initiatives and policies are also discussed, as well as social views, customs, and practices related to the problem or social issue. Discussions about how the countries plan to deal with these social problems are also included.

These volumes present a comprehensive and engaging approach for the study of international social conditions and problems. The goal is to provide a convenient framework for readers to examine specific social problems, how they are viewed, and what actions are being taken by different countries around the world.

For example, how is a problem like crime and crime control handled in third world countries? How is substance abuse controlled in industrialized countries? How are poverty and homelessness handled in the poorest countries? How does culture influence the definition and response to domestic violence in different countries? What part does economics play in shaping both the issue of and the response to women's rights? How does a national philosophy impact the definition and response to child abuse? These questions and more will be answered by the volumes in this series.

As we learn more about our counterparts in other countries, they become real to us, and our worldview cannot help but change. We will think of others as we think of those we know. They will be people who get up in the morning and go to work. We will see people who are struggling with relationships, attending religious services, being born, growing old, and dying.

This series will cover issues that will add to your knowledge about contemporary social society. These volumes will help you to better understand social conditions and social issues in a broader sense, giving you a view of what various problems mean to different people and how these perspectives impact a society's response. You will be able to see how specific social problems are managed by governments and individuals confronting the consequences of these social dilemmas. By studying one problem from various angles, you will be better able to grasp the totality of the situation, while at the same time speculating as to how solutions used in one country could be incorporated in another. Finally, this series will allow you to compare and contrast how these social issues impact individuals in different countries and how the effect is dissimilar or similar to your own experiences.

As series adviser, it is my hope that these volumes, which are unique in the history of publishing, will increase your understanding and appreciation of your counterparts around the world.

Andrew L. Cherry
Series Adviser

PREFACE

This book looks at teen violence in fourteen countries around the world. Our intent is to provide greater insight into the problem of teen violence in our own country. Since the world we live in is essentially a global village, perhaps we can learn from each other's mistakes and progress. When even one child becomes a victim or when even one child commits a violent crime, it is one too many.

Our challenge is to bring ourselves back to an era where the school library once again is characterized by thoughtful silence, broken only by the occasional cough, as opposed to the horrific maiming and killing that we witnessed in Littleton, Colorado. Perhaps through international collaboration, we can share insights and meaningful approaches to helping our youth become healthy citizens of tomorrow.

We have the greatest respect and admiration for the chapter authors who have made this their mission.

ACKNOWLEDGMENTS

We express our sincere gratitude to the chapter authors and especially to Emily Birch for her guidance in making the production of this book possible.

INTRODUCTION

It was Tuesday about midday. The eerie silence and the occasional sunbeam glancing down from above gave the appearance of a surreal painting. Suddenly this dreamy ambiance was interrupted by rapid gunfire, bombs everywhere, booby traps, chaos, fear, screaming, and then the chilling sounds of agony from the wounded. Fifteen lie dead, and many more were wounded and shocked by the massacre.

This is not an account of the battlefield in Kosovo or Desert Storm or the killing orgy in My Lai in Vietnam. It is April 20, 1999, at the site of the school library of Columbine High School in Littleton, Colorado. Twelve students and a teacher were murdered, and twenty-three were wounded. The two teenage attackers committed suicide following their deadly rampage.

ARE TEENS OUT OF CONTROL AND BECOMING MORE VIOLENT?

It would seem so if we look back to the recent past and find similar tragedies just since 1997: a fifteen-year-old opened fire and wounded six classmates in Conyers, Georgia; in Jonesboro, Arkansas, an eleven-year-old and a thirteen-year-old killed four students and a teacher; three students were killed in Paducah, Kentucky; and in Springfield, Oregon, a teen killed two classmates and wounded twenty others. These extreme cases give the impression that teen violence in our schools is running rampant. In fact, it is true that multiple murders by teens have increased in the past few years;

however, violent crime involving a single victim has actually decreased in the last five years in the United States.

This book provides a glimpse into teen violence in fourteen countries around the world, in vastly different geographic regions and with different cultures. They vary from modern industrialized societies, where media frenzy explores every sordid detail of crime and tragedy, to tiny islands where tourism abounds, but its children are the "lost youth." Each chapter presents a brief historical perspective on teen violence in that country and then provides information related to the incidence or extent of teen violence and the specific programs and approaches that have been taken to prevent and control it.

WHY ARE CHILDREN KILLING?

Is it the result of the influence of violent media (TV, movies, computer games, publications)? The lack of parental supervision? The availability of drugs and easy access to weapons? Is it because troubled individuals need help, but adults are slow to react to the warning signs? Is it lack of education, poverty, unemployment, or hopelessness and despair? Is it dysfunctional families, communities, or schools?

There are many contributing factors to teen violence. Each country varies in respect to its explanation of what contributes to its teen violence problems. For example, Jamaica and St. Lucia view the lack of education, abject poverty, drugs, and the helplessness of its youth as being significant contributing factors. On the other hand, Russia, Germany, and Slovenia identify major political changes as being the heart of its teen problems. Despite our knowledge of the contributing factors, the fact remains that schools and teens reflect the social, economic, moral, and ethical problems in the larger society. Historically, children have killed; tragically, they will continue to kill.

ARE WE UNIQUE IN REGARD TO TEEN VIOLENCE?

The underlying theme in this book begs the question, "Are we—that is, the United States—unique in regard to teen violence?" Chapter 14, which addresses teen violence in the United States, suggests that we live in a violent society. For example, every thirty seconds, someone is stabbed, clubbed, or shot. Every day fifteen Americans ages fifteen to twenty-four commit suicide and twenty-three are murdered. Every day 100,000 teens bring weapons to school. Homicide is the leading cause of death for Hispanic males and African Americans ages fifteen to twenty-four. These statistics indicate that the United States *is* the most violent industrialized country in the world.

Teen Violence Trends

Country	Increase	Same	Decrease
Australia	X		
Canada		X	
England	X		
Germany	X		
Israel	X		
Italy		X	
Jamaica	X		
Russia	X		
St. Lucia	X		
Slovenia	X		
South Africa	X		
Spain		X	
Thailand	X		
United States	1988–1994		1995–1999

WHAT ABOUT OTHER COUNTRIES?

Meaningful comparisons of crime information among countries are difficult, if not impossible. There are no uniform measures that are used worldwide to record the type of crime or its incidence. Interpol does collect data and publish the Interpol International Crime Statistics; nevertheless, it is difficult to obtain valid or current information from countries such as Russia that are experiencing major political changes. In addition, although the chapter authors visited the countries in question, reliable data sometimes were nonexistent or unavailable.

Despite these difficulties, a cursory view of the fourteen countries suggests that teen violence has increased in almost all of the countries studied. With respect to the homicide rate, it is ten times higher in the United States than it is in Canada and twenty-eight times that of Germany.

IS THERE ANY SIMILARITY IN THE NATURE OF TEEN VIOLENCE AROUND THE WORLD?

As we review teen crime in the various countries, a number of similarities appear:

- Most youth crimes are property offenses, not violent acts.
- There is a pervasive fear of youth crime (with the exception of Spain).
- The perpetrators are predominantly male.
- Drugs are associated with most violent offenses.
- There are strong links between gangs and violent acts.
- There is a strong association between weapons and violent acts.

- The targets of violent acts tend to be minorities, foreigners, or immigrants.
- School dropout and subsequent unemployment seems to be the norm.
- Bullying at an early school age appears to be associated with delinquency in later years.

One interesting finding relates to moral panic—the media-induced exaggerated perception of the extent and seriousness of youth violence. Countries such as the United States, Canada, Australia, England and Wales, Israel, and Russia all indicate the presence of media sensationalism when it comes to youth crime. This moral panic causes a ripple effect throughout society. When the media contribute to popular fear, they put pressure on politicians, who respond with "get tough laws" that typically have a punitive focus. Many countries report that this phenomenon has led to a lowering of the age at which children can be transferred to adult courts and tried as adults. This is not a progressive step in dealing with teen crime. On the other hand, moral panic often results in positive effects, such as increased funding for intervention programs and renewed awareness by parents and schools with respect to their significant roles in preventing juvenile crime.

DO THE CONTRIBUTING FACTORS TO TEEN VIOLENCE VARY BY COUNTRY?

There are a number of contributing factors involved in teen violence and crime. In the countries reviewed in this book, it appears that certain factors play a larger role than others. For example, the association of groups, gangs, and peers with teen crime appears to be fairly significant in the United States, Spain (urban tribes), and Russia. The authors of the Russian chapter report a racketeering epidemic; they indicate that 25 percent of the racketeering is done by youth gangs.

Deterioration of the family seems especially pronounced as a contributing factor in Jamaica and St. Lucia. The chapter authors contend that approximately 49 percent of families have absentee fathers. Interviews with teens in a boys' training school in St. Lucia found that 80 percent of them were abused by a parent. Still other contributing factors appear significant, such as the unemployment rate for those ages fifteen to twenty-four, which runs at 55 percent in St. Lucia and 34 percent in Jamaica. This is also a significant factor in South Africa, where the unemployment rate for those ages sixteen to twenty-five runs at 60 percent. The availability of education was significant in St. Lucia and Jamaica. Their schools are overcrowded, and with the exception of a select few students, the typical dropout or leaving-school age is eleven.

Victimization seems to be a frequently occurring contributing factor in most of the countries. This might range from children being bullied (77 percent of the boys and 68 percent of the girls age eleven in Russia reported being bullied) to the ultimate violent extreme: homicide. In the United States, children are more likely to be killed by an adult (75 percent of homicide victims are ages twelve to seventeen).

Most countries also reported that any increase in juvenile crime seems to be associated with the proliferation of drug trafficking and abuse. This was particularly evident in the Caribbean countries, the United States, and Russia (estimated to have 2 million drug addicts, most of whom are teens).

In respect to individual psychopathy as a contributing factor, Israel reports the highest suicide rate (13 per 100,000, ages fourteen to eighteen).

Australia and Canada have struggled with issues associated with their native populations. It would seem that just as minorities are overrepresented among those incarcerated in the United States, so too with the aborigines and native Indians of, respectively, Australia and Canada.

A final contributing factor worth mentioning is that of political system changes. Germany, Slovenia, South Africa, Russia, and even Jamaica all report a high price to pay for freedom and modernization: dramatic increases in teen crime. Prior to the fall of the Berlin Wall, East Germany strictly controlled firearms and drugs, and 50,000 parent volunteers were active in the schools. This seemed to keep teen crime at a minimum. After the wall came down, there was a dramatic increase in juvenile crime; 25 percent of all crime is now done by youth. Similarly, political liberation in Russia and Slovenia involved the abolishment of social structures that controlled youth deviance, resulting in rapid increases in youth crime. In South Africa, freedom is closely associated with violence. In the apartheid era from 1950 to 1994, there was considerable state-condoned violence. The first democratic election took place in 1994, but high unemployment and violence persist. The situation in Jamaica is not so much political change as modernization. The colonial legacy emphasized family, tradition, the church, and school; teen violence was rare. With the introduction of modernization, the destruction of the family began with the migration to the cities and both parents working. The religion and traditions that once provided social controls eventually became replaced by hours of television viewing and ultimately a shift to a penal system to control the increase in teen crime.

1

AUSTRALIA

Christine Alder and Nichole Hunter

PERCEPTIONS OF TEEN VIOLENCE

From anxiety over "larrikins" to more recent fear of youth "gangs," Australia has a history of concern about youth behavior. In the late nineteenth century, Australian media reports of gang warfare and violence created the larrikin as a folk devil, a violent threat to the community. Larrikins (and larrikinesses) were working-class youth whose personal presentation was considered loud. They "loitered" on street corners, "taking possession" of "waiting sheds" and making suggestive remarks to passers-by (Finch, 1993). Finch concludes that larrikins were "working-class youth [who] experienced the streets of their cities and towns as multifunctional—that is, as places for socializing as well as for travelling from one place to another." This clashed with middle-class notions about the appropriate use of streets.

Despite newspaper accounts of violence and mayhem, documented accounts of the larrikins' behavior rarely included anything more serious than throwing stones onto roofs and at windows, and claims that their public behavior "outraged decency in all our parks" (Finch, 1993, 78). Nevertheless, Finch notes, legislators debated the suitability of whipping as a fitting punishment, and a constable told the Victorian Commission on Police that a "thief is not so bad as the man who interferes with a respectable lady or gentlemen in the street" (p. 78).

There are many parallels between this situation and concerns about teenage violence in Australia today. The congregation of young people in public spaces, in particular, shopping malls, causes public concern. These concerns, and a general fear of youth crime and violence, are fanned by "negative, inaccurate, exaggerated and sensational characterization of young people's street behavior and involvement in criminal activities" (Buttrum, 1998, 63). Official statistics, however, indicate that such a high level of fear is not warranted. Youth crime in Australia consists primarily of property offenses, and there has been no significant increase in offending in recent years. Nevertheless, in the 1990s, public concern about youth violence generated government inquiries and legislative reforms across Australia.

For many Australians, youths are a source of fear. Media depictions of young people as alienated, unemployed, and drug users contribute to their being perceived as "unpredictable strangers." Certain youths, such as "homies" and "gangs," are particularly likely to arouse feelings of trepidation, and a recent study revealed that public spaces and public transport are among locations perceived to be most risky (NCAVAC, 1998).

CURRENT TRENDS IN TEEN VIOLENCE

Public fear of youth is shaped to some extent by media representations that portray youth as a threat to law and order (Bessant and Hill, 1997). "Words such as 'gang,' 'hooligan' and 'vandal' are often used in articles about youth and have connotations of disorder and destructiveness" (Youth Justice Coalition, 1990, 46). Within this public discourse, "crime" and "violence" become synonymous, and the behavior in public spaces of homeless, unemployed, aboriginal, and Asian young people is understood as particularly problematic.

Public fear of crime and violence, however, is not necessarily related to the actual incidence of criminal behavior (Brown and Polk, 1996). This is particularly the case in relation to fear of youth violence in Australia. For example, in response to growing concerns about youth violence in 1993, the New South Wales (NSW) government established an inquiry into youth violence, which concluded that there was no youth violence "crime wave" (Standing Committee on Social Issues, 1995, 64). Examining trends in officially recorded youth crime in six Australian jurisdictions, Wundersitz (1993) concluded, "There is no evidence from any of the jurisdictions of a massive blow-out in official intervention rates, which must cast some doubts on media claims that juvenile crime is 'out of control' " (p. 58). Furthermore, most juvenile offending in Australia consists of property offenses. "Serious crimes involving violence and drugs are not commonly committed by juveniles" (Buttrum, 1998, 64; see also Juvenile Justice Advisory Committee, 1997; Youth Justice Coalition, 1990).

CONTRIBUTING FACTORS

A New South Wales inquiry (Standing Committee on Social Issues, 1995) identified certain groups of young people as particularly likely to face problems in their contact with the justice system: the homeless, the unemployed, and aboriginal young people who are visible in public places where they often gather due to the lack of alternative recreational and leisure activities. Their public visibility and "difference" can contribute to their being perceived as a threat by other community members, and they are easily targeted as "troublemakers" by police, security officers, and other authority figures (Standing Committee on Social Issues, 1995). The relatively high level of aboriginal and homeless youth stopped by the police has been highlighted in a number of studies (Alder, O'Connor, Warner and White, 1992; Youth Justice Coalition, 1994).

The Youth Justice Coalition report (1994) found that young people from a non–English speaking background were also particularly vulnerable to being approached, searched, and questioned by the police. Language barriers and cultural differences were acknowledged as increasing the likelihood of misinterpretation and conflict. Asian youth in particular are the subjects of racist stereotypes that equate them with illicit drug markets or organized criminal behavior.

Certain young people, particularly those of Asian backgrounds and those wearing "home boy" or "grunge" clothing, have been construed as engaging in "gang" behavior (Youth Justice Coalition, 1994). The NSW Youth Violence Inquiry (Standing Committee on Social Issues, 1995) concluded that the term *gang* should be used cautiously. They noted that although gangs involving youths do exist, the media often exaggerate their prevalence, and by speaking loosely of youths involved in "gangs," they engender fear within the community.

Aboriginal young people in particular are often represented and understood as constituting a threat to the community. The racism of Australia's colonial history continues in aboriginal young people's experience of the juvenile justice systems. Despite the recommendations of the Royal Commission into Aboriginal Deaths in Custody (RCIADIC), indigenous youths continue to be overrepresented in juvenile justice systems across Australia. For example, in South Australia in 1995–1996, aboriginal young people constituted 14.3 percent of police apprehensions, although they were only 1.7 percent of the youth (ages ten to seventeen) population (Juvenile Justice Advisory Committee 1977, 3). The overrepresentation was even higher for aboriginal girls (Wundersitz, 1996, 12).

The extent of overrepresentation of indigenous young people increases as they progress through the system. Aboriginal juveniles are 24.2 times more likely to be imprisoned than nonaboriginal juveniles in Australia (Harding, Broadhurst, Ferrante, and Loh, 1995, 81). In Western Australia the figures are even higher, with aboriginal young people almost 48.3 times more likely to be placed in detention than their nonaboriginal counterparts (Harding et al., 1995, 81; see also Ferrante, Loh, and Maller, 1998, and Beresford and Omaji, 1996).

Although aboriginal young people have long been depicted as criminal and a threat to the community, concerns about violent teenage girls are more episodic. Reminiscent of the late 1970s, the late 1990s witnessed Australian media interest in the "new" violent teenage girl. There is some indication of an increase in the number of girls in the juvenile justice system for violent offending, but a more detailed analysis in Queensland revealed that the offenses were of a "less serious" nature, frequently involving fights between girls in public spaces such as shopping centers (Beikoff, 1996). In a third of cases, the police were named as victim, a finding that perhaps indicates that common public order offenses for juveniles, obscene language, resisting arrest and assaulting police are replacing the "care and protection applications," or status offenses, of the past. Aggression is most often viewed as unacceptable when displayed by girls. Onlookers, including juvenile justice personnel and welfare officers, may feel more outraged, threatened, uncomfortable, and uncertain about how to handle such scenarios involving girls than when boys engage in similar levels of violence. Consequently their responses may be more punitive in relation to girls' violence.

RESPONSES TO THE PROBLEM

Talk of youth crime and violence has underpinned law-and-order campaigns in various recent state elections. (The Australian criminal justice system is divided into a number of jurisdictions based on state and territory borders, and the definition of *youth* varies by jurisdiction.) Consequently, a range of "get-tough" measures have been implemented. Although such responses are intended to be fundamentally punitive, other juvenile justice reforms in Australia have been directed more toward keeping young people out of the juvenile justice system. Nevertheless, the "get-tough" measures are the ones that have dominated media and public discussion of juvenile justice reform. These range from the introduction of individual programs, frequently drawing on models derived from the United States, to legislative reform.

Some of these reforms have been introduced in response to the community's fears of crime, which are expressed through concerns about young people congregating in public spaces. For example, the NSW Children's (Parental Responsibility) Act of 1994 gave police the power to remove young people under fifteen years of age from public spaces if they considered them likely to commit a crime or to be exposed to some risk. In Tasmania, draft juvenile justice legislation, the Youth Justice Bill 1997, will allow courts to sentence children with an "exclusion order," which will prohibit them from being in certain places for an allotted time. "In other words, a young person may be banned from anywhere in Tasmania for any length of time" (Mackie, 1998, 7). The bill applies to youths ages ten to seventeen and has been supported by the Tasmanian Retail Shop Trader's Association, which argued that young people loitering in public caused a nuisance and threatened the tourist industry.

Such strategies ignore the circumstances of young people who often lack alternative places to meet and have limited budgets and transport options. The fact that there is no evidence indicating that such isolated measures will reduce youth crime and violence is of no consequence for such initiatives, which are fundamentally founded in political objectives of appearing to address the community's fear of crime.

There has also been an increasing trend to hold parents accountable for the misdeeds of their children. Some states have enacted legislation that requires parents of juvenile offenders to indicate whether a lack of adequate care and supervision contributed to the young person's crimes. In other states, adults can be asked to pay restitution for their children's crimes (Hill, 1996). Such schemes have attracted considerable criticism as simplistic and ineffective responses that serve to punish parents for the behavior of their offspring (Hill, 1996). They also put increasing pressure on families already under stress, a factor that is itself sometimes related to the young person's offending.

The most extensive legislative reforms in the "get-tough" mode have been introduced in Western Australia. In the early 1990s a number of people died in high-speed police car chases involving juveniles who were driving stolen vehicles (Harding, 1993, 1). The ensuing public outcry fueled by media coverage of these incidents was coupled with the already existing incorrect assumptions that not only were levels of juvenile crime increasing, but that the juvenile justice system was too soft on offenders. Further, it is not irrelevant to the level and nature of the response to these incidents that they most often involved aboriginal young people. As one commentator noted, "The juvenile justice debate in Western Australia over the last two and a half years has been characterized by intensely dramatic and emotive reporting, where criminality has become synonymous with Aboriginality" (Stockwell, 1993, 279).

In response, the Western Australian government passed the Crime (Serious and Repeat Offenders) Sentencing Act, 1992, which introduced mandatory custodial sentences for repeat violent offenders. This act was initially aimed at juveniles and was later expanded to include adults. The intent was to incapacitate and deter "hard-core" offenders and, more important, to signal to the community that the government was taking a tough stance on juvenile crime (Harding, 1993). This Act (accompanied by the Criminal Law Amendment Act, 1992) targeted two specific groups of offenders: (1) serious and repeat offenders and (2) offenders who committed a range of violent offenses associated with driving a stolen vehicle (Wilkie, 1992). A number of offenses were defined as violent, including murder, assault, robbery, and offenses relating to dangerous driving of a stolen motor vehicle. Repeat offenders—those convicted of a number of the prescribed offenses— were subject to a minimum eighteen months in custody.

These reforms were the subject of much controversy. Beresford and Omaji (1996) suggest that this act merely removed youths from society rather than attempting to address the underlying causes of their offending. It has also been suggested that the legislation breached Australia's international obligations as set out in the United Nations Convention on the Rights of the Child, which indicates that detention should be applied only as a measure of last resort and for the shortest appropriate time. Contrary to the principle that juveniles require special consideration in sentencing, the legislation basically treated juveniles and adults in the same manner. The legislation was also criticized as working in opposition to the recommendations of the RCIADIC, which highlighted the importance of keeping aboriginal offenders out of detention.

The legislation was hastily drafted and this led to some difficulties in implementation (Harding, 1993). Research conducted to evaluate the success of the reforms found the legislation failed on a number of grounds. Harding (1993) concludes, "This Research Report demonstrates that the Western Australian laws of 1992, particularly the Crime (Serious and Repeat Offenders) Sentencing Act, 1992, failed according to every criminological criterion by which they can properly be evaluated" (p. 13). It was therefore not surprising that when the sunset clause expired, a new sentencing regime was introduced.

In 1997 the Western Australian government again turned to legislating punitive responses to youth crime when it introduced its "three-strikes" legislation (section 401 of the Western Australian Criminal Code). Under this legislation a person convicted of home burglary for a third time must be sentenced to a minimum of twelve months detention at either a youth training center or an adult prison.

Similarly, the Northern Territory has introduced mandatory sentencing as part of a law-and-order campaign. Since 1997, a young person sixteen to seventeen years of age can be incarcerated for a second property offense regardless of the seriousness of the offense (Schetzer, 1998). Now, youths who would otherwise have received a noncustodial sentence can be placed in detention. Again, this legislation is likely to affect aboriginal young people in particular.

At the same time as these punitive measures have been introduced, juvenile justice policy in most states has been concerned with diverting young offenders away from the juvenile justice system and implementing crime prevention initiatives. Recognition that juvenile offending is frequently transitory in nature and that the majority of youth will "grow out" of offending underpins a movement to minimize juvenile contact with the formal juvenile justice system. There has therefore been a bifurcation of responses to youth crime and violence in Australia. On the one hand, legislation, policies, and programs have been introduced with the intent of dealing with "serious offenders" more harshly. On the other hand, there are moves to divert less serious young offenders from the formal juvenile justice system (Cain, 1998).

Conferencing: An Alternative

With the intent of diverting young people from the more formal juvenile justice system, the introduction of family group conferencing has been the most discussed and widely implemented reform in recent years in Australia. Drawing on earlier New Zealand reforms of this nature, most Australian juvenile justice systems now use some form of this model at some point in their system. In the general climate of concerns about youth crime and violence, the call for juvenile justice reform and conferencing has been a significant, although still contentious, part of the rethinking of juvenile justice in Australia.

Family group conferences were introduced into the New Zealand juvenile justice system in 1989 (see the Children and Young Persons and Their Families Act, 1989, and Morris, Maxwell, and Robertson, 1993). The fundamental idea of the conferences, based on Maori tribal practices, is to bring the offender, the victim, the families, and the community together so that through a process of mediation, the conflict can be resolved and appropriate measures to reconcile all parties can be negotiated.

In Australia the idea of family group conferencing was first piloted in 1991 by the police in the town of Wagga Wagga in New South Wales (Moore and O'Connell, 1994). This model was influential in the early development of conferencing throughout Australia. Unlike the New Zealand approach, this form of conferencing is primarily a police process: police decide which cases should be conferenced and are responsible for their organization and administration, and police officers are the conference facilitators. The level of police involvement in and responsibility for conferencing has been a highly contentious issue (Sandor, 1994), and later implementations of conferencing have somewhat moved away from this model. For example, in South Australia (under the Young Offenders Act, 1993), conferences are conducted by youth justice coordinators (YJCs) and are the responsibility of the Courts Administration Authority. The conferences involve the youth, any guardians or other family members, the victim, the victim's guardian if the victim is under seventeen, a support person for the victim, police, and any other appropriate individuals, such as a social worker or a legal practitioner (Wundersitz, 1996). In Western Australia, juvenile justice teams (JJTs) consist of a youth justice coordinator, a police officer, a Ministry of Education officer, and an aboriginal community worker (Young Offenders Act, 1994). The teams deal with cases deemed too serious for a police caution but not serious enough to require a court appearance and generally attempt to resolve matters by conducting a family meeting. Meetings can be attended by the team members, the young offender, members of the young offender's family, the victim, and the victim's supporters (Hakiaha, 1994).

Since 1991 some form of conferencing has been introduced in every Australian state and territory. However, in each jurisdiction, there are significant differences in the level of police participation, the decision-making point in the juvenile justice system at which conferences are used, the restrictions on the youths able to become involved, the scale of implementation, and other objectives and processes (Bargen, 1996). Nevertheless, a number of common factors have contributed to its implementation: concerns that young people were not being held adequately accountable for their offending; concerns that the traditional juvenile justice system has been "too soft" on juvenile offenders; concerns about threats to the community of increases in youth crime and violence (even though this is an incorrect observation); identification of the need to revise quite dated juvenile justice legislation; pressures to do more for the victims of crime; and fiscal constraints.

Most legislation introducing some form of conferencing into the juvenile justice process has the intent of diverting young offenders from the traditional juvenile justice system, facilitating the greater involvement of victims in the decision-making process, and enabling community involvement in determining appropriate outcomes for young offenders. Such principles may be considered indicative of a restorative justice process. However, at the same time, these changes are also part of a movement to hold young people more accountable for their behavior and are fundamentally intended to ensure that a punishment is enacted as a deterrent to further offending. For example, some of the original objectives for the introduction of conferences by police in Wagga Wagga were "to ensure that the young offender understands the seriousness of his/her offending behavior" and "to provide the juvenile offender with an opportunity to accept responsibility for his/her offending behavior" (Moore and O'Connell, 1994, 55).

Aside from contention about the level and nature of police involvement in conferencing, another set of concerns relates to problems in ensuring the equity and fairness of the process and the outcome decisions. Such criticisms include concerns that the rights of the offender may be sacrificed, due process considerations may be neglected, the issue of guilt may not be adequately considered, the outcomes may be inconsistent, and the process may lack appropriate appeal mechanisms (Warner, 1994). These issues are of particular concern when there is a risk that conferencing may result in more punitive responses to juvenile offending (Bargen, 1996). O'Connor (1998) suggests the shift toward restorative justice at a time of concern to get tough on offenders may not really be a different response but merely a "refinement of punishment" (p. 6).

Cunneen (1997) argues that conferences, introduced, as they often have been in Australia, in the context of punitive law and order responses to youth crime and violence, are likely to result in harsher treatment of aboriginal youths. Conferences are being implemented without consultation or negotiation with the aboriginal community (Cunneen, 1997). While it was anticipated in South Australia that the introduction of family conferencing might be more sensitive to the situation of indigenous young people, thus far aboriginal young people are not being referred to them (Wundersitz, 1998). They are therefore continuing to be dealt with by the more formal procedures of the juvenile justice system, which have the more punitive outcome options. Wundersitz (1998) concludes in relation to South Australia:

Despite the optimism with which the new system was introduced and despite trends which are now emerging for other youths, it is clear that Aboriginal young people continue to be over-represented in their contact with the criminal justice system. They are more likely to be directed straight to court rather than being given the option of diversion to either cautioning or conferencing, are more likely to be sentenced to detention and are more likely to be placed in custody. (p. 42)

Conferencing has been the subject of much debate. Although evaluations are in process, we do not have the results of any rigorous evaluations in Australia upon which to rest final conclusions.

CONCLUSION

Recommendations for the implementation of more punitive measures are often a response to calls to "get tough" on crime. Such responses are fueled by misconceptions about increasing levels of youth crime and violence perpetuated by the media. In fact, research indicates that the majority of young offenders do not reoffend (Cain, 1998). Most young people appearing in juvenile courts are not violent offenders, and generally those appearing for property offenses do not escalate into violence. Contrary to popular beliefs, those who receive the more severe sentences for their first offense (custody, supervised probation or community service order) are *more* likely to reoffend than a first offender who is given a lesser penalty (Cain, 1998). Punitive responses to first and minor offenses do not necessarily reduce further crime and violence.

Calls to get tough on offenders tend to generate punitive and coercive strategies that have a high public profile and can be implemented quickly. Such responses are popular despite the evidence that they are ineffectual at best, and often counterproductive in terms of reducing crime. At a national conference in 1997 (Alder, 1998), there was consensus across the papers delivered that Australia is going dangerously astray in both its overall youth policy and the coercive trends in current juvenile justice reform. The general situation is one in which we have abandoned our youth (Polk, 1997).

The punitive reforms do little to address the underlying social and personal problems young offenders experience. In fact, they exacerbate the exclusion of youth from society. Also, in focusing on crimes committed by youths, the fact that young people are very likely to be victims of violence (National Committee on Violence, 1990) can be overlooked.

The influence of unemployment, lack of income, school exclusion, and family disruption on young people cannot be ignored, and has sparked calls for recognition that "it is only by continually seeking to reconnect young people to major developmental socializing institutions that we provide them with pathways of participation in society and strengthen social bonds" (O'Connor, 1998, 10). O'Connor (1998) points out that accompanying a return to punitive frameworks for juvenile justice has been the collapse of the youth labor market, disrupting the transition from school to work for increasing numbers of young people. The response to the situation of young people—out of work, out of school, and out of income—has been to introduce policies that further exclude them from public places and communities.

Talk of restorative justice and the implementation of conferencing, with its inclusionary rhetoric, held the promise for a way out of the punitive and coercive darkness. However, as O'Connor (1998, 5–6) points out, its translation into practice has been distorted by the "strength of the punitive and exclusionary discourses" that have frequently transformed reconciliatory objectives into "making the offender pay" and "letting the victim get his pound of flesh."

The tendency to impose family group conferences on indigenous communities without consultation and the likelihood of harsher outcomes for indigenous children are also issues of concern (National Inquiry into the Separation of Aboriginal and Torres Strait Islander Children and their Families, 1997). Cunneen (1998) argues that the high level of criminalization and incarceration of indigenous young people "effectively amounts to a new practice of forced separation of Aboriginal and Torres Strait Islander children and young people and their families" (p. 43). Such approaches fail to address the underlying issues that contribute to offending behavior.

Across Australia there is a growing awareness that increasing levels of punishment and exclusion from public space are not solutions to juvenile crime. Policies need to connect and involve young people in their communities. Further, it is important to value young people and help them to recognize and develop their potential, while acknowledging and responding to their economic and social marginalization. This is the biggest challenge in juvenile justice in Australia today.

REFERENCES

Alder, Christine. (Ed.). (1998). *Juvenile crime and juvenile justice*. Griffith, ACT: Australian Institute of Criminology.

Alder, Christine, O'Connor, Ian, Warner, Kate, and White, Rob. (Eds.). (1992). *Perceptions of the treatment of juveniles in the legal system*. Hobart, TAS: National Clearinghouse for Youth Studies.

Bargen, Jenny. (1996). Kids, cops, courts, conferencing and children's rights: A note on perspectives. *Australian Journal of Human Rights, 2* (2), 209–228.

Beikoff, Leanne. (1996). Queensland's juvenile justice system: Equity, access and justice for young women? In Christine Alder and Margaret Baines (Eds.), *And when she was bad? Working with young women in juvenile justice and related areas* (pp. 15–25). Hobart TAS: National Clearinghouse for Youth Studies, 1996.

Beresford, Quentin, and Omaji, Paul. (1996). *Rites of passage: Aboriginal youth crime and justice*. South Fremantle, WA: Fremantle Arts Centre Press.

Bessant, Judith, and Hill, Richard. (Eds.). (1997). *Youth crime and the media: Media representations of and reaction to young people in relation to law and order*. Hobart, TAS: National Clearinghouse for Youth Studies.

Brown, Mark, and Polk, Kenneth. (1996). Taking fear of crime seriously: The Tasmanian approach to community crime prevention. *Crime and Delinquency, 42* (3), 398–420.

Buttrum, Ken. (1998). Juvenile justice: What works and what doesn't! In Christine Alder (Ed.), *Juvenile crime and juvenile justice* (pp. 63–68). Griffith, ACT: Australian Institute of Criminology.

Cain, Michael. (1998). An analysis of juvenile recidivism. In Christine Alder (Ed.), *Juvenile crime and juvenile justice* (pp. 12–15). Griffith, ACT: Australian Institute of Criminology.

Cunneen, Chris. (1997). Community conferencing and the fiction of indigenous control. *Australian and New Zealand Journal of Criminology, 30*, 292–311.

Cunneen, Chris. (1998). The new stolen generations. In Christine Alder (Ed.), *Juvenile crime and juvenile justice* (pp. 43–53). Griffith, ACT: Australian Institute of Criminology.

Ferrante, Anna M., Loh, Nina N. S., and Maller, Max. (1998). *Crime and justice statistics for Western Australia: 1996*. Nedlands, WA: Crime Research Centre, University of Western Australia.

Finch, Lynette. (1993). On the streets: Working class youth culture in the nineteenth century. In Rob White (Ed.), *Youth subcultures: Theory, history and the Australian experience* (pp. 75–79). Hobart, TAS: National Clearinghouse for Youth Studies.

Hakiaha, Matt. (1994). Youth justice teams and family meetings in Western Australia: A trans-Tasman analysis. In Christine Alder and Joy Wundersitz (Eds.), *Family conferencing and juvenile justice: The way forward or misplaced optimism?* (pp. 103–119). Canberra, ACT: Australian Institute of Criminology.

Harding, Richard W. (Ed.). (1993). *Repeat juvenile offenders: The failure of selective incapacitation in Western Australia*. Nedlands, WA: Crime Research Centre, University of Western Australia.

Harding, Richard W., Broadhurst, Roderic S., Ferrante, Anna, and Loh, Nina. (1995). *Aboriginal contact with the criminal justice system and the impact of the Royal Commission into Aboriginal Deaths in Custody*. Perth: Hawkins Press.

Hill, Richard. (1996). Crime by default: Legislating for parental restriction in Queensland. *Alternative Law Journal, 21* (6), 280–283.

Juvenile Justice Advisory Committee. (1997). *Annual report for the year ended 30th June 1996*. Adelaide, SA: Juvenile Justice Advisory Committee.

Mackie, Craig. (1998, Jan.). Exclusion orders: Banning young people from public space in Tasmania. *Rights Now*, p. 7.

Moore, David, and O'Connell, Terry. (1994). Family conferencing in Wagga Wagga: A communitarian model of justice. In Christine Alder and Joy Wundersitz (Eds.), *Family conferencing and juvenile justice: The way forward or misplaced optimism?* (pp. 48–86). Canberra, ACT: Australian Institute of Criminology.

Morris, Allison, Maxwell, Gabrielle M., and Robertson, Jeremy P. (1993). Giving victims a voice: A New Zealand experiment. *Howard Journal, 32* (4), 304–321.

National Campaign Against Violence and Crime (NCAVAC). (1998). *Fear of crime.* Barton, ACT: NCAVAC, Attorney-General's Department, Commonwealth of Australia.

National Committee on Violence. (1990). *Violence: Directions for Australia.* Canberra, ACT: Australian Institute of Criminology.

National Inquiry into the Separation of Aboriginal and Torres Strait Islander Children and Their Families (NISATSIC). (1997). *Bringing them home.* Sydney, NSW: Human Rights and Equal Opportunity Commission.

O'Connor, Ian. (1998). Models of juvenile justice. In Christine Alder (Ed.), *Juvenile crime and juvenile justice* (pp. 4–11). Griffith, ACT: Australian Institute of Criminology.

Polk, Kenneth. (1997). The coming crisis of abandoned youth: A look at the future of juvenile justice in Australia. In Allan Borowski and Ian O'Connor (Eds.), *Juvenile crime, justice and corrections* (pp. 489–501). Melbourne, VIC: Longman.

Sandor, Danny. (1994). The thickening blue wedge in juvenile justice. In Christine Alder and Joy Wundersitz (Eds.), *Family conferencing and juvenile justice: The way forward or misplaced optimism?* (pp. 153–166). Canberra, ACT: Australian Institute of Criminology.

Schetzer, Louis. (1998). A year of bad policy: Mandatory sentencing in the Northern Territory. *Alternative Law Journal, 23,* 117–120.

Standing Committee on Social Issues. (1995). *A report into youth violence in New South Wales.* Sydney, NSW: Standing Committee on Social Issues, Legislative Council, Parliament of New South Wales.

Stockwell, Charlotte. (1993). The role of the media in the juvenile justice debate in Western Australia. In Lynn Atkinson and Sally-Anne Gerull (Eds.), *National Conference on Juvenile Justice: Conference Proceedings* (pp. 279–290). Canberra: Australian Institute of Criminology.

Warner, Kate. (1994). The rights of the offender in family conferences. In Christine Alder and Joy Wundersitz (Eds.), *Family conferencing and juvenile justice: The way forward or misplaced optimism?* (pp. 141–152). Canberra, ACT: Australian Institute of Criminology.

Wilkie, Meredith. (1992). WA's draconian new juvenile offender sentencing laws. *Aboriginal Law Bulletin 55* (2), 15–17.

Wundersitz, Joy. (1993). Some trends in officially recorded youth offending: A state-by-state comparison. In Lynn Atkinson and Sally-Anne Gerull (Eds.), *National Conference on Juvenile Justice: Conference Proceedings* (pp. 52–66). Canberra, ACT: Australian Institute of Criminology.

Wundersitz, Joy. (1996). *The South Australian juvenile justice system: A review of its operation.* Adelaide, SA: Office of Crime Statistics, Attorney General's Department.

Wundersitz, Joy. (1998). Aboriginal youth and the South Australian juvenile justice system: Has anything changed? In Christine Alder (Ed.), *Juvenile crime and juvenile justice* (pp. 32–42). Griffith, ACT: Australian Institute of Criminology.

Youth Justice Coalition. (1990). *Kids in justice: A blueprint for the 90s.* Sydney, NSW: Youth Justice Coalition.

Youth Justice Coalition and Youth Action and Police Association. (1994). *Nobody listens: The experience of contact between young people and police.* Sydney, NSW: Youth Justice Coalition of NSW.

2

CANADA

*Raymond R. Corrado, Irwin M. Cohen, and
Candice Odgers*

PERCEPTIONS OF TEEN VIOLENCE

In Canada, as in most other countries, there is a growing assumption that
the behavior of youth is significantly worse than it has been in the past. In
addition, there is a fear that not only has the amount of youth crime increased, but that youth have become more violent than ever before. This
chapter examines these beliefs in an attempt to explore the quantity and
quality of youth crime in Canada.

In historical terms, contemporary youth behavior is not much different
from that of the past. The homicide rate for youths has not changed significantly in the past decade, and teens have always been disproportionately
represented in property crimes. While the Canadian media has focused national attention on youths engaged in violence against others based on ethnicity recently, violence by youth against immigrants or minority ethnic
groups has been recorded since 1875 in Canada (Tanner, 1996). And although the Stanley Cup riots in Montreal in 1993 and Vancouver in 1994
remain particularly fresh in the memories of most Canadians and serve to
increase concerns about youth participation in crime and violence, teen participation in violent mass riots is not a modern or recent phenomenon.

The notion of race and the influence of the media have traditionally contributed to a distorted view of the quality and quantity of teen crime in
Canada. Similar to the United States, Canada receives immigrants from virtually all countries. The actual individual ethnic group does not seem to be
as important as the concept of the "other" or the "immigrant" in creating

and supporting a moral panic about youth crime. In eastern Canada, the focus tends to be on young blacks, be they Jamaican or Haitian. Expressed in a variety of ways is the belief that these young black immigrants account for a disproportionate amount of violent and drug-related offenses. In western Canada, the focus of attention is on Asian youths. In addition, from coast to coast, there exists a discriminatory view of aboriginals as constituting a disproportionate amount of Canada's criminal element. As Tanner (1996) suggests, merely the sight of large numbers of immigrant or aboriginal youth congregating has the effect of increasing fears about juvenile crime.

It has been well established by researchers that the media play a prominent role in constructing society's understanding and evaluation of youth crime (Cohen, 1973; Perrone and Chesney-Lind, 1998; Schissel, 1997). By choosing to report and sensationalize only the most serious of offenses committed by teens, Canadians are left with the impression that teenagers are out of control and that anyone is likely to be victimized by a gang of youths at any time. Many researchers have concluded that there is a significant gap between the actual level of youth crime, specifically the level of violent youth crime, and the perceived level of crime held by most Canadians (Carrington, 1995; Doob and Sprott, 1998; Markwart and Corrado, 1995; Silverman, Teevan, and Sacco, 1996; Tanner, 1996).

Still, Doob and Sprott (1998) contend that even some of those who believe that the rate of violence committed by youth has not increased in Canadian society argue that the nature or quality of the violence has become more serious. In an analysis of youth court records in Canada from 1991 to 1996, Doob and Sprott found no changes in the crime rates of the most serious types of violent offenses. This conclusion is consistent with the earlier work of Frank (1992), who suggested that although the per capita rate of youth violence doubled from 1986 to 1992, it was uncertain whether this increase was a result of changes in official youth crime statistics, the public's increased willingness to report teen crime to the police, advances in police techniques, or reforms to youth justice laws.

CURRENT TRENDS IN TEEN VIOLENCE

Although it seems certain that regardless of whether crime rates increase or decrease for any given period of time, those in their teens and early twenties will be disproportionately represented among the criminal population. Canadian crime statistics support this assertion. In Canada, the majority of offenders are under the age of twenty-five. Younger people are more likely to engage in property crime, while violent crime is usually perpetrated by individuals in their twenties. For example, in 1991, 51 percent of all property offenders were either sixteen or seventeen years old (Tanner, 1996). In addition, offenders are overwhelmingly male (although the rate of female offenders is increasing). In 1990, 88 percent of all youths charged by the police were male; by 1997, this number had dropped to 75 percent.

In an analysis of youth court statistics in Canada for the 1992–1993 fiscal year, Leonard (1995) points out that eight of ten young offenders were male and that half of the courts' caseload involved offenders who were sixteen or seventeen years of age. In terms of the types of offenses committed, Leonard indicates that theft under $1,000 was the charge for 27 percent of those young offenders between the ages of twelve and thirteen, and that this rate decreases with age. Moreover, offenses such as breaking and entering, minor assault, and mischief also tended to decrease with age. Older youths, on the other hand, account for a higher proportion of charges involving failures to appear or comply, breaches of probation, theft over $1,000, drug offenses, and serious violent offenses, such as sexual assault and assault with a weapon (Leonard, 1995). In other words, when teens do engage in violence, the older they are, the more violent their offenses are. Still, it must be kept in mind that violence by teens is an infrequent event.

In Canada, the collection of data on crime and delinquency is the responsibility of the police and courts. Data on crime are collected using a system of uniform crime reports in a manner pioneered in the United States. Although this system of data collection exhibits the same problems as its American counterpart in terms of indicating the actual amount of crime, it does serve to illustrate the distribution of offenses dealt with by the Canadian criminal justice system. According to this process of counting crimes, only the most serious offense charged is recorded as the actual offense, and only this recorded offense is used to calculate crime rates.

The 1990 Canadian uniform crime report indicates that the number of criminal code violations committed by juveniles was 188,808 (Canadian Crime Statistics, 1990). Of those violations, 12 percent well classified as violent offenses. The overall majority of violations (62 percent) represented property crimes. Of those property crimes, 53 percent were for petty theft. Overall, petty theft represented 32.9 percent of all offenses committed by youth in 1990. Moreover, 61 percent of all petty theft violations were for shoplifting. As such, shoplifting accounted for 20 percent of all criminal code violations. In other words, one of every five crimes known to the police and committed by juveniles involved shoplifting, and only a small number were categorized as violent.

Of the violent crimes committed by teens in 1990, 88 percent took the form of common assault. In Canada, there are three levels of assault. The most frequent type is referred to as common assault, or assault level 1. Assault level 2 is assault with a weapon or assault causing bodily harm, and assault level 3 is defined as aggravated assault (Cunningham and Griffiths, 1997). In 1990, 63 percent of all juvenile assaults were classified as level 1. This accounted for 10.5 percent of all criminal code violations for youths. In terms of seriously violent juveniles, or those charged with assault level 2,

Table 2.1
Criminal Code Offenses, 1993–1997

	1993	1994	1995	1996	1997
Adults charged (all criminal code offenses)	456,241	422,509	408,791	409,894	383,833
Youths charged (all criminal code offenses)	126,887	119,625	120,663	119,410	111,736
Adults charged (violence crimes)	128,853	125,442	117,409	117,246	114,961
Youths charged (violence crimes)	21,477	21,629	22,441	22,521	22,252

assault level 3, sexual assault, robbery, attempted murder, or homicide, a relatively small percentage, 1.44 percent, fell into this category. Nevertheless, it is this group that receives the majority of the public's attention.

The Uniform Crime Statistics for 1991 tell a similar story. The vast majority of criminal charges against youth (70 percent) were for property offenses. Within this category, 42 percent of property offense charges were for theft under $1,000, and 27 percent were for breaking and entering. In a slight increase from 1990, 14 percent of all criminal code charges were for violent offenses.

According to the Canadian Department of Justice, 14 percent of all the charges laid against youth in 1992 were for violent offenses. Almost 50 percent of all violent offense charges against teens were for minor assaults, such as slaps or punches. Again, the vast majority of young offenders were charged with property offenses, with 57 percent of all property offenses being categorized as theft. In terms of the disproportionate view of the public about the extent of youth crime, the Department of Justice concluded in 1992 that the crime rate for youth in Canada was similar to the rates ten years previously. In addition, it was found that of all violent offenses committed in Canada, only 14 percent were committed by individuals ages twelve to seventeen. In 1993, trends in the types of offenses committed by youths remained similar: 17 percent of all charges against youths were for violent crimes, and 59 percent were for property crimes (Uniform Crime Reporting Survey, 1993).

Between 1993 and 1997, there was a decrease in the total number of youths charged with a criminal code offense. Except for 1995, when there was a marginal increase in the overall number of youths charged with criminal code offenses, the overall number of young offenders has decreased, with a significant reduction in 1997 (see Table 2.1). It should be kept in mind that the decrease in youths charged may represent not an actual drop in the participation of youth in criminal behavior but the impact of crime control measures or the philosophy of diversion and alternative measures embedded in Canada's Young Offenders Act (Leonard, 1995).

Of significant interest in the debate concerning the rate of violent crime among youths is that the overall level has not significantly changed over the five years illustrated by Table 2.1. In fact, the rate remained rather consistent. Of significant concern, however, is that youth violence has not diminished in accordance with the overall rate of juvenile crime, nor has it complemented the corresponding reduction in adult violent offenses. Therefore, while youth violence continues to account for a small portion of the total number of violent offenses committed in Canada, and the prevalence of violent acts by youths that are coming to the attention of the police also remains rather constant, juvenile violence is making up a larger percentage of the total number of violent offenses.

In terms of defining the quality of youth crime, 1995 will be used as an example. Cunningham and Griffiths (1997) point out that in 1995, the number of teens charged with homicide was sixty-five, or 13 percent of all the homicides in that year. In terms of the homicide rate, the youth rate was 2.7 per 100,000. In terms of violent crime, 19 percent of youths charged with an offense had at least one charge for violence. As in previous years, the majority of violent charges were for level 1 assault, or common assault. Once again, youth were disproportionately represented in the category of property crimes, where roughly 30 percent of all property offense suspects were under the age of eighteen. In addition, 40 percent of all suspects charged with breaking and entering were young offenders.

Still, even with these readily available statistics, the public's perception of youth violence does not seem to correspond with its reality. Approximately one of every four criminal code offenses is committed by a young offender, with the vast majority being property offenses, and fewer than one of every five violent offenses in Canada is committed by a youth. As such, the belief that one is likely to be attacked by a young offender, or the belief that if one is going to be a victim of some type of crime, it will be a young person who perpetrates it, is exaggerated.

With respect to general long-term trends in juvenile crime between 1970 and 1990, Schissel (1995) contends that fluctuations and increases in youth crime rates may have more to do with law reform than an actual increase in the level of criminal activity by teens. In 1984, the Canadian government abolished the Juvenile Delinquents Act and replaced it with the Young Offenders Act. This reform of the law was accompanied by a sharp increase in the number of youths charged with criminal offenses in all crime categories. Schissel (1995) suggests that this increase is due in part to the inclusion of seventeen- and eighteen-year-olds in the restructured youth justice system and the law's crime control initiatives. Schissel suggests that the quantity of youth crime has not increased, but that the augmented crime rate is a product of the fact that the number of individuals who fall under the umbrella of the youth justice system has dramatically increased. Nonetheless, as suggested by Tanner (1996), the implication of an analysis of official crime statistics is that while these statistics may support the popular perception of the quantity of crime, these statistics do not substantiate the contention and fear that a significant degree of youth crime is violent in nature.

There have been very few studies of the quality of violent crime, specifically homicide, in Canada. However, one such study was conducted by Meloff and Silverman (1992). In their longitudinal study of Canadian youth homicide between 1961 and 1983, 80 percent of teen homicides involved one offender and one victim. When the victim was a family member, 95 percent of the cases involved a single victim. Moreover, the rate of youth homicide for those thirteen years of age was 0.29 per 100,000 and 2.71 per 100,000 for those seventeen years of age. Although the most frequent means of committing a homicide in Canada is with the use of a handgun, only 35 percent of homicides between 1961 and 1983 involved a gun. Unlike in the United States, for example, most acts of teen violence in Canada (60 percent) do not involve any kind of weapon (Tanner, 1996).

In terms of the relationship between the offender and the victim in youth homicides, Meloff and Silverman found that 14 percent of the victims were a parent to the perpetrator, 19.5 percent involved other family members, 35 percent were acquaintances, and strangers accounted for approximately 31.5 percent. When homicides were committed in conjunction with another crime, 70 percent were theft related, and 21 percent involved sex. In returning to the notion of race and the belief that certain minority groups are responsible for a disproportionate amount of violent youth crime, Meloff and Silverman found that Caucasians commit 66 percent of youth homicides, natives represent 30 percent of homicide offenders, and 5 percent are classified as "other." Furthermore, Canadian juvenile homicide is overwhelmingly intraracial. In other words, when Caucasian teens commit homicide, 98 percent involve Caucasian victims.

In an analysis of youth homicide trends, Frank (1992) demonstrates that in 1989, only 9 percent of all homicides were committed by youth, and that 0.04 percent of all cases heard in youth court involved homicide. Moreover, Silverman (1990) argues that the homicide rate for young offenders has actually decreased over the past several decades. An analysis of Canadian crime statistics for 1994 indicates that the number of teens charged with murder, manslaughter, and attempted murder decreased from previous years. These statistics led Tanner (1996) to conclude that homicide is not, and never has been, a significant feature of youth crime and violence in Canada. Instead, the vast majority of youth crime consists of minor property offenses without the use of force. As such, the public's fear of youth violence may be escalating at a faster rate than the actual level of teen violence.

Corrado and Markwart (1994) nevertheless suggest that there have been substantial increases in the level of youth violence that cannot be accounted for by the traditional explanations of an increased willingness of victims of youth crime to come forward, changes in police discretion, improvements in police techniques, or law reform. Although they agree that the number of youths charged in level 1 assaults has risen dramatically over the years, Markwart and Corrado (1995) contend that between 1986 and 1992, there were significant increases in most other categories of youth violence as well, such as assault causing harm, robbery with firearms, and robbery with other weapons. They argue that these kinds of offenses routinely result in police charges and that increases in the overall rates of these crimes by youth represent a real increase in teen violence. They also posit that there is no systematic evidence to support the position that specialized youth squads in urban police forces to deal with teen violence have resulted in more frequent apprehension of violent young offenders.

Moreover, they assert that there is no evidence to support the claim that victims of violent crimes are more willing to report their victimization than in the past (Corrado and Markwart, 1994). As such, they suggest that with the exception of homicide, there was a significant increase in teen violence in Canada over the studied period but that the rate of incidence remained relatively low. Of those charged with offenses, 85 percent were charged with nonviolent crimes, and a substantial amount of youth violence involved minor assaults (Markwart and Corrado, 1995). Still, their interpretation of the statistics suggests to them that the quantity of youth violence had increased and that there was a significant escalation of seriousness and severity of the offense when violence was used.

CONTRIBUTING FACTORS

Setting

There is also a growing concern in Canada, sparked by media attention, regarding the location of youth violence. Increasingly, there is the pervasive feeling among Canadians that there has been a dramatic shift in the quantity and quality of violence in schools by teens. In an analysis of the location of violent youth crime between 1988 and 1991, Tanner (1996), using official Canadian statistics, demonstrates that more minor assaults and aggravated assaults occurred in dwellings as opposed to schools, public institutions, commercial places, and streets. In fact, for these kinds of offenses, schools ranked third (15 percent for minor assaults and 13 percent for aggravated assaults) behind dwellings (28 percent minor assaults and 26 percent aggravated assaults) and the streets (24 percent for minor assaults and 24 percent for aggravated assaults). Overwhelmingly, sexual assaults by youths occurred in dwellings as well (74 percent).

Youth seem more likely to be involved in violence on the streets and in dwellings than to encounter violence at school. Moreover, statistics that suggest a dramatic increase in the levels of school violence may not reflect actual violence levels but the willingness of schools to involve the authorities in matters that previously were dealt with informally and internally by the schools themselves. While this decision to use the police to deal with minor forms of violence in the schools may be a reaction to the real increases in the quality and quantity of school violence, it may simply be a reaction to the moral panic created by the media concerning the risks and dangers of teen violence.

Gender

Another significant issue in the study of youth violence in Canada is that of gender. Undeniably, violent offenses committed by juveniles are heavily gendered. Proportionally more male than female teens commit violent crimes, a relationship that has held true across time in Canadian society (Rowe, Vazsonyi, and Flannery, 1995) and is supported by official data sources (Tanner, 1996). However, in recent years, female young offenders have received an inordinate amount of attention due to a reported increase in violence. Not only are female offenders the focus of media attention (Schissel, 1997), but academics and policymakers are also paying closer attention to the changing tides of female violence (Alder, 1975; Artz, 1998; Chesney-Lind and Sheldon, 1998; Reitsma-Street, 1991).

One of the central issues relating to female violence in Canada is whether it is actually escalating. Although official police charging statistics are consistently indicating an increase, there is concern as to how accurately these measures capture the reality of offending. An additional consideration relates specifically to the nature of the violence. Recent media portrayals of "girl gangs," "swarmings," and "brawls" (Chisholm, 1997) have arguably led to the impression that female violence is not only out of control but becoming increasingly violent (Schissel, 1997). This type of media depiction of females in sensational cases has been linked to the analogy of fallen angels (Perrone and Chesney-Lind, 1998; Campbell, 1990) and, in turn, the idea that youth are running wild. Thus, in order to ensure the most accurate description of female youth violence, it is necessary to review a combination of official statistics and contemporary research, as well as undertake a critique of recent media responses.

Official statistics have consistently indicated either a steady level or an upward trend in violent teen offending for both sexes. Statistics Canada reported a 190 percent increase in charges of female violence between 1986 and 1993, as compared to a 115 percent rise among boys (Artz, 1990). It should be noted that due to the low base rate among females who commit violent crimes, raw figures must be viewed in combination with reported percentages in order to avoid distorting the increase. For example, in 1986 there were only 1,728 females charged with a violent crime, as compared to 5,096 in 1993. The total number of charges laid against males during that same time frame jumped from 7,547 to 16,375, representing an increase of 8,828 charges for males, as compared to the 3,368 new charges for females. Thus, although charges for females have increased at a higher rate in terms of percentages, the greatest absolute increase in terms of raw numbers falls significantly to the males.

Table 2.2
Youth Charges by Sex

	1993	1994	1995	1996	1997
Violent crimes					
Male	16,381	16,747	17,288	17,206	16,613
Female	5,096	4,882	5,153	5,315	5,639
Property crimes					
Male	59,232	54,656	52,956	51,930	46,234
Female	15,749	14,251	15,149	14,772	13,298
Other criminal code offenses					
Male	24,954	24,027	24,405	24,051	23,686
Female	5,475	5,062	5,712	6,136	6,266
Federal statutes					
Male	5,003	6,166	6,758	7,467	7,509
Female	1,093	1,304	1,388	1,665	1,877

Source: Statistics Canada, CANSIM.

The next time frame to consider, spanning 1993 through 1997, paints a somewhat different picture of the relationship between gender and youth violence (see Table 2.2). Although the total number of violent offenses has again risen for both males and females, the charges against female teens are greater in terms of both percentages and raw numbers. The rate for females jumps 11 percent as a result of a 543-charge increase, whereas male violence increases a mere 1 percent, with 232 new charges. Interestingly, between 1996 and 1997, male charges actually decreased by 3.5 percent (593), whereas female charges increased by 5.7 percent (324). Not surprisingly, these statistics have received a substantial amount of attention from criminal justice agents, the media, and scholars.

Despite the fact that the number of females charged with violence has been increasing at twice the rate as the number of males charged over the last decade (Statistics Canada, 1998), the world of violent crime continues to be a distinctly male one (Hatch and Faith, 1990). For example, in 1997, despite the rate of increase among females, males still accounted for 75 percent of all violent crime committed by youth (Statistics Canada, 1998). The overwhelming majority of males in this category reaffirms the importance of distinguishing between relative and absolute numbers when considering the gender gap in teen violence. When young women are charged with violent crime, it is most frequently for a minor assault, which implies a relative absence of violence. However, it is not the minor cases of assault involving females that fill the front pages of Canada's newspapers or make the breaking news story. Rather, it is the isolated incidents of extreme violence, such as the 1997 beating death of a fourteen-year-old Victoria girl by a group of her female peers and the 1995 slaying of a seventeen-year-old pimp by three teenage girls, that are recycled through the media. A portrait of the typical female youth involved in violence is rarely introduced to the public. Hence, it is necessary to take a closer look at not only the official rates of violence committed by females but also the related context, intensity, and damage caused by female teen violence.

Those studying teen violence in Canada hold conflicting views, and as would be expected, the situation is no different with regard to females. One general criticism of analyzing female violence solely on the basis of police charging, which involves a substantial degree of discretion, is that it does not provide an accurate picture of reality. For example, Mawby (1980) argues that girls are perceived more positively than boys are by police officers and thus are more likely to be "let off" for any offense. Other researchers contend that the reverse is true, suggesting that females are treated more harshly by the criminal justice system (Bergsmann, 1989; Chesney-Lind and Sheldon, 1998; Reitsma-Street, 1993). So although the potential for bias within the system is recognized, there is a tremendous degree of controversy surrounding which direction it takes.

Measures such as sentencing data and self-report studies also assist in gauging female teen violence. Despite the fact that these measures may aid in clarifying the picture, they have not been immune from criticism. Judicial and crown discretion are alleged to distort measures at the disposition stage, and the bias inherent in self-report data arguably creates a problem in tapping into the dark figure of female violence. However, when these two approaches are integrated with alternative measures, such as charging statistics, contemporary research, and a critique of media depictions, they serve to sharpen the edges of our profile of female violence.

The majority of the research dealing with female offending cites it as a grossly underdeveloped area (Artz, 1998; Chesney-Lind and Sheldon, 1998). Historically, research on females has amounted to nothing more than a footnote, subset, or minor variation of the delinquency among males. In short, female criminality, and in turn violence, appears to have been seen as almost exclusively a male problem in Canada (Artz, 1998). In a sense, contemporary researchers and practitioners are observing a relatively new phenomenon and are equipped with a fairly limited knowledge base. Consequently, the current mechanisms in place to deal with female violent offenders may be ineffective or inappropriate. The quick response to rising statistics and concern expressed by criminal justice personnel regarding the "girl problem" may be attributed in part to the tendency in the past to associate violence only with males (Bergsmann, 1989). In other words, the acts of female violence that we are witnessing today appear to carry with them a certain shock value that observers are unprepared for.

With regard to the proportion of violent crime committed by girls, the distribution of offending among property offenses, violent crimes, and other criminal code infractions is similar to that of their male counterparts (Tanner, 1996). The differences in overall charges appear to be more in relation

Figure 2.1
Offense Type by Gender, 1997

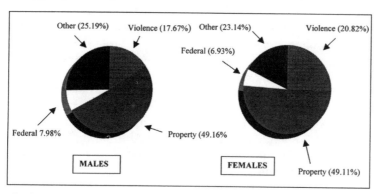

Source: Statistics Canada, Canadian Centre for Justice Statistics.

to the quantity, as opposed to the quality, of offending (see Figure 2.1). For example, in 1997, the percentages of charges for females and males who committed violent crimes were 20.8 percent and 17.7 percent, respectively, for a difference of only 3 percent, whereas property crime was virtually identical for both groups, comprising 49 percent of the total offenses. Despite the rising rates of violence among both groups, the majority of charges laid against youth are for property offenses and other more minor criminal code infractions (Statistics Canada, 1998).

The context of violence is also a relevant consideration in assessing female violence in Canada. Studies (Artz, 1998; Bibby and Posterski, 1992) have examined the increase in violence among school girls. This literature is crucial in that it taps into an area that may previously have been dealt with informally, such as school yard fights. In addition, it targets a population largely ignored by official crime statistics: females who engage in violence but are not detected by the youth justice system. Artz (1998), who recently conducted a study on violent school girls in Victoria, British Columbia, states that violence committed in a school setting is on the rise at an unprecedented rate, with the types of violence being committed becoming more intense, vicious, and deadlier than ever before. These recent findings coincide with a growing body of literature pointing to the overall greater involvement of girls in violence but, more specifically, their increased participation in more serious assaults and those involving the use of weapons (see also Bibby and Posterski, 1992; Ryan, Mathews, and Banner, 1994).

Street Life

A second setting of concern for teen violence is the streets. Hagan and McCarthy (1997) present a comprehensive overview of social worlds of both male and female street youth in two major Canadian cities: Toronto and

Vancouver. The model of violent street crime developed in this study leads to the conceptualization of violence as an integral part of street life as it arises in a variety of contexts. Notably, the most common use of violence in this context involves the instrumental use of force. Violence committed by youths was often cited as being necessary for protecting themselves and their friends, for economic gain, or as a deterrent to others sharing the same social environment. Arguably, the insights provided by Hagan and McCarthy's work are especially relevant to female teens due to the increased probability that they will engage in violence, coupled with the high visibility of young females on the street. Thus, it is not unlikely that they will be well represented in the official charging statistics. Also, in the light of the motivations expressed by these youths, the reported history of abuse, and dangers associated with being on the streets (Badgley, 1984), the perception of the violent female moves from that of aggressor to victim.

Clearly the forms of violence exhibited by youths of both genders are not homogeneous. Rather, both the type and extent of violence among Canadian youths appear to vary in accordance with social class, setting, and a host of other intervening factors. Although official statistics indicate a consistent increase in the involvement of youth in Canada's overall rates of violent crime, and the media constantly bombard the public with vivid pictures of violent youths, cautionary measures must be taken in addressing this issue. The quality of violence did not increase in Canada over the decade 1988–1998, nor did the raw number of youths charged with violent offenses increase. Instead, the picture of youth participation in violence that one is left with is that of general stagnation with the emergence of distinct trends.

Females are slowly catching up to their male counterparts in terms of their participation in violence and how often they are being charged with violent offenses by the police. Moreover, the most serious offenses—homicide, aggravated assaults, assaults with a weapon, and robbery—are no longer the sole domain of male young offenders. Instead, the number of females who are charged with these kinds of offenses continues to rise, although the base rate remains relatively low. Finally, as a whole, youths are being charged with violent crimes at a rather consistent rate, while the rates for adults have been decreasing. In other words, each year a greater proportion of Canada's total number of individuals charged with violent offenses is composed of people under the age of eighteen. Again, it must be kept in mind that the rate is still relatively small, ranging from 12 to 14 percent of the total number of violent offenses in Canada.

RESPONSES TO THE PROBLEM

There is a growing debate on what should be done to curb serious teen violence, with little consensus on this matter in terms of the most effective and appropriate way of dealing with it. The debate in Canada is generally polarized between those advocating rehabilitation and restorative justice ideals and those who believe in the protection of the public through deterrence and incapacitation. Still others contend that the Canadian youth justice system must be better integrated with existing social services, such as child welfare, mental health, and special needs, because many teen offenders are multiproblem youth.

In 1984, Canada instituted the Young Offenders Act (YOA), which placed more emphasis on youth responsibility for their actions while recognizing the special rights and needs of youths. Due to the perception that the quality and quantity of teen violence has increased, and significant criticism of the YOA's ability to protect the public from young offenders, there have been several amendments to the act. For instance, in 1992, amendments increased the maximum length of sentences in youth court for murder from three years to five years. In 1995, in another series of amendments to the YOA, the maximum sentence for murder in youth court was increased to ten years, sixteen- and seventeen-year-old youths became eligible for transfer to adult courts for serious violent offenses, and victim impact statements were introduced to the youth court.

In addition to changes in youth justice legislation, the increasing rates of youth incarceration fostered the search for alternative forms of custody and control. Following the U.S. example, Canada has begun using boot camp prisons and wilderness camps as alternatives to traditional youth incarceration facilities. One boot camp prison is Project Turnaround in Ontario. This program, which began in 1997, can accommodate up to fifty male juvenile offenders. It is used with offenders who have received a youth court disposition of open custody or probation following a custodial sentence. Staff members are clinicians, youth workers, drill instructors, and administrative staff. The focus of this program is on physical fitness and hard work as a way of achieving academic success, life skills, literacy training, and problem-solving techniques.

In 1994, the province of Manitoba changed its youth justice model for secure custody. Under these changes, all teens housed in secure custody participate in programs that closely resemble U.S.-style boot camps. The emphasis in these institutions is on education and exercise. As is the case with most other boot camp facilities, education focuses on academic skills, interpersonal and problem-solving skills, and literacy, while the exercise programs attempt to create overall personal health in these youths through physical training. As with the Ontario project and U.S. boot camps, the main criticism is that there is an overemphasis on discipline and punishment, with little attention being paid to educational, psychological, and social counseling.

In addition to boot camps, Canada has begun to explore the feasibility of wilderness camps as an alternative to incarceration. Wilderness camps attempt to meet youths' need for adventure, excitement, and challenge in a

socially acceptable manner while providing an opportunity for them to develop self-esteem and self-reliance (Roberts, 1988). Two such programs are
Camp Trapping in British Columbia and Project Dare in Ontario. These
programs combine the challenge of outdoor survival with learning to live
through cooperation with counseling, self-esteem building, self-awareness,
and self-confidence.

The literature on boot camps and wilderness programs suggests that these
programs do not demonstrate a consistent reduction in recidivism among
young offenders or reduce the level of teen violence. Moreover, the research
suggests that these alternatives do not teach significant work skills or positive
attitudes toward work and that they can be abusive or damaging to youths.

Another important issue currently in Canada is the practice of transferring
youths to adult court. The main arguments for the more frequent use of
transfer include the general deterrence notion of youth being less likely to
commit violent acts if they knew they would be raised to adult court and
the specific deterrence argument that longer sentences incapacitate the offender for a greater length of time and provide greater protection for the
public. Other arguments for the use of transfer focus on the relationship
between the offense and the punishment by suggesting that the shorter
dispositional length available in the youth system does not sufficiently reflect
the severity or gravity of certain heinous offenses.

Those who oppose the use of transfer are grounded in the rehabilitative
role of the youth justice system. These arguments focus on the unique rehabilitative services offered by the youth justice system, the youth system's
retention of the principle of diminished accountability for teens, the belief
that placing youths in facilities with adult criminals increases the likelihood
of recidivism and the possibility of abuse, and the fact that there is no evidence to support the notion that transfer results in lower youth crime rates.

The 1995 amendment to the YOA, bill C-37, established that teens who
are sixteen or seventeen years old and charged with first- or second-degree
murder, attempted murder, manslaughter, or aggravated sexual assault will
be transferred to adult court unless the youth court decides that the teen
should be tried in youth court. The onus is on the young person to convince
the court that he or she should be tried in the youth justice system for these
types of crimes. The test for transfer involves what is best for the youth and
what is necessary for the protection of the public. This bill also increased
the sentence for murder if a young person is not transferred. It should be
noted that even with this amendment to the YOA, transfers to adult court
occur infrequently.

In 1998, as a result of public and political disapproval of the YOA, the
minister of justice and attorney general of Canada announced a new strategy
for youth justice and the abolishment of the YOA. The new Youth Justice
Act (YJA) may be seen as a consequence of the fear of increasing youth
violence. Some of the key proposals of this new act recommend expanding

the kind of crimes that a youth may be transferred to adult court for to include a pattern of serious violent offenses. Moreover, the age that a young offender may be transferred to adult court will be lowered from sixteen years to fourteen years. Other proposed changes to the youth justice system include allowing for the publication of names of all young offenders who have been given an adult sentence and establishing a special sentencing option for the most violent young offenders. This sentencing option would require convicted violent young offenders to participate in intensive rehabilitative and treatment programs, and subject these youths to extended periods of controlled supervision in the community once they are released from custody.

CONCLUSION

As in most other Western societies, the vast majority of teen crime in Canada involves property offenses without the use of force; only a small percentage are categorized as violent. Although the media focus attention on these relatively few cases of teen violence, resulting in a general fear of violence by youths, teens account statistically for a small proportion of Canada's violent offenses and engage only rarely in violence, individually or collectively. Still, this growing concern over teen violence in Canada has resulted in the increased fear among the public about youth, and new legislation, heavily influenced by crime control principles, to deal with teen violence.

The heightened sense of fear that Canadians feel about adolescents does not seem to reflect the reality. Teens are not more violent than before, and their rate of criminal activity is not increasing. Rather, the quality of youth violence in Canada over the past decade has remained rather consistent. One area for concern may be that youth violence has not decreased in the same manner as the adult statistics have. Consistent with the general trend in Canada, youths rarely engage in homicide or other crimes of extreme violence. Instead, when they are charged with violent crimes, they tend to involve minor assaults without the use of a weapon.

REFERENCES

Alder, F. (1975). *Sisters in crime.* New York: McGraw-Hill.

Artz, S. (1998). *Sex, power, and the violent school girl.* Toronto: Trifolium Books.

Badgley, R. (1984). *Committee on Sexual Offences Against Children and Youths.* Ottawa: Supply Services Canada.

Barron, S. (1995). Serious offenders. In R. Silverman, and J. Creechan (eds.), *Canadian delinquency.* Ontario: Prentice-Hall Canada.

Bergsmann, I. (1989). The forgotten few: Juvenile female offenders. *Federal Probation, 53,* 73–78.

Bernard, T. (1992). *The cycle of juvenile justice.* New York: Oxford University Press.

Bibby, R., and Posterski, D. (1992). *Teen trends.* Toronto: Stoddart.

Campbell, A. (1990). *The girls in the gang* (2nd ed.). New York: Basil Blackwell.

Carrington, P. (1995). Has violent youth crime increased? Comment on Corrado and Markwart. *Canadian Journal of Criminology, 37* (1), 61–73.

Chesney-Lind, M., and Sheldon, R. (1998). *Girls, delinquency, and juvenile justice.* Pacific Grove, CA: Brooks/Cole.

Chisholm, P. (1997, Dec. 8). Bad girls. *Macleans,* pp. 13–15.

Cohen, A. (1973). *Folk devils and moral panics.* London: MacGibbons & Kee.

Corrado, R., and Markwart, A. (1994). The need to reform the YOA in response to violent young offenders: Confusion, reality, or myth? *Canadian Journal of Criminology, 36* (3), 343–378.

Cunningham, A., and Griffiths, C. (1997). *Canadian criminal justice: A primer.* Toronto: Harcourt Brace.

Doige, D. (1990). Young offenders. In C. McKie and K. Thompson (eds.), *Canadian social trends.* Toronto: Thompson Educational Publishing.

Doob, A., and Sprott, J. (1998). Is the "quality" of youth violence becoming more serious? *Canadian Journal of Criminology, 40* (2), 185–194.

Fagan, J. (1990). Social and legal policy dimensions of violent juvenile crime. *Criminal Justice and Behavior, 17,* 93–133.

Frank, J. (1992). Violent youth crime. In C. McKie and K. Thompson (eds.), *Canadian social trends.* Toronto: Thompson Educational Publishing.

Hagan, J., and McCarthy, B. (1997). *Mean streets.* Cambridge: Cambridge University Press.

Hartnagel, T., and Baron, S. (1995). "It's time to get serious": Public attitudes toward juvenile justice in Canada. In R. Silverman and J. Creechan (eds.), *Canadian delinquency.* Ontario: Prentice-Hall Canada.

Hatch, A., and Faith, K. (1990). The female offender in Canada: A statistical profile. *Canadian Journal of Women and the Law, 3* (2), 432–456.

Hill, B. (1996). Analysis of boot camps: What does the research say? Paper presented at the Alternatives to Boot Camp conference.

Juristat. (1992a). Female young offenders, 1990–1991. In *Juristat.* Statistics Canada, Canadian Centre for Justice Statistics.

Juristat. (1992b). Youth property crime in Canada. In *Juristat.* Statistics Canada, Canadian Centre for Justice Statistics.

Juristat. (1994). Trends in criminal victimization, 1988–1993. In *Juristat.* Ottawa: Statistics Canada, Canadian Centre for Justice Statistics.

Juristat. (1995a). Public perceptions of crime. In *Juristat.* Ottawa: Statistics Canada, Canadian Centre for Justice Statistics.

Juristat. (1995b). Youth court statistics. In *Juristat.* Statistics Canada, Canadian Centre for Justice Statistics.

Juristat. (1997). Youths and adults charged in criminal incidents, criminal code, and federal and provincial statutes by sex. In *Juristat.* Statistics Canada, Canadian Centre for Justice Statistics.

Leonard, T. (1995). Youth court statistics. In R. Silverman and J. Creechan (eds.), *Canadian delinquency.* Ontario: Prentice-Hall Canada.

Markwart, A., and Corrado, R. (1995). A response to Carrington. *Canadian Journal of Criminology, 37* (1), 74–87.

Marron, K. (1992). *Apprenticed in crime.* Toronto: McClelland, 1992.

Mathews, F. (1994). *Youth gangs on youth gangs.* Ottawa: Solicitor General Canada.

Mawby, R. (1980). Sex and crime: The results of a self-report study. *British Journal of Sociology, 31,* 326–543.

Meloff, W., and Silverman, R. (1992). Canadian kids who kill. *Canadian Journal of Criminology, 34,* 15–34.

Perrone, P., and Chesney-Lind, M. (1998). Media presentations of crime in Hawaii: Wild in the streets? Available at: *http://www.cpja.ag.state.hi.us/rs/cts/mediajuv/.*

Reitsma-Street, M. (1991). A review of female delinquency. In A. Lescheid, P. Jaffe, and W. Willis (Eds.), *The Young Offenders Act: A revolution in Canadian juvenile justice.* Toronto: University of Toronto Press.

Reitsma-Street, M. (1993). Canadian youth court charges and dispositions for females before and after the implementation of the Young Offenders Act. *Canadian Journal of Criminology, 35,* 437–458.

Roberts, A. (1988). Wilderness programs for juvenile offenders: A challenging alternative. *Juvenile and Family Court Journal, 39* (1), 1–12.

Rowe, D., Vazsonyi, A., and Flannery, D. (1995). Sex differences: Do means and within sex variation have similar causes? *Journal of Research in Crime and Delinquency, 32,* 84–100.

Ryan, C., Mathews, F., and Banner, J. (1994). *Student perceptions of violence.* Toronto: Central Toronto Youth Services.

Schissel, B. (1995). Trends in official juvenile crime rates. In R. Silverman and J. Creechan (eds.), *Canadian delinquency.* Ontario: Prentice-Hall Canada.

Schissel, B. (1997). *Blaming children: Youth crime, moral panics, and the politics of Hate.* Halifax: Fernwood.

Silverman, R. (1990). Trends in Canadian youth homicide: Some unanticipated consequences of a change in law. *Canadian Journal of Criminology, 32* (4) 651–656.

Silverman, R., Teevan, J., and Sacco, V. (1996). *Crime in Canadian society.* Toronto: Harcourt Brace.

Statistics Canada. (1998, Mar.). Canadian dimensions—youth and adult crime rates. Available at: *http://www.statcan/english/Pgdb/State/Justice/legal14.htm.*

Tanner, J. (1996). *Teenage troubles: Youth and deviance in Canada.* Scarborough: Nelson Canada.

West, G. (1984). *Young offenders and the state.* Toronto: Butterworths.

3

ENGLAND AND WALES

Shirley Rawstorne

PERCEPTIONS OF TEEN VIOLENCE

In the United Kingdom today we appear to have developed a negative attitude toward our young people, which appears to have been guided by successive dominant views of history that have gained strength over time. The idea that circumstances of today are always worse than those in the "golden age of the past," which is often twenty years previous, is not new. Contrast this recent quotation,

People seem to forget so easily the reality of the past . . . the profound amnesia whereby young people in the past were orderly, disciplined and well behaved. (Pearson, 1983)

with this one from Socrates:

Our youths love luxury, they have bad manners, contempt for authority and disrespect of older people. Children nowadays are tyrants, they contradict their parents and tyrannize their teachers.

The quotations help to lend perspective to contemporary issues. In more recent history than the wisdom of Socrates, it was as early as 1815 in England that a society was formed for "investigating the causes of the alarming increase in juvenile delinquency." The role of children began to change significantly during this early period, and by the end of the century, children had been marginalized from the workforce and from the center of economic production. The Factory Act of 1833 was seen as a watershed, preventing children under age nine from working in the factories and limiting the working hours of those older.

This process of exclusion of children from the factories to protect them from exploitation was perceived as dangerous by the middle classes, in the sense that if children were no longer controlled by work, idleness would make them vulnerable to disorder and debauchery. This sparked the zeal of education that took hold through the remainder of the century. Piecemeal attempts to distinguish between adult and child in the treatment of offenders also continued. It was the reformatory schools and industrial schools instituted in the 1850s that were the most significant developments. The reformatory schools became the standard disposal for a second offense under the Youthful Offenders Act of 1854, in order for punishment to be inflicted and the child suitably disciplined into submission. The industrial schools were initially for those "at risk" who were nonoffenders. It is clear that theories of some kind of preventative input were gaining ground; if juveniles could be reached before they became involved in crime, then crime could be eradicated altogether.

An official report of 1896 (*Report of the Dept: Committee on Reformatory and Industrial Schools*) argued that there were no significant differences in the regimes of or in the children held in the two kinds of school. This initiated a process culminating in the merging of schools themselves in later legislation, to become Approved Schools for offenders and nonoffenders alike. (The Children and Young Persons Act, 1933, introduced the Approved Schools.)

The distinction between children and adult offenders was formally sealed in the 1908 Children Act with the establishment of juvenile court and the end of imprisonment of children. This represented a major step in the development of the belief that children represent a special category of problem. There followed many initiatives on how to deal best with young people who became involved with crime. A significant piece of legislation, the Children and Young Persons Act of 1933, placed a duty on the court to consider the welfare of the young person. This established a contradiction between welfare and punishment, blurring the youngsters' needs and the punishment of the criminal behavior. The Criminal Justice Act of 1963 continued with the emphasis on welfare. However, the measures had widened the net of social control to register more children and young people as delinquent. The consequence was an inflation in the level of recorded crime, which stimulated yet another moral panic about youth crime. During the 1960s, politicians surrounded themselves with social scientists as advisers, and the first cracks in the postwar optimism of the welfare state were beginning to be seen.[1]

During this period, politicians began to use the law-and-order issue as a voting tactic, and this has remained on political-party agendas ever since.

Cohen and Taylor (1972) write about the mounting anxiety after 1963 of groups of young people calling themselves mods and rockers:

The mods and rockers symbolized something far more important than what they actually did. They touched the delicate and ambivalent nerves through which postwar social change in Britain was experienced. No one wanted depressions or austerity but messages about "never having it so good" were ambivalent in that some people were having it too good and too quickly. Resentment and jealousy were easily directed at the young, if only because of their increased spending power and sexual freedom. When this was combined with a too-open flouting of the work and leisure ethic, with violence and vandalism, and the (as yet) uncertain threats associated with drug-taking, something more than the image of a peaceful Bank Holiday at the sea was being shattered. (p. 192)

The backlash ultimately resulted in the mid-1970s swing from welfare to a somewhat punitive approach to juvenile offenders, the punitive approach gaining ground throughout the 1970s and into the 1980s. The use of care orders and supervision orders declined, and attendance center orders and custody increased. From 1970 to 1978 custodial sentences for young people rose from 3,000 to 7,000. The links between social conditions and crime were rejected as the movement of social responsibility was placed back on the individual and morality back on the family. The rehabilitative ideal had collapsed before it had gathered any real ground; the partial implementation of the 1969 act had been a bitter disappointment to welfare proponents. People were led to believe the juvenile criminal justice system had become softer and softer, while in reality it had become harder and harder.

The widespread feeling that social life was moving and changing faster than people could comprehend throughout the 1960s had created both excitement and anxiety. These changes were taken up by the swiftly growing media that were using circulation tactics in competition for readership. Concern about the activities of youth became a dominant theme in the mounting anxiety evident in newspaper accounts after 1963. The supporters of traditional values and the established order grew anxious about the vandalism, hooliganism, and drug use that increasingly commanded the attention of news reporters and leader writers, who raised concerns that they were merely the more visible symptoms of a deeper social malaise.

The true stories of complex humanity are transmitted into popular fiction by the tabloid press, which is self-imposing and self-justifying and acts as the arbiter of popular morality and helps create moral panic. Fear of crime is out of all proportion to reality, and this fear has risen sharply in recent years. Tales of villains sell newspapers, and the popular press is accomplished at turning messy reality into simple, recognizable moral tales. It appears that the political ideology and professional imperatives of popular journalism guide the journalists into how they view violence. Violence within the family, unsafe working conditions, industrial poisoning of the environment on a large scale, and the violence of inequalities in society are of little interest to the popular press, which focuses predominantly on interpersonal violence involving sudden physical injury to apparently innocent strangers, especially in public places, and invokes what is termed "stranger danger" (of which there is in fact very little). Any adequate explanation of violence must pay some attention to the life situations of people; simply to attribute crime and violence to wickedness is to ignore all this and to reduce the complexities of human motivation to the simplest of tautologies. "Newspapers generally do not draw a direct causal link between wickedness and violence, but rather look for contributing factors such as lack of parental control allowing violent impulses to develop unchecked; and the entertainment media with vicarious violence, which encourages imitation and renders us immune to its actual horrors" (Harris and Timms, 1993).

For those of us reading popular literature or the press, it is necessary to identify what is not said as well as what is, and consider whether the story could have been told differently—in short, to evaluate what we read. For instance, if we seek an explanation, not a justification, that entitles us to view with compassion rather than contempt, we are engaging in a more complex form of moral evaluation than what is normally characteristic of popular literature and tabloid press. Popular literature is tuned into the superficiality of learning the outcome—the predictable and reassuring discovery of the identification of the murderer or the fate of the heroine. The more people are accustomed to this, the more the experts who are considered to complicate things are accused of offering feeble excuses or sociological jargon or even of condoning the act itself. Social workers are often accused of this in their efforts to consider the welfare of children as well as recognizing that a crime may have been committed.

CURRENT TRENDS IN TEEN VIOLENCE

Violent behavior of children and young people in England and Wales causes great difficulty for the judicial process in apportioning justice and welfare considerations.

The disproportionate amount of crime committed by young people in the United Kingdom is property crime. Contrary to media portrayal, violence among teens in England and Wales is not a significant problem. Only a few young offenders commit the most serious types of crime. Even in the 1990s only four were held in secure care or custody for murder or manslaughter; fewer than 400 ten- to seventeen-year-olds were sentenced for serious offenses in 1994.

However, when young people or children do commit serious crime, it generates unprecedented publicity.[2] In 1993, for example, two boys, Robert Thompson and John Venables, both aged ten years, were responsible for the death of two-year-old Jamie Bulger. The publicity surrounding the case highlighted the readiness of people to condemn them as evil monsters or devil children. Thompson and Venables were sentenced under section 53 of the Children and Young Persons Act of 1933 and detained on Her Majesty's pleasure in secure accommodation. The crime itself was unusual, and the camera images of the child being taken away by the other two children remains fixed in our minds. Although the case was extreme, it was not unique. Throughout history in the United Kingdom and around the world, children have killed. Over the past 250 years, there have been just twenty-seven recorded cases in the United Kingdom of children under age fourteen killing other children and four who killed adults. Ironically, in the past, children and young people who had killed were dealt with more leniently than they are today. Although the distinction between children and adults was established only from the mid-1800s, the *doli incapax* ruling (incapable of guilt)[3] had been in force throughout the 1700s, allowing the acquittal of three young girls aged eight, nine, and ten, who had killed a three-year-old girl. In 1855, two nine-year-old boys who had killed a seven-year-old were found guilty of manslaughter and sentenced to twelve months in prison.

CONTRIBUTING FACTORS

In 1968, under current legislation from the Children and Young Persons Act, 1933, the Mary Bell case was a significant landmark. Mary, a ten-year-old, had murdered two toddlers and was sentenced under section 53 of the act and detained under Her Majesty's pleasure, but there was no appropriate accommodation to place her in. The stark differences in these brief examples of sentences over the centuries raise questions regarding the historical development of the way in which society deals with young people and children. Have we made our young people more vulnerable with fewer rights than adults through the creation of a particular image or concept of childhood?

The commonsense notion of what we expect in childhood is shattered by events such as the Bulger case, which we find so hard to understand because they destroy our image of innocence in young children. To attempt to understand the behavior of youngsters, we must consider what it means to grow up in the United Kingdom today. The period from childhood to adulthood is a turbulent period, and the teen years are fraught with risks and difficulties. It is a time of risk taking, a time of exploration, a time of discovery, a time of self-absorption, and a time to question the adult world of rules and regulations. Children learn to fit into society as they develop into adulthood, learning the differing cultural rituals that are in tune with their own environment. The transitional period from child to adult is fraught with risks created by society that young people must manage. They need encouragement and positive input from the adult world at this crucial time.

RESPONSES TO THE PROBLEM

The legislation that has been implemented over the past century has been far from clear on how best to deal with young offenders and even less clear on how to deal with youngsters who commit serious offenses. A long-running tension between welfare and justice, influenced by popular culture, has prevented any real progress. This tension becomes clear through brief reference to the key pieces of legislation during the nineteenth century. (It is worth remembering that most crimes committed by young people are less serious and are property related. There are a very few children or young people who are found guilty of grave crimes.)

The 1908 Children Act established the juvenile court, a criminal court in procedure but with jurisdiction over "care" and "protection" issues as well as criminal cases. For the first time, the state could intervene directly into family life when children were deemed immoral or unruly, blurring the boundaries between criminal and neglected child.

The 1933 Children and Young Persons Act placed a duty on magistrates to consider the welfare of the young person and brought together provisions for the treatment of the delinquent and the neglected. The dominant theme was welfare, but the act also made special provision for juveniles convicted on indictment by the crown court of murder or other serious offenses, through section 53.

Section 53(1) provided that a person under the age of eighteen years, convicted of murder, be detained during Her Majesty's pleasure, and if so sentenced shall be liable to be detained in such place and under such conditions as the secretary of state (home secretary) may direct. This sentence is indeterminate, controversially often treated as a life sentence, and has not been significantly varied or amended by any subsequent legislation. It is the only sentence that a court can disperse in respect of ten- to seventeen-year-olds convicted of murder.

Section 53(2) provided for longer terms of detention with no statutory minimum but up to the adult maximum (life) for those under the age of seventeen (then the minimum age of adult criminal responsibility). This was for the specified offenses of attempted murder, manslaughter, and wounding with intent to do grievous bodily harm.

The Criminal Justice Act of 1961 extended the provision of section 53(2) to any offense punishable in the case of an adult with imprisonment for fourteen years or more. The net result was to bring offenses such as robbery, arson, and burglary within the scope. Burglary became one of the areas of uncertainty, and the Criminal Justice Act of 1991 removed this by reducing the maximum penalty for burglary from fourteen to ten years. However, a further offense was introduced, that of indecent assault on a woman, which qualifies even though it carries a maximum of ten years. In the case of juveniles aged fourteen or over, two further offenses qualify despite carrying a maximum sentence of ten years: causing death by dangerous driving or causing death by careless driving while under the influence of drink or drugs. In 1994 ten- to thirteen-year-olds were included under section 53(2).

The development of section 53(1) since 1933 has barely changed. The mandatory sentence of life detention during Her Majesty's pleasure is prescribed for murder by young offenders under age eighteen at the time of the offense. The sentencer has no power to make a minimum recommendation. Young persons sentenced to detention during Her Majesty's pleasure for murder under section 53(1) are to be treated as persons serving life imprisonment; they are not affected by early-release procedures initiated by the Criminal Justice Act 1991. Section 53(2) has broadened considerably over time with the prevailing climates in the criminal justice system.

In the 1940s two acts were introduced simultaneously: the 1948 Children Act, which addressed welfare issues, seeing young people as victims, and the Criminal Justice Act of 1948, which increased the punitive element for young offenders. The different approaches adopted in the two acts reflected and strengthened societal ambivalence concerning troublesome youth.

By the 1960s welfare had become the dominant language in relation to juvenile offenders. The age of criminal responsibility was raised by the Children and Young Persons Act of 1963 from seven to ten (still very much lower than many other countries around the world). The act was a limited measure to give local authorities the duty to engage in preventative work with children and families thought to be at risk.

During the 1960s, the alliance of social scientists and political parties had a profound impact on juvenile justice policy. The government in 1964 sought radical changes beyond raising the age of criminal responsibility. They sought to reform the treatment of young offenders, the intention being to transform the functioning of the juvenile court in England and Wales, while retaining the structure of the court (Pitts, 1988). With welfare as the dominant language throughout the 1960s, it was the Children and Young Persons Act of 1969 that incorporated the philosophy of these radical reforms, summarized in the statement "that children who were in trouble were not radically different from other children." The act itself provoked much opposition, and the election of a new government in 1970 meant that only part of it was ever implemented.

Throughout the 1970s, there was a massive increase in the use of custody for young people, from 3,000 in 1970 to 7,000 in 1978. By the early 1980s, concern at the use of custody had led to some local initiatives to develop a noncustodial ethos. These local initiatives both informed and were encouraged by deliberate policies, underwritten by provisions in the Criminal Justice Act of 1982. The Criminal Justice Act of 1988 encouraged the decline in the use of custody for young defendants with the increasing range of community-based programs offering an alternative to custody (e.g., supervision orders, probation orders, and attendance center orders). The watershed of the Criminal Justice Act of 1991 formalized community sentences as "sentences in their own right," not alternatives to custody, as in the 1980s. The community sentences carry with them restrictions of liberty at various levels most suitable for the offender. The aims were to put the probation service at the heart of the criminal justice process rather than on the periphery and to provide a whole new sentencing framework.

The media coverage of the Bulger case and other cases of young people who were seen to "get away with crime," through lack of knowledge by the public of community sentences and the reporting tactics of the media, led to the changes in the Criminal Justice Act of 1993, which gave courts more power to impose harsher sentences on young people. This was followed by the Crime and Public Order Act of 1994, which introduced more punitive elements into dealing with young offenders and a new secure training order (in effect a two-year custodial sentence) for twelve- to fourteen-year-olds and doubled the young offender institution maximum sentence to two years.

In 1997, the newly elected government announced that it would implement a comprehensive and wide-ranging reform program aimed to get the youth justice system in England and Wales working more effectively. In tune with the words of Mary Carpenter over a century ago, an audit commission report was produced, titled *Misspent Youth*, which seriously considered the resources necessary to prevent children and young people from becoming involved in crime, or stop it at an early stage. The Crime and Disorder Act of 1998 incorporated the philosophy of *Misspent Youth* and introduced parenting orders, local child curfew orders, and child safety orders. One of the most significant inclusions of the new act was replacing the old cautioning for young offenders with a new final warning scheme.

Youth Court

The youth court is a magistrates court established for the purpose of dealing with criminal proceedings against those under the age of eighteen. Almost every case against a person of that age starts and finishes in the youth court, with five exceptions:

1. The juvenile is charged with homicide (death caused by murder, manslaughter, or dangerous driving).
2. An adult or youth court has equal power to remand the juvenile. An adult court remanding to the care of the local authorities may also grant a secure accommodation order at the same time.
3. The juvenile is jointly charged with an adult.
4. A crown court has the power to deal with juveniles committed for trial or sentence.

5. A court other than a youth court has started to deal with a person, believing him or he to be an adult, but then discovers that the person is under age eighteen.

Institutional Provision

While it is important for youngsters committing such offences to be punished it is not right for all hope to be taken away and for them to be put into a situation in which they cannot help but be corrupted. (Boswell 1996)

Boswell's commentary is appropo to the Mary Bell case. In 1968, at the age of ten, she murdered two toddlers. She was sentenced and held under Her Majesty's pleasure. The irony was that although provision for such a disposal had been implemented as early as 1933, there was in fact no suitable institution or accommodation in which to place such a young girl who had committed such an act. The 1933 act stipulated that section 53 detainees may be detained "in such a place and under such conditions as the Secretary of State may permit," which left the discretion of including a Prison Department establishment. A hospital order was considered for Mary, but she was too young under the Mental Health Act, and she was finally placed in one of the newly set up regional secure units (three such establishments had been set up to provide special units for boys only in 1964, 1965, and 1966). Whether such a punitive element played a part in sentencing, it certainly played a part in her years of custody. Mary was subjected to abuse in the secure unit by staff and the boys.

Today secure accommodation is available to and normally provided by the local authority. Criteria for secure accommodation are children committed to care, those remanded awaiting trial or sentence, and those serving sentences of detention. Since 1983, in order to hold a youngster in secure accommodation for more than seventy-two hours in any twenty-eight-day period, a local authority must obtain an authorization from a juvenile court. The criteria to be met are a history of absconding, likely to abscond again, and if so, likely to put his or her physical mental or moral welfare at risk or likely to harm others.

The length of time a child may be held in secure accommodation is specified by regulation: three months at a first hearing and six months on renewal. In embracing not only different categories of offender but also nonoffenders, secure accommodation seeks simultaneously to meet the needs of disturbed or unfortunate youngsters and to inject discipline and structure into the lives of the deviant young. The intention was to solve the problems of both deviant children (after they have resisted other forms of persuasion) and needy desperate children whose response to kindness is to run away. The security is psychological and physical—to help each individual youngster. The difficult youngster is contained, and efforts to address the problems are made. It is a response to the insoluble, a space at which to take pause. In the consideration of secure accommodation, courts are confronted with dilemmas, paradoxes, and contradictions.

Secure accommodation is perhaps perceived naively in that it is benign, caring, and therapeutic, designed to meet the best interests of the child who is forever running away from problems. Skilled and caring staff provide the youngster with a secure framework within which confidence and maturity can be gained. Somewhat more cynically, secure accommodation is, or may be, a fraudulent attempt to make us forget that secure accommodation is a form of imprisonment of the young, and one without the safeguards that attend other custodial provision. By this view, it can be seen as a form of insidious state power designed less to enhance the well-being of the child than to control the deviant and provide job opportunities for professionals.

Secure accommodation constitutes a particular conjunction of the therapeutic and the penal, the welfare (positive) and punitive (retributive), which are bound so inextricably together in the culture of dealing with young offenders, and is a conjunction that produces many problems. The behavior of children and young people can include mischance and naughtiness simultaneously. Governments have sought to change legislation and, by analyzing that change historically, theoretically, and empirically, have highlighted the complexity and ambiguity embedded in secure accommodation. If young offenders occupy this bridging position between neediness and criminality, the question of how the individual youngster is to be processed is key. To study how the immature are incarcerated—not exactly as criminals but on the basis of factors that relate to their actions as well as their youthful status—is especially illuminating. Secure accommodation is a particular form of locking up that stands not primarily as custody but, ironically, as an alternative to more punitive intervention. "Secure accommodation can be both punishment and care simultaneously, neither hospital nor prison but between the two" (Harris and Timms, 1993).

Custodial Career Planning

[A] young person who enters the Child Care system, say at age 14 or 15, transfers to a Young Offender Institution (YOI) at age 18, and to an Adult Prison at 21 years. (Boswell 1996)

When children are taken into custody at such an age and detained during Her Majesty's pleasure, they grow up in custody and are moved through the system accordingly. Secure provision around the country is provided by local authorities and is usually within community homes. There are also two youth treatment centers, which were designed for therapeutic care of difficult, disturbed children who cannot easily be detained elsewhere in the child care system. The centers house fourteen young offenders. The various secure units around the country differ in the number of beds they provide but usually amount to no more than five. Approximately 100 are in secure provision. The small numbers in the units and high staffing ratio allow the individual care that is required for such children and young people. They are person-centered establishments where staff view appropriate treatment as a priority.

A long-term section 53 offender begins a sentence with a focus on treatment and education. Education and training are found in the secure units, as is privacy and the possibility of forming relationships (Ditchfield and Catan, 1992). The stark differences become evident when the young person progresses into the young offender institution, which is under the direction of the prison system, as he or she grows into early adulthood. The young person moves into a system-centered institution where the focus is on punishment and retribution. The stark differences are visible not only in numbers of inmates but in the staffing ratio. The regimes, culture, and philosophy are at opposite ends of the spectrum. One-third of the population of section 53 offenders reach the adult prison system, where the young lifers must move as they grow into adulthood.

The therapeutic regime that these youngsters have encountered from a very young age is replaced overnight with a punitive regime, which they are often unprepared for. The validity of the therapeutic work carried out in a secure environment, where it has been clearly recognized and accepted that violent youngsters are or have been themselves victims of violence, often in a home where safety and security are a norm for most youngsters, is lost. There is no attention to explaining the implication of an indeterminate sentence; the psychological effects have usually taken their toll well before they move. There is little motivation with the uncertainty so these youngsters get more depressed than necessary. It is hard for staff in secure accommodation to know how to treat youngsters in preparing them for prison. Progress and rehabilitation with the ongoing outside links are lost once the move takes place. It is not surprising that reconviction rates are high: for section 53(2) offenders, 72 percent, and for section 53(1) offenders, 29 percent (of whom a high proportion are first offenders and therefore statistically unlikely to reoffend, and a high proportion are transferred to the prison system for indefinite periods and whose progress is uncharted). The need for consistency and continuity should be paramount, but prison staff concerned with the containment and needs of a large population of prisoners have no separate policy for offering section 53 offenders special facilities and treatment when they are transferred. Until this changes, the process of transition will remain fraught with difficulties for the young lifers.

There is without doubt a need to understand children and young people who commit violent crimes, but there is also a need to understand how these youngsters fit into the wider social world they are part of. The age of criminal responsibility is higher in most other countries than in the United Kingdom. Criminal inquiry for those under age fourteen is inappropriate and should not take place in the adult court or within the public glare. There is now a family court that could be expanded for such a purpose.

Juveniles are excluded from a mandatory life sentence by application of the term of detention during Her Majesty's pleasure. The abolition of section 53 may provide a more equitable system for children, young people, and adults, so that they are not doubly punished.

CONCLUSION

The State grapples with the often unanswerable problem posed by deviant and distressed children and secondly with the unintended consequences of their earlier and unsuccessful endeavors. (Harris and Timms, 1993)

The state concerns itself in the upbringing of children and is willing to control when families have failed or refused. When the state ceases to turn a blind eye to misery, deviance, or self-harm, increasingly decisive forms of control become necessary to deal with problems that have defeated the best efforts of others. In the social world, things are seldom what they seem; attempts at creating change can often go wrong, and the repercussions of these attempts affect the powerless in society, who are least able to bear the consequences. In a complex and ambiguous situation, a simple way forward cannot work. The situation does not remain static but is different in different areas, and within each area it is constantly shifting as a result of social interventions.

The separation of adult and youth courts has done little to improve the court process for youngsters. The basic rule is that all those under age eighteen prosecuted for criminal offenses are dealt with by a youth court in the first instance but in the case of grave crimes will be transferred to crown court. The criminal justice system is an adult system with all its theater and pomp, and this is imposed upon children and young people, often with complete bewilderment, in the youth court and crown court.

NOTES

1. Abel-Smith and Townsend produced their findings from the first major study of poverty in the United Kingdom based on a concept of relative poverty. It claimed that in 1960, over 7 million people, that is, 14.2 percent of the population, lived in poverty: "Individuals, families and groups in the population can be said to be in poverty when they lack the resources to obtain the types of diet, participate in the activities and have the living conditions and amenities which are customary, or at least widely encouraged or approved, in the societies to which they belong."

2. Children and youngsters and young people are used synonymously to include from toddlers to those eighteen years old.

3. The *doli incapax* is a centuries-old ruling that means "incapable of guilt." The *doli incapax* ruling in the convictions for the Bulger case was crucial because the two boys fell into the ten to thirteen inclusive age group for which prosecution has to prove that they knew the difference between right and wrong. The *doli incapax* ruling did not seem to be treated as seriously in this case as in less serious offenses. The judge stated that the boys did not set out that day with the intention of killing a child, but that the act became unstoppable once they had assumed the three-way interaction that allowed them to assert a high degree of power over this small child.

REFERENCES

Abel-Smith, B., and Townsend, P. (1965). *The poor and the poorest: A new analysis of the Ministry of Labour's Family Expenditure Surveys of 1953–54 and 1960.* London: Bell.

Boswell, G. (1996). *Young and dangerous.* Brookfield, VT: Avebury.

Brown, S. (1998). *Understanding youth and crime.* Philadelphia: Open University Press.

Chibnall, S. (1977). *Law and order news.* London: Tavistock.

Cohen, S. and Taylor, L. (1972). *Psychological survival: The experience of long-term imprisonment.* Harmondsworth: Penguin Books.

Ditchfield, D. and Catan, L. (1992). *Juveniles sentenced for serious offences: A comparison of regimes in young offender institutions and local authority community homes.* Research and Planning Unit Paper 66. London: Home Office.

Haines, K., and Drakeford, M. (1998). *Young people and youth justice.* London: Macmillan.

Harris, R., and Timms, N. (1993). *Secure accommodation in child care (between hospital and prison or thereabouts?).* London: Routledge.

Pearson, J. (1983). *Hooligan: A history of respectable fears.* London: Macmillan.

Pitts, J. (1988). *The politics of juvenile crime.* London: Sage.

Pitts, J. (1990). *Working with young offenders.* Britain and South Wales: Macmillan.

Prins, H. (1982). *Criminal behavior: An introduction to criminology and the penal system* (2nd ed.). London: Tavistock.

Sereny, G. (1974). *The case of Mary Bell.* London: Arrow Books.

Townsend, P. (1974). Poverty as relative deprivation: Resources and styles of living. In D. Wedderburn (Ed.), *Poverty, equality, and class structure.* Cambridge: Cambridge University Press.

4

GERMANY

Christopher R. Williams, Bruce A. Arrigo, and Stephanie Klaus

PERCEPTIONS OF TEEN VIOLENCE

Watts (1997) notes that the most common perpetrators of xenophobic violence are juveniles—in particular, male youths. Contrary to popular belief, however, these individuals or groups have little, if any, affiliation with neo-Nazi groups. Further, there is often an absence of political ties. Approximately half of all xenophobic actors who were prosecuted were not directly linked with political motives. Only a fraction of such youths are associated with extremist groups and subcultures. In general, Watts establishes that young males accounted for an astonishing 97 to 98 percent of all documented aggressive acts against foreigners in Germany in the early 1990s. Additionally, 70 percent of those acts were committed by youths aged fifteen to twenty-one. Given the lack of political and extremist affiliation among these youths, Watts supports the notion that these acts of youth violence against foreigners are attributable to informal group dynamics and male aggression.

CURRENT TRENDS IN TEEN VIOLENCE

Discussing the issue of teen violence—its presence, prevalence, and magnitude—in contemporary Germany requires coming to terms with a number of difficulties. Germany, unlike many other Western countries, is marked historically by significantly differing political climates, which affect the nature of social, cultural, and economic relations among other things. Thus, the issue of violence, be it general or specific to the teenage population, must be addressed relative to the political climate of that time. Further, we run against the problem of measuring juvenile violence. In other words, differing opinions as to what constitutes juvenile violence, the causes of juvenile violence, and precise statistics regarding its prevalence are difficult, if not impossible, to come by. This problem is confounded by politics. For example, different political powers have been more or less reluctant to release accurate information relative to one another. Thus, for certain time periods, accurate information may be available, while for others, it may not.

We are left, then, with the issue of what information on teen violence in Germany is most accurate, unbiased, and available. Provided this, we have chosen to concentrate on contemporary (postreunification) Germany. We have concluded that this information will be most helpful to those seeking information on the problem of teen violence throughout the world. This is not to say that teen violence was nonexistent, less prevalent, or less severe in the years prior to 1990, but that information on post-1990 German crime is more widely available in accurate form. Although we briefly comment on teen violence in the years prior to 1990, this information is noted only in an incomplete and often speculative form.

The problem of juvenile violence is not specific to Germany. It is a worldwide concern necessitating worldwide attention. The nature of the problem within Germany is not unlike many other contemporary countries. The staggering rise in juvenile crime, particularly violent crime, has been the cause of substantial concern on behalf of the German government and citizens alike.

Germany's criminal code did not implement specific clauses for juvenile offenders until 1871. Thus, statistics regarding juvenile crime and violent juvenile crime begin in the late 1800s. In general, we find a substantial increase in overall juvenile crime between 1871 and 1914 (Johnson, 1995, 191). At this time, a majority of youth crimes were property crimes rather than crimes against persons. Nevertheless, the number of youth crimes against persons was rising, while those by adults were declining. At times, acts of violence by juveniles were even more frequent than those by adult males (Johnson, 1995, 191). Thus, in general, we find a significant rise in both overall juvenile crime and number of violent crimes committed by youths during the period prior to World War I.

The period between 1918 and 1933 was highlighted by substantial changes with regard to juveniles and the law. Foremost, the national legislation of 1922–1923 incorporated more specific criteria as to what constituted unacceptable juvenile behavior. Further, specific codes of practice were enacted for dealing with youth who broke the code (Stachura, 1989, 133). In 1923, for example, Germany created a separate court system for juvenile offenders. Prior to this, children were often dealt with in special chambers of the adult courts (Wolfe, 1996, 125). The statistics for this period are often inexact. Measurement of juvenile crime in records often did not reflect the true extent of juvenile crime. What can generally be said, however, is that an increasing number of juveniles were being convicted during this period. As noted by Stachura (1989, 133), however, this increase could be attributed to "more efficient detection methods, better cooperation between police and the general public, and more successful prosecution in courts." Thus, what becomes important about the period spanning 1918 through 1933 can be characterized by its treatment of juvenile crime rather than any specific numbers or descriptions. It should be noted, however, that World War I, accompanied by periods of profound instability in Germany (1918–1923 and 1929–1933), created issues for German youth and the problem of juvenile criminality that were very specific to that period.

The next significant era pertaining to youth criminality in Germany is that of 1949 through 1989. In 1949, Germany divided into two politically divergent segments: the German Democratic Republic (East Germany) and the Federal Republic of Germany (West Germany). Because specific information regarding crime statistics and trends in East Germany have been released only in censored form, we must speculate based on the limited information that is available. We will look briefly at juvenile crime during this period, paying particular attention to the 1970s through early 1980s. This is not to suggest that between 1950 and 1970 juvenile crime was less significant, but that the trends in juvenile crime, social and political views, and efforts to confront the problem in the 1970s and 1980s serve as a necessary historical vantage point for the progression into the 1990s.

In general, youth delinquency in the Federal Republic of Germany was high (Knolker, Shuler-Springorum, and Nissen, 1981). Although juvenile criminality was on the rise in the 1970s and 1980s, the rate of convictions for juvenile offenders was not. In other words, there was some question as to whether juvenile delinquency was increasing or whether petty offenses, which had not been recorded prior to this time, were being included as delinquency. The types of offenses being committed by juveniles in West Germany at that time were somewhat consistent with other industrialized nations. In other words, less severe crimes such as property offenses were high, while more serious offenses (e.g., violent offenses) were relatively rare. What we do observe in West Germany in the 1970s and 1980s is a significant increase in drug use by juveniles and a significant increase in unemployment of juveniles. Some observers have suggested that these trends were intricately linked to the overall rise in juvenile deviance. It should also be noted that as early as the 1970s treatment or rehabilitation programs for juvenile offenders were conspicuously lacking. Although West Germany implemented some rehabilitative programs, such as therapy, training, and drug counseling, the rate of success was far lower than had been hoped (especially for juveniles not involved in a long-term incarceration). This failure of the rehabilitative system at that time has been linked in part to a lack of resources (e.g., sufficient numbers of staff and technological resources). In general, there is some debate as to whether the number of juvenile offenders in West Germany had actually increased or had simply appeared to increase. What we can be sure of, however, is that efforts to rehabilitate troubled youths at that time were inadequate at best.

East Germany presents us with a different picture of delinquent youth. East Germany heavily emphasized the role of rehabilitation and a concern for the general welfare of children. Researchers note that as many as 50,000 volunteers worked in the schools and community organizations to help juveniles (Buchholz, 1982, 61). Although specific information on juvenile crime in East Germany is unattainable, there is some suggestion that these rates were far lower there than in West Germany and other industrialized countries. This absence of serious juvenile criminality has been linked to the overall system of socialism that governed the Democratic Republic of Germany. In other words, the guiding philosophy of East Germany emphasized peace, cooperation, education, work, and a general concern for the welfare of all human beings. It has also been suggested that East Germany strictly controlled firearms and drugs, so violent crimes and drug-related offenses were essentially nonexistent. These professions are difficult to confirm or deny. We can, however, presume that the presence of the state in the lives of children had some effect on the rates of troubled teens. This seemingly positive state of affairs concerning crime, however, may have come at the expense of a lower quality of life in other areas.

After 1989, when West and East Germany were reunified, the system of juvenile justice underwent significant changes. The effect of reunification on juvenile delinquency is perhaps best regarded as an integration of the two opposing political systems. In other words, we see many of the same issues now that were noted in West Germany in the 1970s and 1980s, yet we also see the influence of the East German philosophy of child welfare. We will discuss this in more detail. For now, a look at the problem of juvenile crime in contemporary Germany is in order.

The most recent statistical analysis of age and crime in Germany was conducted by the German government using figures from 1993 (Bundeskriminalamt, 1994, 71). Overall, the age breakdown with regard to juvenile crime in Germany is described as follows: children younger than thirteen years of age account for approximately 4 percent of criminal activity; juveniles between the ages of fourteen and seventeen years account for approximately 10 percent and adolescents between the ages of eighteen and twenty years are responsible for approximately 10 percent of all crime as well. Thus, overall, about twenty-five percent of crime in Germany is committed by youthful offenders. Of these offenses, the most frequent are vandalism and fraud (Wolfe, 1996); the most disconcerting are those involving violence.

In the years spanning 1984 to 1998, the number of juvenile suspects in violent incidents in Germany tripled (Supp, 1998), with these numbers showing the greatest increase after reunification. For example, in the 1990s, the number of juvenile suspects in violent crimes rose 600 times in Sachsen, 400 times in Mecklenburg Vorpommem/Brandenburg, and over 200 times in Thurnigen. In addition, violence committed by children against children was significantly higher. Many of these incidents involved such crimes as robbery, extortion, and blackmail in the schoolyards and when children are on the way home from school. Many acts of juvenile violence are more serious and not school related. Some of the most violent and deadly of these juvenile incidents involve violence against foreigners. The extent of this problem in contemporary Germany requires special treatment in this chapter.

CONTRIBUTING FACTORS

Xenophobia and Violence Against Foreigners

Juvenile violence in contemporary Germany assumes a number of forms, but particular attention has been paid to violence against foreigners. Recent statistics regarding youth crime in Germany indicate adolescents as responsible agents in a high percentage of the violent acts committed against foreigners (Viehmann, 1993; Wassermann and Weber, 1993). One approximation (Ostendorf, 1993, 545) estimates that number to be in the range of 70 percent. In other words, of all crimes against foreigners in contemporary Germany, approximately 70 percent are committed by juvenile or youthful offenders. Thus, the high rate of violent acts against foreigners in Germany, as well as the fact that the majority of these offenses are committed by juveniles, makes the issue one of significance for any study of teen violence in Germany today. Questions emerge as to why such acts are being committed and what the government has done to control such hostility.

The reunification of Germany that marked the end of confrontation between opposing political forces of the East and West prompted significant transformations in social relations (Schubarth, 1997, 143) as very different forms of society precipitated, or, perhaps, forced, Germans into new social experiences. The aftermath of such transformation has included a rise in negative attitudes toward foreigners (Otto and Merten, 1993). Such right-wing extremism and violence was for the most part absent in the everyday experiences of East German youth. Although some would attribute this absence to socialist education that promoted friendship and love and respect of others (Buchholz, 1982), the reality was that only about 1 percent (160,000) of the East German population was of non-German origin (Schubarth, 1997, 144). Thus, reunification (and a number of resultant social changes) forced East Germans into more consistent contact with non-German peoples. It is not surprising that many are quick to attribute such negative attitudes toward foreigners and the accompanying violence as an

East German problem. It is perhaps more accurate to say that such attitudes are problems that affect all of Germany (Schubarth, 1997, 143).

The period extending from World War II to reunification has been termed one of "innocence" for the youth of Germany (Breyvogel, 1993). At that time, crimes against foreigners were much less common in both East and West Germany. Beginning in the early 1990s, however, Germany witnessed a significant increase in the extent of these crimes. Several incidents of right-wing violence against foreigners in both East and West German cities (Hoy-erswerda in 1991, Rostock and Molln in 1992, and Solingen in 1993) were responsible for a large number of casualties and attracted attention world-wide. Thus, the reunified Germany became known for its problem of right-wing violence. Some, however, have argued that this form of violence was in fact a problem throughout German history, yet was "covered-up" and, thus, not regarded as such (Breyvogel, 1993).

Nonetheless, the problem of violence against foreigners has become more pronounced in recent years. In 1992, for example, the BfV[1] conducted a study on violent incidents that were linked to right-wing (political) motives. It concluded that in 1992, at least 2,285 violent acts were committed that were attributable to such motives (Breyvogel, 1993). A similar study had been conducted in 1991 by the BKA.[2] Suspects in cases of right-wing crimes were broken down demographically, with the following results: 78 percent of suspects were under twenty-one years of age; 47 percent were between the ages of eighteen and twenty-one; 31 percent were seventeen and under; and only 9 percent were over twenty-five years of age. Further, the study revealed that only 2 to 3 percent of suspects in violent acts with right-wing motives were female. Thus, the problem of violence against foreigners largely appears to be one of young males. Further, the study revealed that 95 percent of such incidents were group incidents (committed with other persons), and 70 percent of violent right-wing crimes were committed by persons living in the same cities as the victims. Overall, then, acts of violence against foreigners in Germany appear to be committed by groups of ado-lescent males who live in close proximity to their victims.

Politically Motivated Violence

Based in part on studies such as those of the BKA and BfV, Breyvogel (1993) has offered a typology of youths who commit acts of violence against foreigners. His typology consists of four types of perpetrator groups. The first group is that of the politically motivated juvenile. Such groups are right-wing extremists or affiliated with right-wing political parties. These youths have clearly defined victims; they know whom they are after and have no problem standing behind their cause in court. In other words, they are proud to be affiliated with such a movement and consider their violence to be in the best interest of their society. Members of this category are often of higher intellect and generally in their late teens or early twenties.

The second group Breyvogel identified has no organizational affiliation. They are rarely identified as having political motives for their actions. Their motives appear to be more strongly related to issues of male aggression and involvement with "action-oriented" peer groups. Within this type are many groups such as skinheads whose primary objective is chauvinistic. In other words, although there may exist a strong racial component to their actions, they are rarely officially identified with political causes. Often members of this category are unemployed and experience problems within the home or at school.

The third type of violent offender is identified as the "negative career" offender. This type of actor often has a long history of involvement in crime, with prior convictions for offenses such as theft and, possibly, violent offenses. These youths are more likely to be victims of violence themselves—at home or in the course of their everyday life. They have no political, racial and ethnic motives. Indeed, there is generally no specific reason for their violence. Their actions are more likely to be the result of everyday interactions or situational factors that may provoke violent acts.

Breyvogel identifies the fourth type of violent actor as the "hanger-on." These juveniles merely "run with others." They have no political, racial or ethnic motives for their actions. They are identified as "socially inconspicuous." In other words, they are searching for a group of peers to "run with" and in the process get involved with groups that are prone to violent acts.

Overall, Breyvogel notes, the population of violent offenders is heterogeneous. There does not appear to be a specific type of individual or group responsible for all violent acts against foreigners. Most of these acts are done in groups or peer groups. Further, a majority are of middle-class status. They range from those who are convinced of their "cause" (the politically motivated) to those who are inconspicuous in their selection of victims. Further, there is substantial variety in the physical appearance of these offenders, ranging from relatively "normal"-looking youths to those who identify with groups such as "skinheads" and present themselves as such.

Several other studies have attempted to discern the extent to which the propensity to violence among German male youth is linked to political motives. One study in particular (Watts, 1997) sheds light on this issue by examining xenophobic attitudes and their correlation to violence in German male youth.

RESPONSES TO THE PROBLEM

Perhaps the best way to understand the role of the government and the sociopolitical views regarding juvenile violence in Germany is through the juvenile justice system and its treatment of juvenile offenders. The system of juvenile justice in Germany—its understanding of juvenile crime and its role—is reflective of the general philosophy of the problem of juvenile crime. In other words, the way in which the government operates with regard to juvenile offenders is indicative of an attitude that promotes prevention rather than punishment or intervention.

Consistent with many other countries, the justice system in Germany includes special provisions for juvenile offenders. Generally the goal of the system is to educate, an emphasis that places responsibility for youths in the hands of both the family and the state. This may be considered a "protection" of the family: parents have a right to care for their children, yet the "national community" has a responsibility to watch over the endeavors of the family (Wolfe, 1996).

There are three age categories under German law that apply to teenage offenders (the fourth category is adult). The first is the child. This category includes children under fourteen years of age and also applies to those over fourteen who have not developed sufficient age appropriate intellectual and moral understanding of the wrongfulness of their actions. Youths falling into this category cannot be held criminally responsible for their actions (Supp, 1998; Wolfe, 1996; Bundesministerium fur Frauen und Jugend, 1994). The second category is that of the juvenile. Youths between the ages of fourteen and eighteen can be held criminally responsible. Nevertheless, youths in this category judged to be "immature" may fall into the first category instead. The third category that applies to youths is the adolescent. This category was not added until 1956, when it was intended to allow youths over age eighteen but under age twenty-one to be tried as juveniles (Wolfe, 1996).

It is the under-fourteen age group where Germany is most concerned with prevention methods. These youths are not held criminally responsible for their actions and are diverted into programs intended to rehabilitate. This effort to rehabilitate marks the core philosophy behind Germany's efforts to reduce later juvenile criminality and violence. Thus, the focus is on youths who may display at-risk behaviors (e.g., petty crimes) and intervention before the individual progresses into more serious activity.

The Youth Welfare Office and Juvenile Court Sanctions

The Youth Welfare Office (YWO) is the primary actor in the rehabilitation process when dealing with troubled youths under the age of fourteen years and those over fourteen years of age judged to be "immature." The YWO is governed by the Youth Welfare Code (YWC), which outlines plans for approaching youths and preventing the escalation of criminal behavior. According to the YWC, which was adopted as the guideline for such intervention around the time of reunification, the Youth Welfare Office has the responsibility of "rescuing" youths from a criminal lifestyle (Supp, 1998).

Although the YWC does not allow for imprisonment of youths, it grants permission to the YWO to intervene as it sees fit. Generally YWO employees, such as psychologists and social workers, meet with the families of troubled youths to formulate plans. The ultimate goal is for the child to remain with her or his parents if at all possible. Thus, the family plays a decisive role in the treatment plan. The YWO provides for different intervention and prevention strategies depending on the individual in question. In other words, one of the key factors in the revised law dealing with juveniles is the emphasis on different plans of action formulated to fit the specific needs of the family and child at risk.

In general, Germany's juvenile justice system aims at prevention rather than punishment and focuses on individual needs rather than sanctioning based on severity of the criminal act. If, for example, problems exist within the family that may interfere with the youth's ability to resist criminal activity, measures may be taken to assist the entire family (e.g., through counseling). Thus, the system attempts to draw on the family, the community, and the state both to prevent juvenile crime and to intervene before the child's behavior becomes too serious. This system of juvenile justice in Germany has been in place for only a limited period of time, so it is difficult to ascertain its effectiveness.

CONCLUSION

Our review of juvenile crime and violence in Germany led us to conclude that generally teen criminality and violence are as much on the rise as in many other industrial countries. Although different historical epochs have encountered different types and different degrees of juvenile crime, they all seem to show a general increase in such acts.

In our exploration of one of the more interesting and thought-provoking aspects of this general issue, violence against foreigners, we noted that a majority of these acts are committed by juvenile offenders. This finding is important in that it stresses the different types of crime and different motives for committing offenses that may be present in juveniles as opposed to their adult counterparts. We have not attempted to offer any sophisticated explanation for acts of violence against foreigners by German youth. Rather, we hope to encourage researchers to ask certain questions that we have not answered: Is the problem in Germany truly worse than in other countries? If not, why does it attain more exposure? Further, researchers may wish to explore the possible motivations (e.g., economic, psychological, sociological) for these acts of violence against foreigners. Is there a difference between German youth and non-German youth? Is this difference distinguishable as an attitude against foreigners that is shared by (some) German youth? If so, how does such an attitude compare to those of non-German youths?

Thus, we have drawn attention to one aspect of German youth violence that we feel will be of particular interest to students of contemporary violence. It incorporates not only the issue of violence but other important issues of our time, such as racism and xenophobia. We certainly do not wish to convey that this type of violence by German youth is, in fact, the *only* significant form of violence in the German youth culture. Nor do we mean to suggest that it is more prominent among German youth than non-German youth. We feel, however, that Germany is perhaps the ideal country in which to explore such an issue and strongly encourage research into the issue of violence against foreigners in both Germany and other countries, for it is an abiding problem in most of the world today.

Our glance at the juvenile law and court system of Germany was intended to draw attention to aspects of the German government's method of handling juvenile delinquency that may be different from that in many, or some, other countries today. In general, we found an emphasis on prevention and the role of the family in reforming troubled youth. That is, Germany's approach is to treat youth before their criminality escalates. Again, we encourage research as to whether this approach is truly different than in other countries and, if so, to what extent. We know, for example, that the United States claims as its primary goal the rehabilitation of juveniles rather than punishment. Thus, Germany's claim to prevent and rehabilitate provides material for further investigation into the confrontation of juvenile crime and violence across the world. In general, although our exploration is somewhat limited, we have provided material for further exploration in and contemplation of the issue of juvenile violence.

NOTES

1. The BfV is a government research organization that generally investigates actions that harm people or interfere with their rights as citizens. It can be roughly translated as the Office for the Protection of the Constitution.

2. The BKA is a government research organization that investigates crimes of varying sorts. It can be roughly translated as the Office of Federal Criminology.

REFERENCES

Breyvogel, W. (1993). *Lust auf Randale: Jugendliche Gewalt gegen Fremde*. Bonn: J.H.W. Dietz Nachfolger GmbH.

Buchholz, E. (1982). The German Democratic Republic. In V. Lorne Stewart (Ed.), *Justice and troubled children around the world*. New York: NYU Press.

Bundeskriminalamt. (1994). *Polizeiliche Kriminalstatistik Bundesrepublik Deutschland Berichtsjahr 1993*. Wiesbaden: Bundesdruckerie. [Bundeskriminalamt is the "Federal Criminal Office" in Germany.]

Bundesministerium fur Frauen und Jugend (1994). *Kinder-und Jugendhilfgesetz (Achtes Buch Sozialgesetzbuch)* (6th ed.).

Johnson, E. (1995). *Urbanization and crime: Germany, 1871–1914*. Cambridge: Cambridge University Press.

Knolker, H., Schuler-Springorum, H., and Nissen, G. (1981). Federal Republic of Germany. In V. Lorne Stewart (Ed.), *Justice and troubled children around the world*. New York: NYU Press.

Ostendorf, H. (1993). Jugend und Gewalt/Moglichkeiten und Grenzen der Konfliktregelung. *Strafverteidiger*, *13*, 545–548.

Otto, H., and Merten, R. (1993). *Rechtsradikale Gewalt im verelnigten Deutschland.* Opladen: Leske and Budrich.

Schubarth, W. (1997). Xenophobia among East German youth. In H. Kurthen, W. Bergmann, and R. Erb (Eds.), *Antisemitism and xenophobia in Germany after unification.* New York: Oxford University Press.

Stachura, P. (1989). *The Weimar Republic and the younger proletariat: An economic and social analysis.* New York: St. Martin's Press.

Supp, B. (1998). Die Kleinen Monster. *Der Spiegel, 15,* 127–141.

Viehmann, H. (1993). Was machen wir mit unseren jugendlichen Gewalttatern? *Zeitschrift fur Rechtspolitik, 26,* 81–84.

Wasserman, R., and Weber, V. (1993). Soil das Jugendstrafrecht verscharft werden? *Focus, 26,* 199.

Watts, M. (1997). *Xenophobia in united Germany: Generations, modernization, and ideology.* New York: St. Martin's Press.

Wolfe, N. T. (1996). Germany. In D. Shoemaker (Ed.), *International handbook on juvenile justice.* Westport, CT: Greenwood Press.

5

ISRAEL

Giora Rahav

PERCEPTIONS OF TEEN VIOLENCE

Although there is a prevailing notion in Israel that juvenile violence is widespread, increasing, and becoming more and more severe, there are very few figures to support or verify this belief. Police records are the obvious source of information. Unfortunately, they seem to be quite limited in the information they can supply. One reason is that these records are the end products of a complex social and organizational process. Consequently, only a small number of offenses are recorded, and these are not a representative sample of the whole. This problem afflicts all police records but is even more serious when we try to isolate juvenile records, because this can be done only for records with known (or suspected) offenders. In Israel the problem is even more difficult because of several changes in the age definition of minority (the legal definition of being a juvenile) and of criminal responsibility. Currently, a person is considered a minor until the age of eighteen, and the age of criminal responsibility is twelve. Also there have been changes in the handling and recording of juvenile offenses.

CURRENT TRENDS IN TEEN VIOLENCE

The number of juveniles arrested or referred to the Juvenile Probation Service cannot be compared over long periods because the information available in police statistics is rather limited. Table 5.1 presents the number and

Table 5.1
Violent Offenses with Juvenile Involvement

	Absolute Numbers				Rates		
Offense	1990	1997	Growth		1990	1997	Growth
Against Life	286	105	0.37		52	17	0.33
Against Body	1,100	1,332	1.21		199	214	1.08
All Juvenile	9,307	11,053	1.19		1,685	1,777	1.05
Percent Violent	13.2	11.5	0.87				

rates of offenses against life and against human body in which juveniles were involved as suspects for the years 1990 and 1997. (Offenses against life are mostly homicide, attempted homicide or threats to life. Offenses against body are mostly assaults.) The rates were calculated per 100,000 in the twelve to eighteen age group in the population. The table seems to show a sharp decline in the number and rate of offenses against life. This may reflect the fact that in the years 1988 through 1990, a considerable proportion of the offenses against life were "stone throwing with nationalist background," an offense that characterized the Arab *intifada* in the occupied areas, but has had little presence since then. However, since the majority of the violent offenses are offenses against body, this barely affects the overall picture, which is one of considerable stability in the rate of interpersonal juvenile violence.

In order to assess whether these rates are high or low we may compare Israel with other countries. Table 5.2 presents the proportion of violent offenses by juveniles (minors) in 1995 for the major categories of violent offenses for ten European and North American countries. These figures show that Israel's juveniles were involved in a rather small fraction of the recorded violent offenses (about 9 percent of murders, 6 percent of serious assaults, and 12 percent of robberies). Israel ranks eighth, second, and first, respectively, among these countries (from low to high).

Any reference to these figures must be very cautious, since the figures may be misleading: a high rate of adult offenders automatically decreases the rate of juveniles. Despite this deficiency in the data, I could not find a better set of official statistics. This may serve as a warning concerning the meaning and use of official crime statistics. Obviously, some other type of data seems desirable.

Death rates from murder are generally low among adolescents. During the years 1989 through 1992 (these are the most recent figures), the murder death rate for the age group fifteen to nineteen years averaged about 4.2

Table 5.2
Percent Juvenile among Violent Offenders, 1995

Country	Murder	Assault	Robbery
Austria	4.10	0.80	23.70
Canada	10.70	15.40	35.50
Finland	7.00	21.60	43.20
France	7.10	12.20	30.90
Germany	6.00	17.70	32.30
Israel	9.30	6.10	11.80
Netherlands	8.00	15.00	25.00
Sweden	16.00	—	48.00
Switzerland	6.90	11.70	34.90
United States	5.30	14.70	32.30

Sources: Interpol (1995) and Israeli Police (1995).

per 100,000, compared with twelve to seventeen in the United States (Snyder, Sickmund, and Poe-Yamagata, 1996; Anderson, Ventura, Peters, and Mathews, 1998; Central Bureau of Statistics, 1996a, 1996b). A comparison with European countries was not possible for that age group: UN data are published for the age groups five to fourteen (which is much lower) and fifteen to twenty-four (which is considerably higher). But the rates for these age groups are easily calculated. The rates in the children's group ages five to fourteen are 1.5, 0.4, 0.1, and 0.2 for the United States, Germany, the Netherlands, and Israel, respectively. For the adolescents and young adults (ages fifteen to twenty-four) these rates were 13.9, 1.4, 1.7, and 2.0. Thus, the juvenile homicide rates in Israel are somewhat high compared to those of European countries but an order of magnitude lower than those of the United States.

Surveys

For assessment of the prevalence, circumstances, and characteristics of violence and of violent individuals, a survey is often the choice of preference. Very few studies have assessed the extent and forms of juvenile violence in Israel by means of surveys, either of victimization or of self-reported violence. Frenkel, Horowitz, and Yinon (1990) carried out one of the early studies. They sought to assess juvenile violence by several methods (police files, observation, and surveys) and conducted several focused, small-scale studies in several cities, in classes (grades 10 and 11) from different types of high schools, ranging from academic to vocational, as well as among several groups of juveniles who had dropped out of school. They asked about a wide range of violence victimization during the past three months. The percentage reporting being slapped or kicked in school ranged from 5 percent (girls, academic school) to 23 percent (boys, vocational school) and 40 percent (dropout boys). Up to 15 percent of the boys in school and 35 percent of the dropped-out boys reported being "savagely beaten," and up to 4 percent of the boys in school and 26 percent of the dropouts reported being knifed. Comparable reports were provided for other social settings, but no overall measure was provided. This lack of an overall indicator of violence across situations and youth types, as well as other methodological problems, makes this study hard to compare with others. However, some of the substantive conclusions are worth noting. First, the order of violence across situations was from dropouts, through vocational schools, to academic schools, and boys were always higher than girls. The most violent settings were the school, the neighborhood, and soccer fields.

The Dgani and Dgani (1990) survey, which was conducted at about the same time, was much more limited in its scope. It focused on grades 5, 7, 8, and 10 of the Tel Aviv public schools (all present students) and examined the manifestations and contexts of violence. One of the major products of this survey was a series of maps of the spatial distribution of violence across the city. The survey also yielded a series of tables presenting the distribution of the types of aggressive and violent behaviors across school types and grades. Thus, even if we limit ourselves to incidents of actual (physical) violence, a rather grim picture emerges. Nearly half of the students (47 percent) reported being beaten seriously during the previous year, over 8 percent reported that they were injured in such incidents, and over five percent reported that they were injured with a stick, a knife, or a similar instrument.

From an epidemiologic viewpoint, the most important study so far has been by Harel, Kani, and Rahav (1997). It was based on a representative sample of the students in grades 6 through 11 of the public schools in the Jewish sector (Arab schools were sampled only in the second wave of the survey, still in the initial stages of analysis). Thus, it represents a major part of the school-attending juvenile population. It was a part of a collaborative study of juvenile health behavior that was carried out in twenty-three countries. Thus, many of the indicators used in this study are available for a considerable number of other countries as well (for a description, see King, Wold, Tudor-Smith, and Harel, 1996).

The widest definition was the answer to a questionnaire item indicating being bullied at least once during the school year. Over 50 percent of the students were bullied once or more. The figures show a distinct difference between boys and girls within each age group, with boys indicating considerably higher involvement in violence. Another clear trend is one of declining involvement in bullying as age increases. The rate of bullying victims declines from 69 percent of the boys in grades 6 and 7 to 48 percent in grades 10 and 11, and from 53 percent of the girls in grades 6 and 7 to 29 percent in grades 10 and 11. A rather similar picture emerges if the criterion variable is participation in bullying others, although the percentages are somewhat lower (among boys in grades 6 and 7, 64 percent, and among girls in grades 10 and 11, 23 percent).

Because bullying includes a wide range of behaviors, a stricter criterion for violence may be involvement in physical fights. The percentage of students who reported involvement in physical fights once or more during the past twelve months ranged from 80 percent to 57 percent of the boys in grades 6 and 7 and 10 and 11 (respectively), and from 32 percent to 17 percent in the same grades for girls. That is, the involvement in physical fights declines sharply with age, and at each age it is considerably lower among girls than among boys.

During the school year, 7.9 percent of the students reported being hit with a stick, a knife, or some other object. Like other indicators, this percentage declines with age, from 15 percent of the boys and 7 percent of the girls in grades 6 and 7 to 6 percent of the boys and 5 percent of the girls in grades 10 and 11. The gender difference is maintained, although in this indicator it tends to narrow with age. Finally, 9 percent of the students reported involvement in physical fights (during the past twelve months) in which they were injured and needed some medical attention. Here again the declining trend with age is very clear among boys (from 16 percent in grades 6 and 7 to 4 percent in grades 10 and 11), but much less among girls (where the decline is from 5.3 percent to 4.2 percent).

A Comparative View

Taken together, these figures (which are merely some of the highlights of the report) may leave an impression of a very violent society, at least insofar as adolescents are concerned. However, this conclusion may deserve some further thought. These figures represent a situation that justifies, perhaps requires, some form of intervention. In that sense they *are* high. However, if our evaluation of rates of violence as "high" or "low" is based on comparative assessment, then the picture may be quite different.

Table 5.3 presents the percentage of the surveyed students who reported being bullied once or more during the past year. The countries are ordered by the percentage of girls age eleven, but the ranking by the percentages in the other columns would be rather similar. Israel is listed in the eighth

Table 5.3

Percentage of Students Reporting That at Least Once During the Past Year They Were Bullied at School, by Country, Age and Gender

Country	Age 11		Age 15	
	Boys	Girls	Boys	Girls
Austria	53.5	36.5	24.9	10.5
Belgium (Fl.)	60.4	54.2	32.9	20.7
Belgium (Fr.)	76.7	66.7	55.0	47.2
Canada	39.1	30.0	20.0	18.5
Czech Rep.	55.5	52.4	43.6	30.0
Denmark	62.6	59.6	64.3	50.8
Estonia	71.1	56.0	61.2	52.4
Finland	56.8	46.7	27.2	21.8
France	58.1	63.4	41.1	31.0
Germany	66.3	53.0	28.4	15.5
Greenland	77.3	71.7	43.5	47.1
Hungary	59.2	47.3	37.3	29.2
Israel	67.3	54.8	38.9	35.3
Latvia	58.4	49.4	42.5	45.1
Lithuania	55.9	59.7	53.6	33.9
N. Ireland	40.0	23.0	19.6	16.7
Norway	40.2	33.1	36.0	16.7
Poland	48.8	32.5	30.0	23.2
Russia	75.3	67.9	74.5	58.0
Scotland	29.9	30.7	26.3	20.5
Slovakia	50.7	39.2	46.0	38.0
Sweden	20.4	16.5	15.5	13.2
Wales	37.7	31.2	17.5	11.4

Source: King et al. (1996).

position (its rank would be fifth if ranking was done by the percentage of boys rather than girls). In a list of twenty-three countries, this means that Israel is above the average, but not very much higher (the ranking by percentage of boys would put Israel as the lowest in the top quartile).

In most countries the percentage of girls is lower than that of boys (boys report being bullied more frequently than girls). Another general observation is that in most countries, the percentages at age fifteen are lower than those at age eleven. That is, involvement in bullying tends to decline with age. Israel conforms well with these generalizations: the involvement in bullying declines with age, it is higher among boys than among girls, and the gender gap tends to narrow with age. Bullying is a very wide—perhaps too wide—definition of juvenile violence. However, the picture emerging from the other criteria used for the comparative view is quite similar (Harel et al., 1997).

CONTRIBUTING FACTORS

Age

One of the most prevalent explanations for youth violence is youth itself. Childhood and adolescence are considered periods in which socialization is still going on, with the clear implication that children and adolescents are not adequately socialized. This notion alone may provide an explanation for the repeated finding that the prevalence of violence declined with age. However, this global process provides an explanation only for the general epidemiologic question. It does not explain why certain individuals, or certain subpopulations, are more prone to violence than others.

Another form of the socialization model suggests that the age of adolescence is particularly stressful. Children have to cope within a short period with rapid physiological changes, as well as with changing, and often unclear, role expectations. Some authors emphasize that at that age, students develop many of the requirements for personal independence, yet they are obliged to live in a highly controlled environment. Presumably these stresses find their release in aggressive tendencies and violent behavior.

However, there is another explanation, this one claiming that the age trend is mostly a research artifact. According to this model, the institutional system (which served as the basis for sampling juveniles in all the participating countries in the World Health Organization study) slowly identifies the most violence-prone individuals and gets rid of them. In other words, the most violent juveniles drop out of the school system (King et al., 1996). The age trend, according to this model, is merely a reflection of the long period to achieve the desired selection.

Cultural Divisions

One of the most significant divisions in Israeli society is between the Jewish majority and the Arab minority. This distinction is pervasive and generally encompasses all spheres of life: geographic locations, religion, language, educational attainment, occupational structure, status of women, and so on. On top of that, the ethnic (and in many cases ideological) identification of the Arabs with the Arab nations, with which Israel has had a long series of wars, leads to many mutual suspicions between Jews and Arabs. These conditions seem ideal for the emergence of a subculture of violence, which stems from the structural conditions as well as from the cultural heritage of the Arabs. Blood feuds and murders "for the honor of the family" were rather frequent in Israel's early years. And although these forms of violence have considerably diminished, they are still evident. Under these conditions, it is no surprise that violence rates are much higher among Arabs than among the Jewish population.

Table 5.4 shows murder rates by age and sex in the Jewish and the Arab populations. In almost every age and sex comparison, the Arabs' murder rate is much higher than that of the Jews. With the exception of the lowest group among girls (ten to fourteen years old), the Arab rates are 2.2 to 2.6 higher than those of Jews. The figures should be interpreted with caution, since they are of death rates, and thus reflect victimization more than violent

Table 5.4
Murder Rates by Age Group, Sex, and Ethnicity, 1984–1994

		Ages 10-14	Ages 15-17	Ages 18-21
Males	Jews	0.30	0.87	2.87
	Arabs	1.00	2.34	6.79
Females	Jews	0.32	0.46	1.33
	Arabs	0.17	1.23	2.89

Source: Israeli Police (1995).

behaviors. However, most of the Arab victims were murdered by other Arabs, so interethnic violence cannot explain these differences. Here again, a brief comparison with the United States is instructive: in the United States, the death rate from murder among fifteen- to seventeen-year-olds was 17.1 in 1997 (Anderson et al., 1998).

Juvenile Probation Service (1994) statistics convey a similar message: about 33 percent of the new male cases referred to the service for violent offenses in 1993 were Arab, a clear overrepresentation; their percentage in the relevant age groups was less than 22 percent (overrepresentation of 1.44). Among females, the picture was quite different: only eight of the ninety-seven new female cases were of Arab origin (an overrepresentation of the Jewish girls of 4.02). Thus, both types of official data suggest that Arab males show a considerably higher involvement in violence than their Jewish counterparts. (It should be emphasized at this point that most of the violence is not directly associated with the Jewish-Arab conflict and that most of the violence of each group is carried on within that group.)

The ethnic factor did not find expression in most surveys. Both the Harel et al. (1997) and the Horowitz and Frenkel (1990) surveys sampled only the Jewish population. Sherer (1991) studied norms and values held by street-corner youths and found that Arab boys held more aggressive norms. The major survey reporting Arab juvenile violence was the Dgani and Dgani (1990) survey. Because the survey covered all schools in Tel Aviv (including the ones in the Jaffa area, where most of the Arab population of Tel Aviv resides), it encompassed a number of Arab schools. In their tables we find that Arab students reported being hit by others about as often as students in Jewish high schools did. However, Arab students reported more often being beaten by a group of other students (16.5 percent versus 10.1 percent in Jewish nonreligious schools), being injured by violence (12.9 percent versus 5.3 percent), and being injured with a knife or a stick (12.6 percent versus 4.0 percent). Although each of these studies suffers from considerable methodological problems, the overall picture seems to be consistent with a variety of informal impressions and reports about the prevalence of violence among the Arab juveniles. It is still unknown how much of the difference between ethnic groups may be accounted for by the social and economic differences.

Sherer (1991) provides a partial explanation to the higher violence among Arab youths. Comparing Jewish and Arab youths, high school students, and dropouts on several questionnaires, he found that Arab dropouts were the most aggressive group, while Jewish dropouts were more adept at manipulation.

Another important distinction in Israel, this time only among the Jewish population, is between the Ashkenazi and Sephardi groups—those, respectively, whose origin was in Europe and America and those whose origin was in the Middle East and North Africa. This difference is not only in type of cultural background of the immigrants (mostly the parents or grandparents of today's youth), but is strongly associated with the type and level of educational and occupational attainment, socioeconomic status, attitude toward religious tradition, and a variety of other social characteristics. It is not surprising, therefore, that this variable, or its operationalization in terms of parental country of origin, is often mentioned as a correlate of violence. Official statistics do not allow this type of conclusion because they do not provide the rate of arrest for specific offense categories by country of origin. The surveys, however, tend to check it. Thus, Frenkel and Horowitz (1990) show that juveniles of Asian-African origins tend to have higher scores on scales of macho values, justification of use of violence, exposure to violence, and actual participation in violent behavior. In contrast, Harel et al. (1997) did not find significant differences in violence between the origin groups. The significance of ethnicity is not clear for two reasons. First, its association with violence was not adequately tested. Second, the differences that were found between ethnic groups may be interpreted in terms of cultural background and subculture of violence, as well as in terms of socioeconomic structure, availability of legitimate resources, and open (or blocked) mobility channels.

A reference to ethnicity or to cultural background in Israel of the mid- and late 1990s cannot ignore the massive immigration from the former Soviet Union, which started in 1989. Adolescents from this group comprise about 8 percent of the ten- to nineteen-year-old age group. This may not seem a high percentage, but the visibility of this group is enhanced by the fact that Israel is a highly segregated society in which the most fertile groups (particularly Arabs and ultraorthodox Jews) tend to live in segregated communities and neighborhoods and have their own schools. As a result, the new immigrants comprise a significantly larger proportion of the nonorthodox Jews. This group is distinct because it tends to maintain much of its culture (this holds for the adults much more than for children and adolescents), including language and various cultural institutions. Unlike traditional immigrants, they tend to be well educated and to have a background of upper- and middle-class occupations (it is estimated that 40 percent to 50 percent have a background in scientific, technical, managerial and professional occupations). Thus, this group tends to move rapidly into the middle class. Yet like any other group of immigrants, they include a significant proportion of individuals who do not adjust to the new society. Thus, it seems that while the majority of juveniles of this group tend to be well adjusted and among the better controlled and least violent of their age group, there is a minority of unadjusted youths who are highly involved in violent behavior (Harel et al., 1997; Advisory Committee, 1996).

In a recent draft report to the Knesset's committee on juvenile violence, the Advisory Committee reports that despite the absence of quantitative data, it seems that the recent immigration from the former Soviet Union has brought with it some extreme forms of violence. Some of these forms were formerly unknown in Israel, including highly organized gang activity and systematic extortion. The committee states that while it is impossible to assess the extent of the problem, the impression is that this is a non-negligible phenomenon. However, the Harel et al. (1997) report, which tested the effect of immigration status, did not find a consistent effect. New immigrants were more likely to be victims of frequent bullying, but they were less likely to be involved in physical fighting and to be hit with a stick, stone, or a knife. Consequently, the overall indicator of violence victimization did not differentiate between the groups.

Class and Socioeconomic Tensions

It is generally assumed that lower-strata adolescents, particularly males who have dropped out of school or come from multiproblem families, are a highly violent group. The small number of quantitative studies does not allow a clear confirmation of this assertion, but seems to provide limited support. The Frenkel, Horowitz, and Yinon (1990) study made a point of including such juveniles in its sample. And indeed, they found that on each indicator of involvement in violence, this group ranked highest. The Dgani and Dgani (1990) report did not classify individuals by socioeconomic status. However, the strength of their work lies in their mapping of the spread of violence over the city. These maps show quite clearly that the rate of violence was much higher in southern neighborhoods, particularly those characterized by a high rate of social problems. The third large-scale survey of violence, by Harel et al. (1997), used a single indicator of socioeconomic status: economic condition of the family as assessed by the subjects. This indicator was not consistently related to violence, either because of the weakness of this indicator or because only students participated in the survey, thereby underrepresenting the most deprived strata.

Mass Media

Israeli adolescents, like their counterparts in other countries, spend considerable time watching television. The WHO survey (King et al., 1996) shows that Israeli children are typically in the top half in the percentage devoting four hours or more per day to television and about the middle of the range in the percentage watching videos at least four hours a week and the percentage playing computer games at least four hours a week. It is not surprising, therefore, that there is a concern that the violent scenes, which are so common in commercial television, may affect children's behavior. Despite this concern, little has been done to test this possible effect in Israel, and opinions are usually based on either intuition or American studies. The major exception is a recent study by Lemish (1997, 1998), which examined the effect of watching World Wrestling Federation programs. She reports the presence of a discernible tendency to imitate the behavior presented in these shows, both playfully and seriously. One of the most surprising findings Lemish (1998) presents is that despite the emphasis on masculine, macho-style behavior in the shows, significant proportions of the girls questioned reported watching the shows and imitating behaviors (although these proportions were much lower than those of boys).

RESPONSES TO THE PROBLEM

While police sometimes record offenses committed by younger children, their general tendency is to let the social welfare departments handle these cases. Some of the juvenile cases are handled informally, without court intervention. In the 1980s this was a small proportion of the juvenile cases (presumably many minor incidents were handled even more informally by the officer on the spot). As a rule, these cases were not referred to the juvenile probation service. However, since the end of the 1980s, police have had to refer these cases as well to the juvenile probation service.

CONCLUSION

The extent of juvenile violence in Israel is somewhat high compared to European countries but far lower than in the United States. Despite the paucity of data, this general observation seems to be consistent with the information derived from a variety of sources. The only data that allow some reference to temporal developments are official statistics. These statistics, which reflect only the most extreme forms of violence, seem to suggest that the rate of juvenile violence increased only mildly over the past decade. This observation is in sharp contrast to the common opinion that juvenile violence has increased dramatically. The discrepancy between the data and public opinion may reflect the poverty of the data, but I think that there are more important sources. First, over the past decade, the population of juveniles in Israel increased by about 25 percent. This is a high rate compared to most other industrialized societies and is a result of the presence of several highly fertile groups (particularly Arabs and ultraorthodox Jews) as well as the mass immigration from the former Soviet Union. At the same time, mass media went through a process of rapid proliferation with the introduction of cable TV and local news media. These factors mean that even with a constant rate of violence, the absolute number increased rather quickly, and the exposure to such incidents increased rapidly. The introduction of several extreme or formerly unknown forms of violence (e.g., WWF-style fights or cases of organized extortion), even if they are merely isolated cases, serves to illustrate to the public the fact that juvenile violence has increased dramatically.

The bulk of the problem of juvenile violence seems to comprise two major parts. First, there is widespread, very common, perhaps even playful violence. This phenomenon seems to characterize mostly the lower age groups. It seems to be rather evenly spread over all Israeli society (as it is in many other countries) and to be determined largely by age and sex. This form of violence may be explained by several models, the most common of which is socialization effects, but the alternative model, suggesting a selection and research artifact, cannot be ignored.

The second part of the juvenile violence problem is focused in those locations of the social system that tend to be selected out into the social periphery; school dropouts, the lowest socioeconomic strata, and multiproblem families are various aspects of this part of the population. These youths are often referred to as unattached, as they tend not to take part in the major institutional settings of society: well-organized families, school or work, and (in Israel) military service. Apparently the violence in these strata is considerably more widespread, and its forms tend to be much more extreme than the violence found in the main body of youths. By definition, this subpopulation is extremely hard to locate and interview and has therefore been little studied. Yet judging from a variety of local, sometimes anecdotal reports, they seem to be the hard core of most persistently violent individuals and are often associated with criminal behavior of various forms (including drug use).

It is unfortunate that certain groups, which may be described in terms of cultural background, socioeconomic resources, or religious beliefs, tend to include disproportionate numbers of individuals and families from the social periphery. Consequently, it is very difficult, and perhaps impossible, to decide which of their characteristics are the most significant in the causation of violence.

REFERENCES

Advisory Committee to the Parliamentary Investigative Committee on Juvenile Violence. (1996). *Summary of the committee's work.* Tel Aviv: Elem and Forum on Children and Juvenile Issues, School of Social Work, Tel Aviv University.

Anderson, Robert N., Ventura, Stephanie J., Peters, Kimberly D., and Mathews, T. J. (1998). Births and deaths: United States, July 1996–June 1997. *Monthly Vital Statistics Report, 46* (12), 1–7.

Barash, Miriam, and Mirski, Yulia. (1995). *Behavior problems among immigrant juveniles in the former Soviet Union in Karmiel.* Jerusalem: Falk Institute. (in Hebrew)

Central Bureau of Statistics. (1996a). *Statistical abstracts of Israel.* Jerusalem: Author.

Central Bureau of Statistics. (1996b). *Cause of death statistics.* Jerusalem: Author.

Dgani, Avi, and Dgani, Rina. (1990). *Violence among the school walls: A phenomenon and its dimensions in the education system and the social-urban space of Tel-Aviv–Jaffa.* Tel Aviv: Geocartographia. (in Hebrew)

Frenkel, Eva, and Horowitz, Tamar, with Yinon, Yoel. (1990). *Patterns of juvenile violence.* Jerusalem: Henrietta Szald Institute. (in Hebrew)

Harel, Yossi, Kani, Dafna, and Rahav, Giora. (1997). *Youth in Israel: Social welfare, health and risk behaviors in a cross-national perspective.* Jerusalem: Joint-Brookdale Institute. (in Hebrew)

Interpol (International Criminal Police Organization). (1995). *International crime statistics.* Lyon, France: Author.

Israel Police. (1995). *Annual report.* Jerusalem: Police Headquarters. (in Hebrew)

Juvenile Probation Service. (1994). *Minors in care of the juvenile probation service, 1993.* Jerusalem: Ministry of Welfare and Central Library on Social Work. (in Hebrew)

King, Alan, Wold, Bente, Tudor-Smith, Chris, and Harel, Yossi. (1996). *The health of youth: A cross-national survey.* WHO Regional Publications, European Series, No. 69.

Lemish, Dafna. (1997). The school as a wrestling arena: The modelling of a television series. *Communication, 22,* 395–418.

Lemish, Dafna. (1998). Girls can wrestle too: Gender differences in the consumption of a television wrestling series. *Sex Roles, 38,* 833–849.

Sherer, Moshe. (1990). Criminal activity among Jewish and Arab Youth in Israel. *International Journal of Intercultural Relations, 14,* 529–548.

Sherer, Moshe. (1991). Peer group norms among Jewish and Arab juveniles in Israel. *Criminal Justice and Behavior, 18,* 267–286.

Snyder, Howard N., Sickmund, Melissa, and Poe-Yamagata, Eileen. (1996). *Juvenile offenders and victims: 1996 update on violence.* Washington, DC: Office of Juvenile Justice and Delinquency Prevention.

United Nations. (1997). *United Nations demographic yearbook.* New York: Author.

6

ITALY

Anna Constanza Baldry

PERCEPTIONS OF TEEN VIOLENCE

Because of its relatively low delinquency rate, Italy as a whole has not viewed teen violence as a major issue. It has been primarily concerned with its economic well-being. Therefore, its priorities have been largely on dealing with issues of unemployment and poverty. Delinquency is seen as a result of juvenile hardship. When teen violence occurs, it is believed to have been committed by foreigners. Perceptions vary somewhat by region, reflected in the fact that there are few delinquency prevention initiatives in the south. The northern and central regions of the country, in contrast, are very much involved in the development of a variety of programs, thus reflecting their philosophy of promoting the welfare of juveniles and the prevention of juvenile delinquency.

CURRENT TRENDS IN TEEN VIOLENCE

Rome, October 1997. A boy suddenly opens the windows of a classroom and points a gun at a teacher sitting at her desk. He shouts and insults her and then he shoots three times. The gun was not real, but the terror was.

Brindisi, November 1997. A fifteen-year-old girl is invited by a group of same-age peers to have something to drink. They make her drink, and they kidnap her. Then they bring her to an isolated place and rape her. Subsequently the police find and arrest eight boys all between the ages of fourteen and seventeen.

Bolzano, February 1998. Three sixteen-year-old boys threaten at knifepoint a fourteen-year-old girl, forcing her to undress in front of them.

Violence by teenagers has always been a subject of public concern, but the question of analysis, prevention, and intervention has only recently become the focus of governmental initiatives and attracted the attention of the mass media. Independent programs and laws have been implemented that, although they do not directly address teen violence, deal with young delinquency and the promotion of the welfare of juveniles for the prevention of violence. Projects to tackle the problems and hardships of disadvantaged young people have been only locally developed; it is only in the past few years that the government has established new guidelines and laws to promote the welfare of children and adolescents.

Teen violence is a broad concept that includes violent actions perpetrated against people, as well as acts of vandalism.

The overlap of teen violence with juvenile delinquency is broad. In the Italian juvenile justice system, the age of criminal responsibility is fourteen; young people ages fourteen to eighteen who commit a crime are judged by a special court for juveniles (Tribunale per i Minorenni), which has existed since 1934. Even when juveniles turn nineteen but committed the crime at the age of eighteen or younger, they are still judged by the special court for minors (De Leo and Scardaccione, 1991). However, if any new crime is committed when over age eighteen, the regular court judges them. The age limit for criminal responsibility was increased in the nineteenth century. At the beginning of the century, children committing a crime at the age of ten could be convicted. (In some European countries, including England, this still applies.) This extension of the age limit of criminal responsibility is a reflection of the acknowledgment that criminalizing children ages ten to thirteen is not effective because at that age, children are not aware of the consequences of their actions. In addition, this increase is also a reflection of the extension of the adolescent phase. In comparison with other European or North American countries, young people in Italy live longer with their parents, often until they get married and certainly long after they turn eighteen. This is due both to economic constraints and to unemployment but also to the central role of the family in Italy (Palmonari, 1996). The increase in the age at which teens leave school has also extended the preadolescent and adolescent phase.

According to Bandini, Gatti, Marugo, and Verde (1991), the adolescent phase has changed during the last decade. Young people previously were involved in political movements and campaigns, and some even in terrorist groups. Subsequently their social and political involvement became more oriented toward practical issues, such as school and university matters or unemployment. Therefore, during the 1970s and 1980s they were actively

Table 6.1
Violent Crimes Reported, Committed by Minors, Ages Twelve to Eighteen

	Crimes against the Person[1]	Crimes against the Person[2]	Crimes against Life[3]	Crimes against Personal Safety[4]	Sexual Crimes
1986	3,036	15.39	165	2,644	227
1987	3,268	15.37	179	2,830	259
1988	4,147	16.91	221	3,583	343
1989	4,362	14.98	251	3,848	263
1990	5,989	14.59	292	5,384	313
1991	6,952	15.46	339	6,330	283
1992	7,504	16.75	317	6,742	445
1993	7,638	17.61	257	6,914	467
1994	7,860	17.73	244	7,586	414
1995	8,086	17.56	221	7,865	486
1996	8,481	19.28	250	7,792	439

Notes: [1]Including crimes against life, personal safety, and sexual crimes; [2]Percentage of all crimes committed by juveniles; [3]Homicide and attempted homicide; [4]Personal injury, brawl, and assault.

Source: ISTAT (1994, 1995, 1996); Occhiogrosso (1994).

campaigning on these issues, but in the 1990s, as they themselves became personally affected by unemployment and political instability, they suffered a loss of identity and active involvement. This has led, according to De Leo (1997), to an increase in the use of drugs and alcohol by adolescents.

One of the problems of teen violence is that of definition and measurement. There is obviously a substantial overlap between violence and delinquency, although not all forms of violence are criminal acts (either because they are not reported or detected or because they are not serious enough), and not all forms of crimes include violence (such as possession of drugs, theft, or burglary). In this respect, it is difficult to have a clear and precise description of the prevalence and incidence of teen violence in Italy.[1] In addition, Italy is divided into twenty-one regions. Each region is locally administered, and culturally and socially there are many differences from one region to another in terms of the rate of teen violence and preventive initiatives (Fadiga, 1994).

The criminal records collected by the police and the courts are published yearly by the National Institute of Statistics (ISTAT), although data are usually published only about two years later (see Table 6.1). Official statistics are not always an exact reflection of the phenomenon under investigation because they might indicate different trends in the legal procedures and not the actual crime rate. In addition, the official statistics obviously do not record violent acts that are not reported to the police or those that are not considered serious enough to be reported.

Figure 6.1
Crime against the Person (including crimes against life, personal safety, and sexual crimes committed by teenagers under age eighteen)

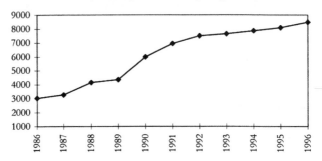

Gathering information on violent crimes perpetrated by teenagers is not an easy task. The system in use distinguishes only between crimes against the person and those against property, without always discriminating different levels of seriousness of violent crimes, and this of course applies to statistics on the rate of crimes committed by young offenders.

Teen violence mainly constitutes crimes against the person, which includes all forms of violent crimes: personal injury, brawl, threat, homicide (attempted), sexual violence, and private violence. Some of the crimes against property can also include violence (robbery with threat, vandalism, destroying goods). Other forms of violence that young teenagers engage in, involving minor aggressive behaviors, can be detected with research studies based on self-reports. In this instance, violence in schools and bullying has been investigated only recently in Italy (Genta et al., 1996; Baldry, 1998a; Baldry and Farrington, 1998).

In order to understand how the problem is dealt with in Italy, it is important to analyze the frequency that juveniles are reported to the police for committing a violent crime. We refer here only to the number of crimes reported, not to the number of convictions, because the latter highly underestimates the proportion of juveniles committing a crime. This is a result of the Italian juvenile justice system's tendency to avoid juvenile convictions.

As indicated by these official statistics, the number of reported violent crimes committed by teenagers has shown a gradual and constant increase from 3,000 in 1986 to nearly 8,500 in 1996 (see Figure 6.1). It is important, however, to indicate that property crimes known to be committed by juveniles have also increased, although not at the same rate. In addition, in the past five years, much of the increase of property crimes (burglary, theft) is due also to the increase of crimes committed by foreign juveniles, especially those from the former Yugoslavia. Italian juveniles, on the other hand, account for up to 90 percent of all violent crimes.

Italy is still far from U.S. crime rates, especially those of young gangs.

Table 6.2
Prevalence of Bullies and Victims, Students Eleven to Fourteen Years Old, Italy

Country/study	% bullies	% victims
Italy. Florence and Cosenza.	*At least sometimes:* Florence: 13.6, Cosenza, 19.3. *Once a week or more:* Florence: 4.3 and Cosenza: 7.1.	*At least sometimes:* Florence: 30, Cosenza, 2. *Once a week or more:* Florence and Cosenza: 10.
Italy. Rome, pre-adolescence.	*At least sometimes:* 25.3 of girls and 34.4 of boys.	*At least sometimes:* 31 of girls and 25 of boys.
Italy. Rome, pre-adolescence.	*At least once or twice:* 25.2	*At least sometimes:* 29.4
North Italy	*At least sometimes:* 10 of girls and 21.7 of boys.	*At least sometimes:* 16.5 of girls and 19.2 of boys
Central Italy. Suburb of Florence.	*At least sometimes:* 15.1 of girls and 28.5 of boys.	*At least sometimes:* 31.2 of girls and 29.2 of boys.
Central Italy, Suburb of Rome.	*At least sometimes:* 12.8 of girls and 20.5 of boys.	*At least sometimes:* 19.4 of girls and 14.4 of boys.
South Italy, Naples.	*At least sometimes:* 31.8.	*At least sometimes:* 30.7.
South Italy, Calabria.	*At least sometimes:* 16.9 of girls and 10.6 of boys.	*At least sometimes:* 8.4 of girls and 10.9 of boys.
South Italy, Palermo.	*At least sometimes:* 20.2 of girls and 19.9 of boys.	*At least sometimes:* 25.7 of girls and 17.5 of boys.

Sources: Baldry (1998a); Baldry and Farrington (1998); Fonzi (1997); Genta et al. (1996).

According to the National Crime Victimization Survey (NCVS), which gathers information on crimes committed against persons age twelve or older, in 1991 juveniles were responsible for 19 percent of all violent crimes (rape, personal robbery, and aggravated and simple assault) (National Center for Juvenile Justice, 1995). Between 1993 and 1996 in the district of Rome, however, there was a constant increase in the number of juveniles committing offenses alone but especially in the number of those committed with other offenders: 40 percent of juveniles committed a crime with at least one other juvenile, 37 percent committed the crime alone, 15 percent committed it with adults, and 8 percent committed it with both adults and juveniles (Scardaccione and Spagnoletti, 1998).

Teen violence does not always constitute a criminal offense. Violence perpetrated in schools, which often is not reported to the police, accounts for a great proportion of teen violence. Only recently has research been conducted in Italy to measure the prevalence and nature of bullying in school (Baldry, 1998a; Baldry and Farrington, 1998; Fonzi, 1997; Menesini, Eslea, Smith, Genta, and Giannetti, 1996; Prina, 1997).

Table 6.2 summarizes the results of studies conducted in different parts of the country, indicating that violence in schools is a widespread phenomenon affecting over one-third of the school population. Most of this research, however, deals only with primary and secondary school students;

there are few studies that investigate, with self-report measurements or other methods, the prevalence of bullying or other forms of violence in school (Gatti et al., 1994) perpetuated by young people ages fifteen to eighteen, which in most cases go unreported to the police.

CONTRIBUTING FACTORS

It is clear that teen violence can be identified as a form of disadvantage for young people who often are not able to count on services that can help them during this difficult phase of life. Teen violence is also the outcome of social-familial hardship and connected with school failure and dropout. School dropout in Italy varies greatly from region to region; some areas in the south have a higher rate of dropout among younger pupils, whereas in the north, most dropouts are older students. This phenomenon can be attributed to several factors, mainly socioeconomic reasons in disadvantaged areas, cultural reasons (attitudes, family perceptions), and personal and scholastic problems (e.g., bullying, low school achievement). According to the minister of social affairs, "Investing in the education of young people means capitalizing on an invaluable patrimony in the development of future society" (Presidency of the Council of Ministers, 1998, p. 35).

Scardaccione and Spagnoletti (1998) found a direct correlation between low level of education and commission of crimes against property, and between crimes against the person and higher level of education and higher socioeconomic status. Crepet (1997) in his study showed that violent crimes are independent of economic hardship. He found that some juveniles have an easy life but lack positive family, social, and personal values. These juveniles attempted to prove their existence and masculinity through violence. Teen violence, including bullying, is mainly committed by males, although there is an increase in violence among girls.

RESPONSES TO THE PROBLEM

The Italian government has implemented several laws for the protection of the rights of juveniles. In addition, it has developed a new criminal procedure that interprets teen violence as an expression of disadvantage and hardship and aims to decriminalize young offenders.

The Criminal Justice System for Young Offenders

The Italian minister of justice established in 1934 the court for minors and a special office for juvenile justice that coordinates all interventions in relation to young offenders. In addition, in 1988 a new Italian juvenile criminal justice system was introduced for young people between the ages of fourteen and eighteen who committed a crime (Decree of the President of the Republic n. 448/88). The decree reflects the United Nations' Standard Minimum Rules for the Administration of Juvenile Justice (United Nations, 1986, p. 18). According to these rules, all juvenile criminal justice systems of countries conforming to these recommendations (Italy included) should favor the protection and promotion of the rights of young offenders by helping them to take responsibility for their actions while paying their debts to society for the wrongdoing. The Italian juvenile justice system reflects the idea that the deviant behavior of the young offender is the result of combined pressures related to society, the family, and the personality of the juvenile. Therefore, the purpose of any sanction imposed should be to protect and reeducate juveniles while holding them accountable for the wrongdoing. According to this system, sanctions can be imposed only if juvenile offenders are held to be responsible, which means that they were aware, when committing the offense, of the illegality and the consequences of the action. Thus, there is a tendency to decriminalize young people who commit a crime.

Incarceration is usually the last resort and is part of the sentence only for very serious cases or, more likely, for cases of recidivism, where no other alternatives are applicable. Prisons for young offenders in Italy are called not "prisons" but "institutions," to emphasize the rehabilitative and reeducative element. When a juvenile is sentenced to incarceration in an institution, the period is rarely for more than two years. Even in these cases, the juvenile can be released after one month of custody and receive alternative sanctions. Some juveniles who commit repetitive offenses stay in an institution as a form of protective custody for six to twelve months while awaiting trial. When the juvenile is sentenced, this period of custody is considered part of the time served. In most cases, however, the judge, together with youth social services, establish the best judicial response or alternative to custody, keeping the interests of the juvenile in mind. The aim is to hold the juvenile responsible for the crime committed. In some cases when a sentence would be less than two years, such as for petty crimes, and in most cases for first-time crimes, the case is dismissed or the juvenile is acquitted.

In the last ten years, there has been a gradual and constant increase in residential communities or day centers that provide accommodation for juveniles who have committed a crime and are required to live in or attend these communities as part of a suspended sentence. In addition, with the new penal code procedure, the judge has the option of suspending the trial with probation before the sentence. In the Italian justice system there are no independent probation services as in the United States or England; this role is played by youth social workers of the Ministry of Justice. During the probation period, the social worker in charge of the young offender prepares a program that the young offender has to follow for a prescribed period of time (decided by the judge in each case). If the young offender follows the program, there is a declaration of *estinzione del reato* ("extinction of the crime"). This form of probation in Italy thus holds the youth responsible for the illegal behavior without criminalizing him or her (Scardaccione and Merlini, 1996). The process attempts to give young offenders an opportunity to provide a "payback" for the harm they caused. Scardaccione and Spagnoletti (1998) found that suspending the trial with probation is prescribed mainly for young offenders who have committed violent crimes, even attempted murder or rape, or in cases of recidivism or when the juvenile has committed several offenses. There is a tendency to avoid custody even for serious crimes. In all these cases, however, there must be an attempt to develop a program that involves social and local services, as well as the family, to promote a network for the implementation and the realization of the project. In this respect, the judge or the social worker also considers the possibility of victim-offender mediation. Only a few experiments in mediation are taking place now in Italy (Baldry, Scali, and Volpini, 1998; Scardaccione, Baldry, and Scali, 1998). Case studies on mediation with violent young offenders have demonstrated a positive outcome for both victims and offenders; the juvenile is held responsible for his or her action and has the opportunity to make retribution (Baldry, 1998b).

Prevention of Teen Violence

Several initiatives developed recently attempt to prevent juvenile delinquency and bullying. These prevention programs are usually local and use local funds. There is often no systematic evaluation of their effects, which limits the opportunity to expand their advantages and create a national plan to prevent teen violence. A brief description of some of these projects follows.

Preventing Violence in Schools and at Home

The Association Differenza Donna (Association of Women against Violence to Women), which runs two shelters for battered women in Rome, initiated a project called Bulli & Pupe ("Bullies and Dolls") to prevent violence against women, specifically focusing on prevention of violence in schools (especially bullying). A three-year research project (Baldry, 1998a, 1998b; Baldry and Farrington, 1998) had shown that bullying among adolescents in Rome is a serious problem that needs intervention. In addition, fieldwork and case studies on sexual harassment and violence by male teenagers against girls also required prevention programs in schools to address violence and develop a culture that respects gender differences.

Violence among teenagers can lead to further violence (Widom, 1989). Moreover, longitudinal studies show that many men who are violent with their partners were bullies at a younger age (Farrington, 1993, 1994).

The intervention project consists of three-day seminars conducted by professional women with experience in the field of violence. There is also an accompanying kit with a video and a booklet divided into three parts. Part 1

"Bullying among Peers," focuses on getting peers to talk about teen violence among peers. The materials point out that forms of bullying may lead to further aggressive and violent behavior. The second part of the program, "Children Witnessing Domestic Violence," analyzes the effects of domestic violence on children—their physical and psychological well-being and the repercussion on school achievement and peer relations. The last part of the program deals with the cycle of violence and the long-term effects of violence on adults who were victims of violence in their childhood: women who might persist in abusive relationships and men who might become violent with their partners and children. The intervention project focuses on secondary and high school students in the city and province of Rome. The project is in its pilot experimental phase, so there are no results yet on its efficacy (in terms of change of attitudes and gender-role stereotypes, and reduction of violent behavior).

Project DETA

Project DETA started in 1988 in Cologno Monzese, in the northern part of Italy, with the support of the region of Lombardia and the Institute of Criminology of Padua. The project aimed to prevent delinquency, drug addiction, and alcohol use among juveniles. The project involved not only adolescents but also adults (parents, teachers, and others) and juveniles who had committed a crime. In the first part of the project, a study was conducted on juvenile attitudes toward violence and crime. Results of the study were used to promote intervention programs and facilitate communication among adolescents and adults (Jani and De Leo, 1997). The subsequent phase of the project included direct intervention in the schools with teenagers to discuss issues of violence and crime. In addition, several meetings with inmates were organized to discuss crime, drugs, and alcohol abuse.

Governmental Initiatives

Governmental initiatives for the prevention of youth violence were previously established. In 1991 a new law for the prevention of the involvement of juveniles in criminal activities was approved. This law renewed efforts to offer services and places where young people can meet and tackle the side effects of isolation and crime in the most at-risk areas of Italy. After seven years of experience with this law, there is still an urgent need to allocate resources better and to promote initiatives to help juveniles already engaged in criminal activities or at risk of doing so.

All of these policies are directed to the prevention of juveniles' disadvantages and can be considered broader ways for the prevention of teen violence.

In 1977, D.P.R. 616/77 (Decree of the President of the Republic) transferred to the local services of each region any civil and administrative procedures for the intervention in favor of juveniles who subsequently had to be dealt with in the juvenile court. All cases that were not crimes but required a civil and administrative intervention on the behalf of social services had to be administered locally. Unfortunately this disposition has failed in its intent because local administrations often refused to intervene and promote services for the prevention and assistance of juveniles at risk. In addition, this decree led to a substantial difference between various parts of the country. In several parts of northern and central Italy, there has been a gradual development of services to assist and promote the welfare of juveniles and prevent juvenile delinquency (Pisapia, 1990). In the South of Italy, on the other hand, services are not always working efficiently or are nonexistent (Fadiga, 1994).

Protection of Youth Welfare

Most of the political and social attention regarding juveniles is in relation to the protection of the rights of children and adolescents. The increase in child abuse and the analysis of the condition of juveniles in Italy has led the government since 1996 to develop new laws and provide new services and funding for the promotion of children's welfare.

In 1996, the Italian government, on the basis of the UN Convention on the Rights of the Child (November 20, 1989), committed itself to implement a program in which the condition of the juveniles is taken into consideration. Several laws and significant financial investments were established to improve the quality of life for children and adolescents. According to the convention, the government has to commit to the promotion of initiatives to protect young people. On this basis, the Department of Social Affairs (the Presidency of the Council of Ministers) developed a plan of action for children and adolescents for 1997–1998. It established a national fund for children and adolescents for the implementation of local, regional, and national initiatives to promote their rights, quality of life, growth, individual maturity, and socialization. The interventions are intended to support services for parent-child relationships, fight poverty and violence, and offer alternatives to the placement of juveniles in welfare and educational institutions.

A subsequent law established the National Observatory on Childhood, which every two years prepares a national plan of action and interventions for the protection of the rights and development of adolescents. In addition, in 1996, the National Center for Documentation and Analysis for Childhood and Adolescents was established in Florence. Its duties are to collect and make public national and international regulations, provide an updated map of services available in the private and public sectors, analyze the health and welfare of children, and formulate proposals for intervention. Moreover, the Ministry of Social Affairs has embarked on a policy of tackling juvenile delinquency and violence by investing substantial sums of money. This is the first time in Italian history that such action has been taken for the promotion of the welfare of juveniles. The implementation of the law is only recent; there is not yet any data or information on the efficacy of the law.

CONCLUSION

Teen violence in Italy, in terms of both bullying and delinquency, has traditionally been researched from a scientific and theoretical point of view with the hope of providing possible explanations of such behaviors (Crepet, 1997; De Leo, 1997; Palmonari, 1996). However, few studies have investigated the problem from the social point of view in terms of legal and governmental initiatives. This chapter has shown that there are no structured organizations that address the problem. Nevertheless, several initiatives have been implemented to address the protection of children and adolescents' rights. Teen violence is viewed and dealt with as an indication of juvenile hardship. This is clearly reflected in the criminal justice procedure for young offenders, which tends to decriminalize juveniles and help them rehabilitate themselves by holding them responsible. Incarcerating juveniles does not reduce the crime rate, although in the last decade there has been an increase of juvenile delinquency, especially regarding crimes against the person. It is not possible, however, to attribute this increase to the change in the criminal procedure. It is more likely that this tendency reflects an increase in social and family problems, and an increase of foreigners (juveniles who commit crime), even if they commit only a small proportion of violent crimes.

The best strategy in dealing with teen violence is prevention. Italy has only recently begun to develop programs that deal with teen violence, and there are no programs of this type for primary school children. Nevertheless, an increasing amount of attention is being directed toward youth welfare in Italy. We hope that it will lead to the development of national programs for the prevention of violence, and that these programs will both focus on intervention in schools and involve families.

NOTE

1. The prevalence rate is the proportion of people committing violence; the incidence rate is the percentage of offenses committed in a given period (e.g., one year).

REFERENCES

Baldry, A. C. (1998a). Bullying among Italian middle school students: Combining methods to understand aggressive behaviors and victimization. *School Psychology International* 9(4), 155–168.
Baldry, A. C. (1998b). Victim-offender mediation in the Italian juvenile justice sys-

tem: The role of the social worker. *British Journal of Social Work, 28*, 729–744.

Baldry, A. C., and Farrington, D. P. (1998). Parenting influences on bullying and victimisation. *Criminal and Legal Psychology, 3*, 237–254.

Baldry, A. C., Scali, M., and Volpini, L. (1998). Mediation in the Italian juvenile justice system: A mediation service project. *VOMA Quarterly, 3*, 6–11.

Bandini, T., Gatti, U., Marugo, M. I., and Verde, A. (1991). *Criminologia* (Criminology). Milan: Giuffré.

Crepet, P. (1998). Cuori violenti. Viaggio nella criminalita giovanile. (Violent hearts. Journey into juvenile delinquency.) Milano: Universale Economica Feltrinelli.

Fadiga, L. (1994). *Quale interazione?* (Which interaction?) *MinoriGiustizia, 2*, 12–23.

Farrington, D. P. (1993). Understanding and preventing bullying. In M. Tonry (Ed.), *Crime and justice: A review of research* (pp. 381–458). Chicago: University of Chicago Press.

Farrington, D. P. (1994). Childhood, adolescent, and adult features of violent males. In L. R. Huesmann (Ed.), *Aggressive behavior: Current perspective* (pp. 215–240). New York: Plenum Press.

Fonzi, A. (Ed.). (1997). *Il bullismo in Italia* (Bullying in Italy). Firenze: Giunti.

Gatti, U., Fossa, G., Lusetti, E., Matugo, M. I., Russo, G., and Traverso, G. B. (1994). Self-reported delinquency in three Italian cities. In J. Junger-Tas, R. Terlouw, and M. W. Klein (Eds.), *Delinquent behaviour among young people in the Western world* (pp. 267–287). Amsterdam: Kugler Publication.

Genta, M. L., Menesini, E., Fonzi, A., Costabile, A., and Smith, P. K. (1996). Bullies and victims in schools in central and southern Italy. *European Journal of Psychology of Education, 11*, 97–110.

ISTAT. (1994). *Satistiche giudiziarie penali. Anno 1994* (Penal satistics, year 1994). Roma: Author.

ISTAT. (1995). *Satistiche giudiziarie penali. Anno 1995* (Penal statistics, year 1995). Roma: Author.

ISTAT. (1996). *Satistiche giudiziarie penali. Anno 1996* (Penal statistics, year 1996). Roma: Author.

Jani, L., and De Leo, G. (1997). Modelli di prevenzione della devianza minorile (Models for the prevention of juvenile offending). In G. De Leo (Ed.), *La psicologia della devianza* (Psychology of deviant conduct). Milano: Cortina.

Menesini, E., Eslea, M., Smith, P. K., Genta, M. L., and Giannetti, E. (1996). Cross-national comparison of children's attitudes towards bully/victim problems in school. *Aggressive Behavior, 23*, 245–257.

National Center for Juvenile Justice. (1995). *Juvenile offenders and victims: A focus on violence.* Pittsburgh, PA: Author.

Occhiogroso, F. (1994). Minorenni e Criminalitá in Italia, oggi (Juveniles and criminality in Italy, today). *MinoriGiustizia, 2*, 90–124.

Palmonari, A. (1996). *Psicologia dell'adolescenza.* Milano: Il Milano.

Pisapia, G. V. (1990). Costruire prevenzione a Cologno (Toward prevention in Cologno). In AAVV (Eds.), *Progetto DETA* (Project DETA). Milano: Decembrio.

Presidency of the Council of Ministers. (1998). *Italian policies for children's rights, 1996–1998.* Florence, Italy: Social Affairs Department.

Prina, F. (1997). *Bullismo e violenza a scuola* (Bullying and violence in school). Citta' di Torino: Progetto Itaca.

Scardaccione, G., and Merlini, F. (1996). *Minori, famiglia, giustizia* (Juveniles, family and justice). Milano: Unicopli.

Scardaccione, G., and Spagnoletti, M. T. (1998). L'attivitá del giudice dell'udienza preliminare presso il TM di Roma: Minori, tipologie di reato, risposte giudiziarie (The activity of the judge for preliminary hearing at the court for minors in Rome: Juveniles, types of crimes, and judicial responses). *Rassegna Italiana di Criminologia*, 3.

Scardaccione, G., Baldry, A. C., and Scali, M. (1998). *La Mediazione penale: ipotesi di intervento nella giustizia minorile* (Penal mediation and opportunities for intervention with juveniles). Milano: Giuffré.

United Nations General Assembly. (1985). United Nations standard minimum rules for the administration of juvenile justice ("The Beijing Rules").

Widom, C. (1989). The cycle of violence. *Science, 244*, 160–166.

7

JAMAICA

Frederick Allen

PERCEPTIONS OF TEEN VIOLENCE

Observers believe that the lack of educational and economic opportunities, the lack of basic amenities and a clean environment, and psychological factors all contribute to the rising teen violence in Jamaica. According to the Jamaica Survey of Living Conditions,[1] the out-of-school population—those persons between the ages of twelve and eighteen—represented 6.5 percent of the school-age population in their sample, and of this population, more than half (54.5 percent) belonged to single-headed households, two-thirds of these households being headed by females. Also, more than half (54.5 percent) belonged to the poorest group, while only 27.2 percent belonged to the wealthiest group. Furthermore, the survey showed a close relationship between socioeconomic group and school achievement. Some 79.0 percent of those from the wealthiest group completed some upper secondary education, compared with only 46.6 percent of the poorest. Jamaica has a faltering educational system, with only 65.6 percent of those between the ages of twelve and eighteen enrolled in secondary education[2] and an unemployment rate of 16 percent, although a recent estimate places the rate at 34.4 percent for young persons.[3]

CURRENT TRENDS IN TEEN VIOLENCE

The image of Jamaica as an exotic tourist location has steadily been tarnished by news of violence. Most of the violence among the adult population is attributed to the drug trafficking, political gang in-fighting, and deteriorating economic conditions, although a relatively new phenomenon, increase in teen violent crimes including homicide, rape, robbery, aggravated assault, and arson has occurred. The Jamaica police records indicate that between January and April 1998, 177 teenagers were arrested. Of that number, 79 were charged with robbery, 47 with shooting, 28 with rape, 12 with murder, and 11 with carnal abuse.[4] According to the minister of justice, 60 percent of persons incarcerated in 1997 were between the ages of seventeen and twenty-four. Taking its size into consideration, the murder rate is among the highest in the world. Jamaica's population is only 2.5 million, but during the first six months of 1998, there were nearly 500 murders.[5] In the inner city there are not many people who have not been personally affected in some way by the surge of violence. Webster Edwards wrote, "I know a 16-year-old girl who has had three brothers murdered on different occasions over the past five years. This is not an isolated instance as this experience is repeatedly shared by many who are living in the war-torn areas of Kingston and lower St. Andrew."[6]

Teen violence is a worldwide problem; few communities have been untouched by the increasing number of violent crimes committed by teens. For example, in the United States, juveniles were responsible for 14 percent of all Violent Crime Index offenses cleared in 1994. Generally a public health approach is adopted based on prevention. Various sociological and economic factors are taken into consideration, such as the increase in troubled families, domestic violence, victimization from neglect, physical abuse, sexual abuse, the availability and prevalence of drugs. Developing countries such as Jamaica present a new focus on sociological and economic factors. The colonial legacy, the pressures of modernization, and the war on drugs have produced new opportunities for teen violence. This framework is based on the concept of a social perspective. Conventional criminological theories sometimes do not relate to the workings of the criminal justice system in these developing countries. To understand teen crime in developing countries such as Jamaica, one has to understand Jamaica's colonial past, the change in respect for state agencies, these agencies' popularity and legitimacy, and the need to establish true social justice.

Jamaica's Colonial Legal Legacy

Jamaica was under British rule from 1655 to 1962. During this period, Jamaica, a traditional colonial society, adopted the legal system of the colonial ruler. Early British law emphasized lay participation. Thus, the legal system in Jamaica was never too far removed from the ordinary people. Furthermore, peacekeeping was not the total responsibility of the formal criminal justice system but a responsibility shared among all citizens. The family, school, and church played important roles in setting the public standard of behavior, particularly with respect to the behavior of the young. The presence of a vibrant, informal peacekeeping enforcement system resulted in a teen population that was essentially law abiding.

The British common law system, under which Jamaica was ruled, emphasized lay participation: justices of the peace were selected from among the citizens, bridging the gap between the community and the courts. Law, as defined by the formal system of justice, was but one mechanism of social control. A vibrant community-based informal system operated alongside the formal system. The informal institutions such as the school, religion, and the family played a significant role in enforcing rules. The following example of the informal system at work during Jamaica's colonial days, when teen violence was rare, illustrates the role the community played in teen behavior:

A young fellow in his teens was involved in a fight with another youth while returning from school. A small crowd of school children gathered to observe the fight. The two boys began throwing punches when an adult male from the house across the street emerged. He held the two boys, verbally reprimanded them, and then, using his belt, went on to apply corporal punishment. During the process he threatened that he would inform their parents of their disorderly conduct on the street. The boys accepted the punishment that was meted out. While begging the gentleman not to inform their parents, they seemed more concerned about the prospect of their parents being informed than the strokes they were receiving from the gentleman. The gentleman promised that he would not inform the parents on condition that no further fighting took place, but later reneged on his promise and contacted the parents. The parents thanked him for intervening, and particularly for applying the corporal punishment and proceeded to apply their own corporal punishment, which they of course applied in a much more forceful manner.[7]

With its ambitious quest for modernization and its newly independent status, Jamaica has slowly abandoned the vestiges of colonial rule and developed new policies that are consistent with the goals and expectations of an independent nation. With independence comes more reliance on formal enforcement mechanisms and less on the traditional, or informal, institutions. With development comes the need for more precision in evaluating misbehavior and ordering sanctions. The Jamaican community has slowly become less of a collective, or common, conscience, with shared values, and more of a penal system that relies almost totally on the formal peacekeeping mechanisms of the police, the courts, and penal sanctions. In the case of teens, emphasis has slowly been placed in the hands of the juvenile justice agencies rather than the family and other informal institutions. This has resulted in the emergence of a new social structure.

The Pressures of Modernization

Jamaica needs to look to developed countries for guidance in addressing the many technical problems it faces. In the area of crime, however, the solution must be found within the context of Jamaica's traditions. Unfortunately, this has not been the case. The Jamaican criminal justice system is slowly beginning to adopt the characteristics of developing countries. In Jamaica, like most modern societies with industrialization and modernization, law enforcement has become a more formal function of the police and other law enforcement agencies.

Following independence, Jamaica saw an erosion of the early police-community partnership. The informal institutions, school, religion, and the family have given way to the formal institutions of law. Industrialization has moved people from rural settings to the cities; economic conditions now require both parents to be employed; and religion is playing a significantly reduced role in the life of teens in Jamaican society. Now teens return to their homes from school to watch television. With satellite and cable services, they receive a constant dose of TV violence. It is not surprising that Jamaica has joined the rest of the world in experiencing an unprecedented amount of teen violence. According to recent reports, young people are the most violent of all age groups and are committing more random violence and killing strangers more frequently than adult criminals.[8]

CONTRIBUTING FACTORS

The War on Drugs and Teen Violence

Studies show that more male teenagers are responsible for the crimes that inflict horror and pain on the Jamaican society than any other group. The prevalent use of hard drugs, including crack-cocaine, has resulted in increased violence, particularly in the capital city of Kingston.[9] It is now widely recognized that drug trafficking and the associated evils of the trade such as gun smuggling, corruption of public officials, and drug abuse constitute a major security threat to Jamaica and the entire Caribbean today.[10] However, the war on drugs has reduced the opportunity for many young Jamaicans to profit from growing marijuana. One Jamaican government study established a clear link between marijuana production and income generation:

A number of farmers and young people have turned to the farming of marijuana to earn a living. The Government's anti–drug eradication program has succeeded in destroying vast areas planted in marijuana, but the socioeconomic problems remain. The small growers in these target communities have been experiencing a worsened situation in generating income or finding suitable employment. Information from a study done prior to the eradication program indicated that the average disposable income was 84 percent above the national level, but since the program, it fell to 18 percent above the per-capita disposable income.[11]

The teen population is becoming very conspicuous in the drug trade and the use of drugs, which has contributed to increased violence. The reduction in the marijuana cash crop has led to trading in other drugs such as cocaine. In the case of cocaine trafficking, guns become necessary; gang feuds, protection of turf, and drugs and money all translate to violence.

Education with Scarce Resources

Criticizing government's administration of the education system, the leader of the opposition party said one-third of the eleven-year-olds were leaving primary school illiterate because of irregular attendance and a deficiency in the early childhood education system.[12] The educational system is based on the reality that the government does not have the resources to provide universal access to education beyond age eleven. Beyond this age, only students who have demonstrated that they can benefit from further academic learning or whose parents have the resources for private schools have the opportunity to continue in an academic track. Up until 1999, students were selected via the Common Entrance Examination (CEE). With the shortage of opportunity for the many children seeking an education, the CEE, like any other selection test, served as an instrument to select the best performers. The CEE tested students in mathematics, English, and mental ability. Critics had long called for a more comprehensive system that would test broader areas and provide a more accurate picture of the student's academic promise. This was accomplished with the introduction of the National Assessment Program (NAP).[13]

The realization that many students may fail to do well at age eleven due to social, economic, and environmental reasons and other circumstances well beyond their control has not been a major issue on the Jamaican educational agenda. Students from poor families are sometimes unable to attend schools with qualified teachers and resources and are therefore doomed to fail the NAP. On the other hand, wealthy families can afford tutoring to increase their children's chances of scoring high enough for placement in the academic track. Finally, it is often not realized that the NAP helps government officials award placements based on the number of academic places available, not based on the passing of the NAP. Thus, a student may obtain a passing grade on the NAP but fail to obtain a place in the academic track due to the number of students competing for the number of available spots and the performance of the top portion of the total population. Let us say that 2,000 students take the examination and 50 percent receive a passing grade; there are only 600 spaces, so 400 passing students will be designated failures even though they passed the examination. According to reports in 1997, a record 17,515 students, or only 33 percent of the 52,581 who sat for the examination, were awarded places in secondary high schools for the beginning of the 1998–1999 academic year.[14] This represents a small increase over the 28.36 percent awarded in 1996 and the 31.01 percent awarded in 1997.

This description of the Jamaican educational system makes it easy to understand how large numbers of teens become prime targets for dysfunctional lives that may eventually lead to crime and violence. With the informal controls having disappeared, formal police controls have not been effective. Failing to join the academic track, many teens see no future. Unemployment is high, and with the absence of legitimate opportunity, many teens turn to drugs, mainly the cultivation of marijuana. In a visit to a small town in Hanover, I was introduced to a Johnny, age eighteen, who had been out of school since he failed to obtain a place after taking the CEE. His parents did not have the money to send him to a private school, where he could prepare for the General Certificate of Education (GCE) or the Caribbean Examination Council Certificate (CXC) or the Jamaica School Certificate. Johnny explained that even after people complete these exams, it is difficult to find a job. Instead, he has been clearing small plots of land in the hills for marijuana cultivation. A tour of the small plot showed that Johnny was involved in a small-scale exotic marijuana cultivation, planting a variety of marijuana. Because the variety was considered more potent than the marijuana that was grown in the United States, there was a good market for his crop.

Due to the war on drugs, specifically interdiction programs, the Jamaican government has received assistance from the United States in acquiring helicopters and other detection mechanisms that have almost wiped out the cash crop for hundreds of small growers like Johnny. According to a police superintendent in Montego Bay, most of the violent crime that occurs in the city can be attributed to these teens, who, like Johnny, have moved to the city. The superintendent explained that the removal of these teens from marijuana plots has also disrupted the food chain, since these teens planted not only marijuana but also food products—yams, banana, potatoes, and vegetables. He also stated that the involvement in drugs in itself is associated with violence. Teens sometime acquire firearms to protect their investments, and the presence of firearms increases the chance of violence.

Other Contributing Factors to Teen Violence

Recent reports state that teenagers living in Jamaica, especially those with visas to the United States, are among those being targeted by narcotics traffickers to smuggle drugs out of the country. Teens are being paid up to $2,000 for their services as couriers. Most of the teens range between ages fifteen and eighteen, are students from prominent high schools in Kingston and western Jamaica, and are from middle-class families. Most of them are recruited by peers who have already been drawn into the business. The drug dons, as they are called, can become so vicious that they threaten the teenager's life if he refuses to carry out their instructions. In newspaper accounts of some of these cases, the teenagers tell their parents or guardians that they will be attending seminars or other engagements and then sneak off the island.[15]

Teen Stress

Caribbean mental health specialists have noted with grave concern the high level of stress among the young people in the Caribbean region. Gloria Keans-Douglas, president of the Caribbean Federation for Mental Health, states, "We feel it is fair to say that young people in all the territories are displaying symptoms of stress. They are acting out, all over the Caribbean and the wider world, in terms of violence, teenage pregnancy and the increased rate of suicide.[16] Symptoms of stress was the subject of a recently released study by the Pan American Health Organization, the *Caribbean Adolescent Health Survey*. This survey, conducted among young people in the region, found that suicide attempts among adolescents are common; 10 percent of ten- to twelve-year-olds, 17 percent of thirteen- to fifteen-year-olds, and 23 percent of sixteen- to eighteen-year-olds reported that a friend had attempted or completed suicide. Gang violence is also a growing problem in the Caribbean, with one out of eleven adolescents reporting that they are gang members and another 10 percent saying that they have been in a gang in the past.

RESPONSES TO THE PROBLEM

On June 3, 1998, Chief Justice Lensley Wolfe addressed what he called the "pulse of a youth problem festering untended for too long." Brandishing two large knives seized from two schoolboys on the verge of a fight, the chief justice said he is on a campaign to rescue the young people of Jamaica. He took this action after the threatening of a school principal, which led to cancellation of the national school football competition. To deal with violence in schools and to ensure that schools in violence-prone areas are able to carry out their function of education, the government has initiated these measures:

1. Additional guidance counselors in schools
2. Training of more teachers in conflict resolution
3. Peace and Love in Schools (PALS), a privately sponsored conflict-resolution program
4. Additional patrols and escorts in schools in the violence-prone areas[17]

In 1975, the Department of Correctional Services, an arm of the Ministry of National Security and Justice, was established with the merger of the three correctional agencies then in operation: the Prison Department, the Probation Department, and the approved schools. Juveniles were designated to approved schools for protection and care. The 1975 reorganization created the Department of Correctional Services, which was designed to develop new approaches to deal with juvenile offenders that were different from those of the adult program. Among the changes that came with the establishment of the Correctional Services were changes in the names of the juvenile departments, from approved schools to juvenile correctional centers. The rationale behind the changes included the department's efforts to eliminate the notion of stigmatization and labeling usually associated with the term "approved school" and to broaden the scope and functions of the new juvenile centers to make them more effective in studying, diagnosing, and treating juveniles.[18]

In 1978, the Criminal Justice Reform Act was passed to provide new sentencing options available to judges for the treatment of adult offenders. The act also provided for special consideration for first offenders, particularly offenders between the ages of seventeen and twenty-three years, for community-based treatment, such as suspended sentence with a supervision order, a community service order, or probation orders.

CONCLUSION

The world has become a dangerous place, and Jamaica is no exception. Jamaica continues to benefit from a vibrant tourist trade because visitors to the tropical paradise rarely glimpse the crime problem. Tourists are whisked from the airport to their hotel, where they are pampered with food, drink, and lavish accommodation, later leaving without ever having seen the real Jamaica. However, with respect to teen violence, there is clear evidence that the violent teens in Jamaica present a major threat to the island's continued development.

Jamaica inherited a community service model from its colonial heritage that presents a more promising solution than the formal penal system that is being copied from rich, developed countries. Developing countries need to borrow selectively in finding solutions to their problems. A case in point is the unproductive colonial educational system that was kept while the community-partnership enforcement was abandoned. Jamaica's crime problem must be viewed from a social justice perspective whereby young Jamaicans are provided with legitimate means to achieve success and are regarded as the most precious national asset; there is a commitment to provide equal access to education and training, whereby all Jamaicans enjoy full respect for human rights, security forces are held accountable without arbitrary arrests and detentions, and the judicial system is improved to reflect justice and fairness. Currently in seven out of ten murders committed in

Jamaica, no arrest is made. Neither deterrence nor detection is working, nor is punishment swift and sure even when arrests are made.[19] Riots in the capital city, killings, and vigilante justice are clear signs of trouble.

Youth represent Jamaica's hope and future for the twenty-first century. Jamaica's teens have been well represented in the world of sports. Twelve-year-old Jody-Anne Maxwell, who won the Scripps Howard National Spelling Bee competition in Washington, D.C., was the first person outside the United States to win the coveted US championship. The Jamaican soccer team, Reggae Boyz, participated in the recent World Cup in France. Jamaica's reggae music contributes to the international music scene. These are examples of the potential of Jamaica's teens.

NOTES

1. Statistical Institute of Jamaica and the Planning Institute of Jamaica, *Jamaica Survey of Living Conditions: Report 1996* (Kingston: United Co-operative Printers Ltd., 1997).

2. Ibid., p. 20.10.

3. Ibid., p. 18.3.

4. G. Sinclair, "Juvenile Lock-Up Opening Doors," *Jamaica Gleaner*, Aug. 27, 1998, p. 1.

5. W. Edwards, "Jamaica's Murder Rate Is Totally Unacceptable," *Jamaica Daily Observer*, July 11, 1998.

6. Ibid., p. 6.

7. "History and Functions: The Department of Correctional Services," *Jamaica Gleaner*, Oct. 28, 1997.

8. S. Dobblin and S. Gatowski, *Juvenile Violence: A Guide to Research* (Reno, NV: National Council of Juvenile and Family Court Judges, 1998).

9. National Security Minister K. D. Knight. "Most Crimes Committed by 15–24 Year Olds," *Daily Observer*, June 26, 1998, p. 4.

10. I. Griffith, *Drugs and Security in the Caribbean: Sovereignty under Siege*, University, PA: Pennsylvania State University Press, 1997.

11. Jamaica, Ministry of Agriculture, *Alternative Systems for an Illegal Crop*, quoted in Griffith, *Drugs and Security in the Caribbean*, p. 182.

12. "JLP Targets Education, Job Creation," *Jamaica Gleaner*, Oct. 27, 1997.

13. The Common Entrance Examination was discontinued in 1998 and the National Assessment Program, which officials say will test a broader area of education, replaced the CEE. See D. Campbell, "Bidding Farewell to the Common Entrance," *Daily Observer*, June 30, 1998, p. 15.

14. "Common Entrance Record," *Jamaica Observer*, June 26, 1998, p. 1.

15. G. Sinclair, "Drug Dealers Courting Teens," *Jamaica Gleaner*, July 28, 1998.

16. "Region's Youth Are Stressed—and It Shows," *Jamaica Gleaner*, July 24, 1998.

17. Available at: http:/Iwwwjamaica-info.com/news/archives/96sep/96sep02.html.

18. "History and Functions: The Department of Correctional Services," *Jamaica Gleaner*, Oct. 28, 1997.

19. "The Crime Challenge," *Jamaica Gleaner*, Dec. 29, 1997. Available at: http://204.177.56.98/gleaner/19971229/cleisure/c.html.

8

RUSSIA

William E. Thornton and Lydia Voigt

PERCEPTIONS OF TEEN VIOLENCE

The problem of youth violence and delinquency in Russia has been proposed as being endemic to a society that is in turmoil and decay:

> When, in what had been the USSR, seven decades of appalling pressure were followed by the sudden and wide-open unchecked freedom to act, in circumstances of all-around poverty, the result was that many were swept down the path of shamelessness with the unbridled adoption of the worst feature of human behavior.

With these words, Aleksandr Solzhenitsyn (1995, 6) summarizes Russia's current situation. He is not alone. Russian as well as outside observers and analysts, including philosophers, journalists, criminologists, and governmental officials, have all claimed that the collapse of the Soviet Union, followed by political and economic instability, has caused a societal crisis and has led to large-scale disorder, as indicated by an epidemic of youth violence and deviance and the growing encroachment of organized crime. Indeed, in the West "the old rhetoric of the evil empire" has been replaced by fears of Russian mafia penetration of Western economies (Handelman, 1995, 95).

Against this backdrop, the problem of youthful violence and delinquency has been viewed as an unfortunate by-product of a society in flux, replete with faltering institutions. Typical discussions of causation include the usual list of suspects—the family, the school, the workplace, peer groups, and belief system—all framed in terms of deficiencies that contribute to the delinquency problem (Melnikova, 1998; Ministry of Internal Affairs, 1997).

Young people are considered to be major targets of the recruitment activities of organized crime groups who offer enticing material gains in the face of dire needs and diminishing economic opportunities. The Russian Ministry of Internal Affairs (MVD), for example, declared in 1992 that the number of racketeering adolescents was rising and posed a major threat to the future of the nation. Officials predicted that the problem of crime and delinquency would only get worse if current social conditions persisted. The report went on to say:

At present, a considerable part of young people is involved in illegal business because they see in it a quick road to prosperity. If five years ago the percentage of people under the age of 24 among profiteers was 13.5% in 1991 it was already 23.6% almost twice more. There is a serious threat that if the market conditions prevail, young people, currently engaged in consumer goods profiteering in the streets, will be without an education and profession, and that will lead to a deepening crime problem. The very young are also actively involved in racketeer activities. Racketeer adolescents account for 25%. (Ministry of Internal Affairs, 1992, 1–2)

During the Soviet era, the incidence of juvenile crime and violence remained a secret to the rest of the world. For the most part, Soviet authorities would not openly admit that there was a crime problem. Prior to Mikhail Gorbachev's policies of *glasnost* (openness) and *perestroika* (restructuring) and the subsequent fall of the Soviet Union, information regarding crime or delinquency was rarely discussed.

Historical accounts, however, indicate that juvenile crime was a problem both prior to and after the Soviet takeover of the Russian imperial state. Millions of detached children, both war orphans and refugees from World War I, roamed the cities and countryside. From the beginning, the new government had to address these problems. After the Russian Revolution, destruction, famine, devastation, and later rapid industrialization and Joseph Stalin's forced program of collectivization were believed to contribute to the growth of crimes committed by wayward children (*besprizorniye*). Of course, what was not reported was how many of these children had done nothing criminal, but either questioned the legitimacy of the new authority or came from families perceived to be enemies of the state. What happened to these children is not known. The belief that criminal activity is rooted in the stubborn bourgeois past may suggest that many children were simply made criminal by the new order and not for any traditional antisocial acts.

By the mid-1920s, juvenile crime was considered a serious problem; an estimated 6 to 7 percent of all criminal convictions involved juveniles. In 1923 and 1925, the total number of adolescents processed or convicted by the commissions and criminal courts increased from about 61,000 to

102,000. The greatest increase in youth crimes was for "hooliganism," a term generally used to refer to public disorderly conduct such as fighting, drunken behavior, and vandalism (Zeldes, 1981, 85). It is quite possible, however, that these high statistics revealed the more rigid order under the rule of Stalin than real increases in youth crime.

The perceived increase in juvenile crime and the inability of the Soviets to control it led to the passage of a 1935 law, On Measures for Combating Juvenile Delinquency. Under this law, juveniles twelve years and older could be convicted for criminal thefts and violent offenses, including murder. Although estimates vary, delinquency rates during the 1930s remained high, perhaps higher than the first years of Soviet control. Some estimates suggest an increase as high as 300 percent. After World War II, there was another marked increase in crimes committed by juveniles. During these years, juvenile delinquency was linked to the direct effects of the war (loss of parents, disruption of schooling, and economic deprivation). It is interesting to note that these same variables are used to explain juvenile crime today.

CURRENT TRENDS IN TEEN VIOLENCE

Both the number of delinquent children and the incidence of crime are reported to have increased in the postwar period, and all major Soviet cities continued to operate their Commissions of Juvenile Affairs (CJAs) to handle juvenile criminality as well as to add special police units to deal with more serious juvenile crime. Solomon (1978) analyzed data on delinquency in Russia for the years 1945 through 1965 and reported dramatic fluctuations in juvenile crime rates. For example, between 1961 and 1963, the number of criminal offenses committed by juveniles increased from about 3 percent to 9 percent. The years through the 1970s revealed a further increase in delinquency, probably because of increased activity on the part of CJAs. Initially, most cases were treated informally. In fact very few of the cases handled by the commissions were maintained on official delinquency records. Juvenile delinquency increased through the 1980s; by the end of this decade, the counts of juvenile offenses began a spiral upward. This upward trend has sparked much concern on the part of contemporary Russian leaders and criminologists.

When Soviet crime statistics first appeared in 1961, only percentages comparing crime incidence with that of previous years were usually given. A typical news release might read: "In the Soviet Union in 1985 murder decreased by 8.7 percent, in 1986 there was a 20.7 percent decrease compared with 1985, and in 1987 there was only a 1.2 percent decrease relative to the previous year" (Voigt, Thornton, Barrile, and Seaman, 1994, 599). Rarely were total crime figures offered, and when they were presented, seldom was any mention made of the relative population size. Moreover, the categories of offenses for which totals were offered usually lacked precise definitions, making comparisons and analysis difficult.

Following Gorbachev's reforms, Russian government statistics reported by the Ministry of Internal Affairs have taken a more comprehensive form. An effort has been made to display actual numbers of "registered" or reported crimes, in terms of various "characteristics" of offenders who committed crimes, such as whether they are students, whether they come from single-parent families, and the like. However, crime classifications and categories still tend to vary from year to year, and the cross-classification of data, especially for juvenile offenders, is virtually nonexistent. Much like the U.S. official crime statistics, timely crime data are difficult to obtain. Despite the weaknesses, including the usual problems of any "official" crime statistics, an examination of current Russian Ministry of Justice data allows us to make some observations about current juvenile offending patterns in Russia.[1]

Figure 8.1 presents a ten-year trend line comparing total registered crimes (e.g., murder, rape, robbery, assault, hooliganism, theft) reported in Russia from 1987 to 1996 (top line) and registered crimes committed by juveniles (bottom line) for the same period. As can be seen, there was a steady increase in total registered crimes in Russia through 1993—a 58 percent total increase. A slight decrease of about 6 percent took place in 1994, followed by an increase of 5 percent through 1995 and then another slight decrease (5 percent) through 1996.[2]

Registered juvenile crimes increased by about 50 percent for the same time period of 1987 through 1993, dropping by about 2 percent through 1994 and continuing to drop slightly through reporting year 1996. Of interest is that since the restructuring of Russia in 1991, the increase in juvenile registered crimes has been relatively moderate—about a 15 percent increase through 1996. This increase almost mirrors the increase in total registered crimes for the same time period of about 17 percent. Over time, the proportion of juvenile registered crimes to total registered crimes has been relatively stable. Juvenile registered crimes comprise about 8 percent (average) of total registered crimes from 1991 through 1996, slightly less than the previous years from 1987 through 1990, averaging about 10 percent of total registered crimes. Russian criminologists argue that only a small portion of the actual number of criminals, especially youthful offenders, are registered or reported, suggesting that the problem is greater than is shown by the statistics (Borbat, 1997, 75). The fact that official statistics represent only the tip of the iceberg is a universal problem, and is not unique to Russia.

However, it is important to remember that the Russian population has been experiencing a declining trend since 1965, and as of 1992 began a negative rate of population change. Despite seemingly moderate increases in juvenile registered crimes over the years, the highest offending age co-

Figure 8.1
Correlation between Total and Juvenile Crime in the Russian Federation, 1987–1996

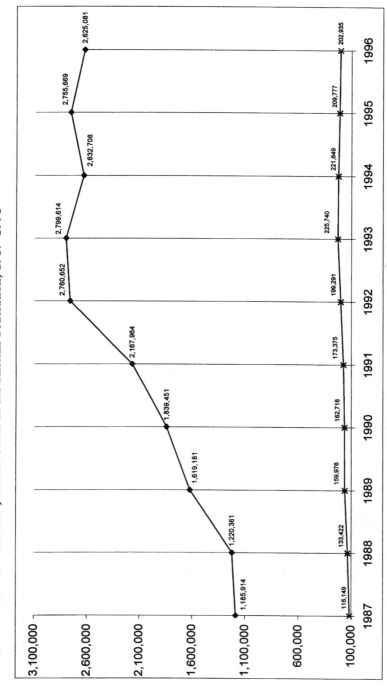

Sources: Ministry of Internal Affairs of the Russian Federation, Main Information Center (1992, 1993); *Crime and Delinquency, 1996* (1997).

Table 8.1
Structure of Crime among Teenagers in Russia (percent of total crime)

	1992	1996
Premeditated Murder or Attempted Murder	0.3	0.6
Rape or Attempted Rape	1.0	0.8
Robbery	8.1	8.1
Hooliganism	5.6	7.7
Premeditated Bodily Injury	0.6	1.0
Theft	65.6	60.4
Muggings	1.7	2.3
Other	17.1	19.1

Source: Crime and Delinquency, 1996 (1997).

horts (roughly fifteen to nineteen years old) have been decreasing in size over the years. For example, in 1993 and 1994, the age cohort fifteen to nineteen years comprised only about 7 percent of the total Russian population) (United Nations, 1997). Given the demographic trends, one would expect Russian "teenage" crime to be substantially decreasing in the Russian Federation, but this is obviously not the case. This situation of fewer juveniles committing more crimes has led some experts to assert that juvenile crime, especially violent crime, is at epidemic proportions in Russia. In order to unravel such claims, we must examine more specific types of crime data to better interpret the dilemma.

Characteristics of Russian Juvenile Crime

An examination fo Table 8.1 shows a percentage breakdown of crimes committed by Russian teenagers (ages fourteen to seventeen) by type compared to the total crimes committed for the years 1992 and 1996. For each year, the percentage of violent crimes (murder or attempted murder, rape or attempted rape, bodily injury, and muggings) committed by juveniles accounts for no more than 12 or 13 percent of total crimes. Much like the United States, the great bulk of crimes committed by Russian juveniles tend to be property offenses; thefts accounts for about 60 to 66 percent of committed crimes. In the past, a distinction was made between theft of state property and theft of private property. This differentiation no longer exists. The crime of "hooliganism" generally refers to rowdy, often group-type offenses involving public disorder and disturbance. This category accounts for 5 to 8 percent of total juvenile crime. "Other" crimes, including drug and alcohol offenses and traffic crimes, account for 17 to 19 percent of juvenile crimes.

Crime statistics on the number of juveniles committing major crimes (e.g., murder, rape, assault, robbery), including certain sociodemographic characteristics about these offenders, have been maintained by the Ministry of Internal Affairs for about ten years (*Crime and Delinquency, 1996*, 1997,

Table 8.2
Persons Ages Fourteen to Twenty-nine Committing Crimes in Russia (per type of crime)

	1992	1993	1994	1995	1996
Total Number of People					
Committing Crimes	1,148,962	1,262,737	1,441,568	1,595,501	1,618,394
age 14-17 %	16.4	16.1	14	13	11.9
age 18-29 %	38.1	38.9	37.9	37.3	39.8
Premeditated murder					
or attempted murder					
age 14-17 %	4	4.8	5.4	6	5.6
age 18-29 %	32.2	32	33	33.5	35.1
Assault					
age 14-17	3.8	4.8	5.4	5.4	5.7
age 18-29	29.2	30	30.7	32	32.2
Mugging					
age 14-17	20	21.6	21	19.7	18
age 18-29	56.5	57	58	58.2	60
Rape or Attempted Rape					
age 14-17	23.9	22.5	22.4	20.8	20.1
age 18-29	55.2	56	56	55.9	55.3
Robbery					
age 14-17	32.2	31.4	29.8	28.2	26.7
age 18-29	44.7	46.2	47.1	47.3	48.9
Theft					
age 14-17	26.8	24	21	19.6	18.5
age 18-29	37	24	21	19.6	18.5
Hooliganism					
age 14-17	15.7	14	12.4	12.4	12
age 18-29	49.9	47	43.3	42.3	42.4
Drugs					
age 14-17	8.7	8	7.06	7.4	7.61
age 18-29	62.5	61.3	61.3	59.8	60.7

Source: Crime and Delinquency, 1996 (1997).

47). Table 8.2 presents information on juveniles who have committed (and been "detected," as the Russians phrase it) select major offenses for the years 1992 through 1996.

The total number of juveniles (ages fourteen to seventeen) who have committed major crimes increased slightly between 1992 (188,186) and 1993 (203,826)—an increase of 8 percent—and between 1994 (200,954) and 1995 (208,096)—an increase of 3 percent. However, there have also been decreases, such as an 8 percent drop between 1995 and 1996 (192, 199).

Murder or Attempted Murder

An examination of juveniles ages fourteen to seventeen who have committed murder (or attempted murder) reveals that in any given year, this population comprises no more than about 6 percent of the total number of murderers or attempted murderers in Russia for the five-year period. Russian criminologists continue to incorporate attempted murder in both their categories of "registered crimes" and "detected criminals," a somewhat misleading practice when attempting to compare cross-national "homicide" statistics. The largest number of juvenile murderers detected was in 1995, with a count of 1,458. There has been a 52 percent increase in juvenile murderers from 1992 to 1996, a point the Russian media have made much of.

Like their adult counterparts, juvenile murderers are mostly males, averaging about 90 percent in any given year. A disproportionate number of juvenile murderers fit a "violence profile" of nonworking, nonstudying juveniles, many coming from conflict-ridden homes, and the offenders are often under the influence of alcohol or drugs (*Crime and Delinquency, 1996*, 1997). There is also some evidence to suggest that each year a larger proportion of juvenile murderers commit their offenses in a group or gang setting—possibly as many as 10 percent. While statistics on the use of firearms in the perpetration of murder by juvenile offenders are sketchy, some studies suggest that juveniles are rapidly becoming armed, much like their American counterparts. In Moscow, about 100 teenagers per year since 1993 have been arrested for possession of illegal guns (Borbat, 1997).

Assault and Mugging

Juveniles who commit serious assault peaked with a count of 2,424 offenders in 1994. While the total number of juveniles committing assaults has increased by 50 percent from 1992 to 1996, the increase has not been steady every year; there has been a moderate decline since 1994. Juvenile assaulters comprise about 5 percent of total individuals committing serious assault in any given year.

Reports of vicious assaults against minority and ethnic groups (e.g., Africans and Asians) by unemployed, poorly educated Russian teenagers identifying themselves as "skinheads" (by their shaved heads) began appearing in the popular media in the mid-1990s. Many of these youth, coming from the workers' districts and lowest social depths of Russian society, espouse racist rhetoric and are quite willing to attack individuals they believe are somehow to blame for their position. According to the Foreign Students Association from Moscow University, every week ten to fifteen foreign and minority students are seriously assaulted by small groups of violent skinheads.

Less serious assaults, usually not involving the use of a weapon, are classified under the general rubric of "mugging" in Russian crime statistics. As Table 8.2 depicts, the number of juveniles who have committed a mugging is substantially higher in both sheer volume and in proportion to the total population of muggers. For example, there were 6,682 juveniles detected for mugging in 1994, comprising 21 percent of the total population of muggers in Russia for the same year. Juvenile muggers increased by about 20 percent during the five-year period, and their characteristics parallel the violence profile noted above.

Rape or Attempted Rape

The total number of juvenile rapists or attempted rapists peaked with 2,934 offenders in reporting year 1993, comprising about 21 percent of the total number of people detected for the crime(s). In absolute numbers, discovered juvenile rapists have declined since 1993, a drop of 30 percent from that year to 1996. There is no doubt that the crime of rape, as in most other countries, is underreported.

Social demographic profiles of youthful rapists, almost exclusively male, indicate that the offenders are often under the influence of alcohol (about one-third), are repeat offenders for the same offense (about one-third), and are group oriented, with multiple offenders operating together to perpetrate the crime (approximately 40 percent of all juvenile rapists or attempted rapists) (*Crime and Delinquency, 1996,* 1997; Chelnokov, 1993; Melnikova, 1998). While most studies report that probably 70 percent of juvenile rapists come from the lower socioeconomic ranks of Russian society (e.g., unemployed or unemployed families, blue-collar workers, educational dropouts), more current statistics indicate that as many as 30 percent of juvenile rapists are schoolchildren or college students, a disturbing trend.

Robbery

Juvenile robbery offenders comprise the largest proportion of total individuals committing robbery—about 30 percent each year. This figure, when coupled with the eighteen- to twenty-nine age group of people committing robberies in Russia, accounting for about 47 percent of total robbers, indicates that the crime of robbery is truly a young person's crime. The total number of juveniles committing robbery peaked in 1993 with 23,612 offenders and declined through 1996, with 18,351 offenders, a drop of 18 percent. Russian analysis of robbery indicates that juvenile robbers are more represented in "street robberies" (in streets, parks, and public squares) rather than in the robbery of commercial establishments or residences. There is, however, some evidence that the armed robbery of apartments is increasing on the part of a hard core of repeat juvenile offenders (Borbat, 1997). Also, robbery of passengers on trains is becoming a serious problem. About 50 percent of all juvenile robbers operate in groups or gangs to perpetrate their offenses, and some type of weapon is used in about 60 percent of street robberies, though firearms do not appear to be highly prevalent based on the number of juveniles who are convicted (less than 1 percent).

About 90 percent of juvenile robbers are male, and well over half come from the nonworking and nonstudent segment of Russian society. At least 20 percent of juvenile robbers are repeat offenders, having committed prior robberies. There is also some recent evidence that as many as one-third of these offenders, as reported in conviction statistics, are now coming from single-parent families.

A common theme often found in the popular Russian press is the belief that crimes such as robbery are becoming an increasingly professional operation. Juveniles operating in groups or gangs are more likely today to plan their crimes and often attempt to disguise themselves with wigs and masks and use firearms to intimidate their victims. Such youth who are willing to fight and be aggressive are eventually recruited into adult organized crime structures (Pronina, 1994).

Hooliganism

Hooliganism is a term loosely used by Russian criminologists and the Russian public to describe a number of offenses, such as disorderly conduct, vandalism, drunkenness in public, and minor interpersonal assaults such as fighting in the streets (Thornton and Voigt, 1992; Terrill, 1997; Melnikova, 1998). Known juveniles committing acts of hooliganism, at least according to Russian crime statistics, decreased slightly from 1995 to 1996 (about 5 percent) but have been steadily increasing since 1992. While the term *hooliganism* is often associated with juveniles, for the time period examined in this analysis, minors committing hooligan acts comprise no more than about 13 percent of the total number of individuals committing hooliganism.

Juvenile hooligans, who are disproportionately found under the influence of alcohol and drugs, come from all strata of Russian society. However, they appear to be overly represented by nonworking and nonstudying youths who engage in seemingly wanton acts of destruction, such as damaging seats in suburban trains, breaking windows and headlights of expensive cars, and engaging in periodic raids as they destroy public and private property (Pronina, 1994).

Kidnappings by Juveniles

Based on legislation introduced in the 1995 Russian Federation Criminal Code, the registered crime of "kidnappings by juveniles" became law partly as a reaction to increases in kidnappings in general (110 in 1993, 499 in 1994, 628 in 1995, and 766 in 1996—an 85 percent increase) and because of actual reported instances of juvenile offenders kidnapping individuals for ransom (4 cases in 1995 and 10 cases in 1996) (Dolgova et al., 1997).[3]

CONTRIBUTING FACTORS

Prior to *glasnost* and *perestroika*, Soviet criminologists were somewhat restricted in their explanations of crime causation, especially violent teenage crime. Early causal explanations of crime and delinquency were rooted in socialist ideology, expounding the view that crime is a bourgeois remnant from the prerevolutionary capitalist past (Avanesov, 1981). It was further argued that in the future under communism, social classes and consequently class conflict would no longer exist, and that eventually many causes of crime would therefore not exist. However, before the breakup of the Soviet Union, party leaders and criminologists were hard pressed to explain why juveniles were increasingly engaging in criminal behavior.

From the beginning, Soviet criminology generally rejected biological and psychological causal explanations of juvenile and adult criminal behavior.[4] Violent juveniles who had mental disorders, for example, were thought to be a rarity. Instead, Soviet criminologists placed major emphasis on social-structural determinants of criminal behaviors or trends. In order to control juvenile crime and other social problems, the Soviets attempted to manipulate and control their basic institutions, primarily the family, school, workplace, and youth organizations, which historically served to inculcate socialist principles and morality. Now Russian criminologists again look to the family, school, workplace, and youth organizations to explain perceived rising juvenile crime and other associated youth problems.

Property Offenders

By far the largest segment of juveniles committing crimes are those youth caught for various types of theft. It is interesting to note, however, that the number of juveniles who commit theft decreased in 1994 (118,620) and 1996 (113,083) to levels lower than 1992 (121,107). Juveniles who commit thefts represent about 21 percent of the total number of offenders committing theft crimes.

Some reports suggest that before the restructuring, youngsters stole items because there was a shortage of goods in Russia. Now, however, merchandise is available in the stores, but the prices are out of the reach of the average person, so juveniles steal things that they need because of the new social class system. According to some Russian criminologists, some career juvenile thieves have adopted the "code" of organized thieves (*Voiy V Zakone*) and are fully socialized into a life of crime in which violence and extortion are an everyday occurrence (Thieves Professing the Code, 1998).

Juvenile Drug Offenders

Juveniles who have committed drug offenses (using drugs and drug dealing) increased by 65 percent from 1992 to 1996 (Table 8.2). However, juvenile drug offenders represent only about 8 percent of the total number of known people committing drug crimes. It is important to remember that only a small portion of juvenile drug offenders are detected by the police. Some reports coming from the Ministry of the Interior indicate that there are as many as 2 million drug addicts in Russia. Heroine use is widespread, and the drug is readily available. Russian amphetamines can be purchased cheaply and are popular among teenagers. The highest percentage of drug addicts are said to be teenagers who turn to drugs due to a sense of fatalism coming from the lack of jobs and opportunities for higher education (Russian Drug Epidemic, 1998). Unfortunately, very few drug prevention programs are operating in Russia. There are no needle exchange programs, and methadone use is against Russian law.

Family

The family has been singled out as a basic institution that can contribute to the delinquency of minors. Blame is placed on parents' inability to socialize their children to values conducive to conformity in Russian society. Lack of parental supervision, excessive drinking in the home and workplace, and violence and criminality in the family are noted in discussions, both scholarly and popular, dealing with Russian juvenile crime (Melnikova, 1998). The prevalence of a large number of single-parent families in Russia—more than 3 million—has been particularly linked to juvenile violence. For example, in 1996, 40 percent (47,973) of the total number of juveniles aged fourteen to seventeen convicted for serious offenses came from single-parent families (almost exclusively female headed) (*Crime and Delinquency, 1996*, 1967). About one in four adolescents and teenagers are raised in abusive homes. More than 160,000 children are raised in orphanages because their parents are in prisons or facilities for alcohol and drug abuse (Dolgova et al., 1997; Borbat, 1997). In 1998 an estimated 50,000 Russian teenagers ran away from home; many end up on the street as victims (e.g., young female and male prostitutes) or as offenders seeking to survive (Signorelli, 1997).

Schools

Russians have long emphasized the importance of the role of the school in the development (and indoctrination) of children. With the apparent increase in juvenile crime, many Russians have criticized schools for not being aggressive enough in teaching juveniles the values and skills that they need to be productive citizens. A long tradition of Russian studies on delinquency indicates a strong correlation between school factors or problems and the prevalence of juvenile crime and delinquency (Voigt and Thornton, 1985). A survey taken by the Ministry of Education reported that the largest group of juveniles who get into trouble with the law were those who dropped out or were forced out of school. According to available data, in Moscow alone, about 80,000 youngsters dropped out or were expelled from school in 1993 (Gleizer, 1993). Nine years of schooling is universal in Russia, and students are accepted into the tenth grade (the final year of secondary school) on a competitive basis. Often those students who have poor grades and subsequently are expelled may have been labeled by teachers as troublemakers or otherwise have had some learning disorders or psychological or behavioral problems that inhibited learning through normal pedagogical channels. Those teenagers (fifteen- and sixteen-year-olds) who do not enter the tenth grade are supposed to apply to trade or vocational schools or learn a trade or occupation through private enterprise. However, many engage in unskilled, often manual labor jobs, or gravitate toward criminal enterprises and get involved in theft, extortion, or worse.

Youth Organizations and Recreational Activities

The disappearance of communist organized youth groups and the prohibitive costs of youth camps and vacations have left, according to Russian child experts, many young Russians idle to roam the streets and get into trouble. Although much of the former Soviet propaganda machine embellished and glossed over flaws in the system, the one thing that was hard to criticize were the resources that were devoted to children. The proper upbringing (*vaspitania*) of children was part of the national agenda and remained a leading priority during most of the Soviet era. Free summer vacations, free summer camps, free hobby and sports groups, free health care, and the like were taken for granted by families. Every city had its own children's circles, sports clubs, and artistic studios. Children paid no admission fees to museums, parks, or other cultural events. Most of these now privatized facilities and activities are beyond the economic reach of the average Russian family with children.

Communist leaders in the past turned the mansions and palaces of czarist nobility into summer camps, orphanages, schools, and sanatoria. The old Soviet government set up a number of youth leader organizations to educate, train, and recruit future managers and leaders for the communist country: the Little Octobrists (children aged seven to nine), Pioneers (children ages ten to thirteen) and the Komsomol (children ages fourteen and up). Children under the socialist regime lived well, especially those who progressed to the Pioneers and Komsomol membership ranks. Every summer, children attended free Pioneer camps. Despite the obvious political indoctrination of children who became enmeshed in the communist track, and the discrimination of children who chose not to follow party lines, the majority of children fared relatively well during this Soviet era.

This is not the case in Russia today. With the restructuring of the society and the redistribution of wealth, the Russian government has sold to private entrepreneurs many of the "state" recreational facilities and schools that were devoted to children in the past. As a result, only the children of wealthier families can afford summer camps, vacations, sports or art schools, and children are often left to their own resources—hanging out in the streets and joining youth groups or unions, many no different from juvenile gangs (Signorelli, 1997).

Poverty and Inequality

Linking poverty to crime and delinquency is relatively new in Russian etiological discussions. Crime in this context is invariably connected with market reforms and the emergence of a wealthy elite class noted for its conspicuous consumption and corruption. Emerging as the most significant factor threatening the social order is the deep divide between winners and losers (Freeland, 1995). Drastic declines in the standard of living and increasing mass impoverishment while the social safety net has been quickly disappearing have resulted in deterioration of public health, declining longevity, increasing mortality and morbidity, and growth in the number of suicides, alcoholism, and crime and delinquency (Silverman and Yanowitch, 1997).

One of the symptoms of severe poverty is the growing number of homeless children. For example, in Moscow, it was estimated that 60,000 youngsters are homeless (UNICEF, 1995). Hundreds of thousands of migrants and refugees add to the problem of homelessness. According to the All Russian Living Standards Center, approximately 30 percent of Russians live below the poverty level (currently defined by an income less than $60 a month). The Russian government recently admitted that at least 12 million children (9 percent of the Russian population) live in extreme poverty.

The growing disparity of income, declining living standards, loss of security, and deepening inequality are believed to be the primary seeds of disorder threatening the democratization of Russian society (Milanovic, 1995).

Anomie

In January 1992, a public opinion poll, which allowed individuals to write in their own statements, asked what people believed to be the greatest hardships facing them in their daily lives. Sixty-six percent of the Russian public who were polled expressed "not knowing what to expect tomorrow" (Zaslavskaya, 1992). Rapid social change, especially in political and economic institutions, is often associated with the transformation of people's lives—suggesting that their routine ways of doing things, traditions, and sets of expectations are disrupted while new social adaptations have not yet evolved and resulting in what has been described in terms of uncertainty and a condition of anomie (Durkheim, 1951/1987). Changes such as those associated with *glasnost, perestroika*, the 1991 coup, the Moscow–White House confrontation in 1993, the collapse of the oil industry, hyperinflation, and the fall of the Russian stock market all have had uncalculated effects on the society. Among other things, these policies and events have led to increases in the division of labor, the growth of occupational and political groups, and the formation of nationalistic and religious factions, resulting in the intensification of competition for dominance, and demand for official protection of a growing number of vested interests.

Such changes are invariably accompanied by expectations of new opportunities, as well as by fears and disappointments. Advertisement by mass media, the arrival of many consumer goods, and the development of commercialism have reinforced both high expectations and deep disillusionment. The mere desire for bigger and better things is not the same as their actual achievement. Although the mass media, largely through advertising, may present material acquisition or wealth as desirable to all members of the society, not all members can partake in the rewards (Melnikova, 1998). Many people are going to be thwarted by their inability to satisfy these aspirations. This disillusionment may promote frustration and anxiety, and eventually lead to norm violation and deviance. (See the classical work by Merton, 1938.) It is interesting to note that Russian crime, especially teenage crime, has been viewed as both a cause and an effect of social disintegration and declining quality of life, even though, logically, something cannot be its own cause and effect at the same time (Thornton and Voigt, 1992). Unfortunately, concepts such as disorganization or the condition of anomie are rarely defined or measured empirically and are usually taken as self-evident, serving more to sensationalize than to clarify the problems of delinquency and crime.

While these social changes with their accompanying sets of rising aspirations and frustrations have been associated with conditions more conducive to crime, it is still worth pointing out that the majority of the Russian population is law abiding. Perhaps more remarkable than the transformation of the political economy is that Russian society has been relatively orderly and peaceful. As formal structures crumble, the informal relationships and routines of individuals remain relatively intact, much as they have for generations.

RESPONSES TO THE PROBLEM

Originating as early as 1918, Commissions of Juvenile Affairs (CJAs) were established to combat juvenile crime. Every village, town, and city had a CJA staffed by volunteers; they operated much like today's juvenile courts and provided a full range of methods for handling both juvenile violent offenders and juveniles who simply needed supervision or treatment. These commissions were predominantly composed of unpaid citizens who heard cases against juvenile lawbreakers and dispensed reprimands, warnings, and sentences of confinements in rehabilitation and residential educational facilities.

Modern Russian law dealing with crimes against the person and property is similar in form to the law of some Western countries, especially those modeled after the Roman Germanic legal system. According to Russian law, persons who have reached the age of sixteen before the commission of a crime shall be subject to criminal responsibility. Conditional criminal responsibility is faced by juveniles ages fourteen to sixteen for selected crimes such as homicide, rape, robbery with violence, intentional battery, and battery. Youngsters below age fourteen who have committed minor offenses such as petty hooliganism, public drunkenness, and drug abuse may be relieved of criminal responsibility or punishment and handled administratively by the CJA, the militia (police), or the regular courts.

Although changes in the constitution and legal codes followed the breakup of the Soviet Union, the handling of juvenile offenders has changed relatively little. Under the former Soviet Union, there were three types of law enforcement systems in existence: state security forces, regular forces, and ancillary forces. State security, originally the old KGB (Committee for State Security), has undergone numerous changes since the collapse of the Soviet Union, most recently the creation of the Federal Security Service (FSS) in 1995, whose duties are counterintelligence and intelligence and protection of state borders (Federal Border Service) of the new Russian Federation (Terrill, 1997).

The militia was developed during the early days of the Soviet state to perform day-to-day police functions such as law enforcement and order maintenance. Current militia efforts are almost exclusively focused on combating street crime, and there have been improvements, including better recruitment and training of officers. So-called *militsia* (inspectorates on juvenile affairs) are part of the militia and are the closest to juvenile officers that the Russians have. However, evidence indicates that relatively little training is devoted to the handling of juvenile offenders, or the problems of juveniles in general, in the more than sixty regional training centers around Russia.

The individuals who are charged with handling and investigating juvenile cases have wide powers in questioning juveniles, making referrals, and the like (Finckenauer, 1996). It is important to note that despite efforts to reform overall criminal procedures for individuals who come into contact with the system, Russian law protecting the rights of juveniles has not changed substantially in more than thirty years (Finckenauer, 1996).

Inspectorates on juvenile affairs also can impose and monitor informal dispositions for minor juvenile law violators. They can arrange for various types of juvenile aid or refer juveniles to representatives from the new Ministry of Social Protection who have assumed the responsibility for placement centers for children.

Most ancillary forces—formal groups of volunteers to assist the militia with law enforcement—disintegrated after the collapse of the Soviet Union. However, vestiges of volunteerism in public safety remain in the Russian Federation, as in the form of volunteer police aides (in Moscow). Volunteers over the age of eighteen with no criminal record assist the police in certain crime-fighting duties, including checking documents, writing reports, and making referrals to appropriate agencies. It should be noted that Russian citizens continue to be skeptical of the role, or ability, of the police to deal with social problems such as crime, especially youthful criminality, which is of special concern in Russia today.

Courts

The judicial system of the Russian Federation remains strikingly similar to the former Soviet judiciary (Solomon, 1997). At the top of the court hierarchy is the Constitutional Court of the Russian Federation, consisting of nineteen judges who for the most part handle cases concerning the Russian Constitution. At the next level, the Supreme Court of the Russian Federation "has the ultimate judicial responsibility for civil, criminal, administrative and other cases from general jurisdiction lower courts" (Terrill, 1997). Regional courts try more serious criminal and civil cases and have jurisdiction on both original and appellate cases. At the lowest level, people's courts handle most minor criminal and civil cases. All cases involving juvenile law violators, especially violent offenders, are tried in both regional and people's courts if the offenders have reached the age of criminal responsibility (which is sixteen or at least fourteen if charged with certain adult type offenses).

Russia has no separate juvenile (or family) court with exclusive jurisdiction over juvenile offenders, although in larger cities such as Moscow, so-called de facto juvenile courts operate. Reports suggest that large numbers of arrested juveniles have led to the informal development of these courts, and there are proposed reform efforts for the formation of formal juvenile courts in the future. Prior to 1991, the CJAs, staffed by volunteers, operated much like juvenile courts and provided a full range of dispositions (e.g., victim compensation, reprimands, probation, supervision by social workers or collectives at place of work, placement in technical schools) (Thornton and Voigt, 1992). Chiefly due to lack of financial resources and changes in infrastructure, most of the CJAs were eliminated in the new Russian Federation, with only a few CJAs remaining in operation in the larger cities such as Moscow and St. Petersburg. Current efforts to revive the CJA are afoot in Russia and probably stand a better chance of passing than a proposal for the establishment of a formal juvenile court system. In recent years, probably no more than 40 percent of arrested juvenile offenders have been referred for formal court processing, the remainder being handled by the *militsia*.

Corrections

Sanctions against juvenile offenders can come from several sources. As noted, the *militsia* can impose and monitor informal dispositions for minor juvenile law violators as well as make referrals for some offenders to agents under the Ministry of Social Protection. Juvenile offenders can, for example, be placed in residential educational institutions designed to rehabilitate and deter them from future criminality. CJAs also have the authority to impose sanctions on juveniles found guilty of certain criminal offenses, including referral to special educational, vocational, or technical schools.

People's courts, however, are the chief sentencing authority for juveniles in Russia today and can impose a number of penalties that are available to adult offenders, including suspended sentences, fines, restitution to the individual or community, incarceration in a prison or a correctional labor colony, probation, and forced treatment for a mental problem or for alcoholism and drug abuse. The death penalty cannot be imposed on individuals below eighteen years of age. The courts may also impose educational or reform measures instead of criminal punishment on juveniles under the age of sixteen who commit crimes (Voigt et al., 1994; *Crime and Delinquency, 1996,* 1997).

The system of special schools in the former USSR was created in 1964 and was for all intents and purposes the backbone of the residential and institutional system for dealing with the juvenile offenders sentenced for stealing, hooliganism, and drug and alcohol abuse. The first signs of crisis appeared in the late 1980s when serious juvenile offenders who had committed crimes like murder and rape were disproportionately placed in facilities along with severely mentally disturbed juvenile offenders. The lack of offense differentiation in referral to these facilities, which destroyed the rehabilitative milieu of the schools, lack of personnel resources (i.e., insufficient staff, especially psychologists), and lack of maintenance of the facilities have led to the decline of the residential institutional system. In recent years, the number of available places in special educational and treatment institutions has been reduced substantially, limiting options for referrals (see Baiduzhy, 1993).

CONCLUSION

It is difficult to know how all of the different factors of change interact or what their influences are on youth. To suggest to an ever-disillusioned public that loss of personal security and decline in the well-being of children are the unavoidable and unfortunate by-products of democratization and the transition of a market economy is not only an insult but is grossly inaccurate. According to the statistical data reported by the Russian Ministry of Internal Affairs, the rise in juvenile crimes over a ten-year period has been relatively moderate, even suggesting a declining trend in several categories of offenses. Clearly, the far-reaching changes with their corresponding impact on the everyday lives of Russian youth have not been subject to the rigors of scientific investigation.

The changes experienced by Russian youth have perhaps not only encouraged some of them to commit crimes (although the majority are law abiding), but to affirm their roots (ethnic and religious) and to reunite with past traditions, customs, and values. In the process of developing a new cultural identity, they have found new opportunities, established new relationships, and formed new social organizations. They have also discovered uncertainties, frustrations, and hardships. The changes have forced the Russian public not only to reevaluate their past but to ponder their future (Yergin and Gustafson, 1993). For some, the march of Russian history seems to have temporarily stalled. Yet as Russians stand at a point at which anything can happen—good or bad—by refocusing their attention on the needs of their youth, they may once again look toward the future.

NOTES

1. Criminologists use the term *official statistics* to refer to crime data collected by criminal justice agents such as the police. Other types of crime data may be collected from either the offenders themselves, referred to as *self-report studies*, or from crime victims, referred to as *victimization studies*. Official data, however, remain the most comprehensive way of gauging crime in a society on a regular basis.

2. The number of registered or reported crimes to the police is always a much larger figure than the number of "detected" offenders by the police. The numbers of juveniles committing specific crimes in Table 8.2 will be substantially smaller than those registered crimes reported to the police in Figure 8.1. The Uniform Crime Reports in America collected by the Federal Bureau of Investigation report, for example, "crimes known to the police" as well as arrest statistics—the number of people actually arrested for the commission of crimes. Arrest figures are always substantially smaller than crimes reported or "known to the police."

3. Juvenile kidnappings are not included in Table 8.2.

4. Some criminologists have attempted to explain certain types of criminality, particularly violent crimes, through biological explanations. For example, recent theories have examined such things as genetic and endocrine gland abnormalities and brain dysfunctions and tried to linked these phenomena with criminal behavior. The results of these types of theories have been questionable over the years.

REFERENCES

Avanesov, G. (1981). *The principle of criminology.* Moscow: Progress Press.
Baiduzhy, Andrel. (1993). Children behind bars: There is no system for working with troubled children in Russia. *Nezavisimaya Gaseta*, Mar. 31, p. 6.
Borbat, A. V. (1997). Problems of juvenile crime in Moscow. In A. I. Dolgova (Ed.), *Crime, statistics, and the law.* Moscow: Criminological Association. (In Russian)
Chelnokov, Aleksei. (1993). Children of the market. *Izvestia*, Aug. 11, p. 8.
Crime and Delinquency, 1996. (1997). Review. Moscow Ministry of Internal Affairs

of Russia, Ministry of Justice of Russia, Statistical Committee of the CIS. (In Russian)

Dolgova, A. I., Vanyushkin, S. V., Evlaova, O. A., llin, O. S., Korleva, M. V., Serebriyakova, V. A., and Yutskova, E. M. (1997). Crime in Russia: Statistics and realities. In A. I. Dolgova (Ed.), *Crime, statistics, and the law.* Moscow: Criminological Association. (In Russian)

Durkheim, E. (1951/1987). *Suicide.* Translated by J. R. Spaulding and G. Simpson. (Originally published in 1897). New York: Free Press

Finckenauer, James O. (1996). Russia. In Donald J. Shoemaker (Ed.), *International handbook on juvenile justice.* Westport, CT: Greenwood.

Freeland, Chrystia. (1995). Capitalism exposes the poverty gap. *Financial Times,* Nov. 10.

Gleizer, Grigory. (1993). Crime won't go away unless schools learn to teach everyone. *Current Digest of the Post Soviet Press, 45* (33), 23.

Handelman, Stephen. (1995). The Russian mafia. *Foreign Affairs, 73*(2), 83–96.

Melnikova, E. B. (1998). *How to protect a teenager from conflict with the law.* Moscow: BEK Publishers. (In Russian)

Merton, Robert. (1938). Social structure and anomie. *American Sociological Review, 3,* 672–682.

Milanovic, Branko. (1995). *Poverty, inequality and social policy in transition economies.* Washington, DC: World Bank.

Ministry of Internal Affairs (MVD) of the Russian Federation. Main Information Center. (1992). *Statistical data regarding juvenile crime in the Russian federation—1987–1991.* Moscow: Author. (In Russian)

Ministry of Internal Affairs (MVD) of the Russian Federation. Main Information Center. (1997). *Statistical data regarding crime and delinquency, 1996.* Moscow: Author. (In Russian)

Pronina, Lidia. (1994). Juvenile crime skyrockets. *Current Digest of the PostSoviet Press, 46* (1), 8.

Russian Constitution of 1993. Article 49.

Russian drug epidemic. (1998). *Crime and Justice International, 14*(2).

Signorelli, Lara. (1997). The most privileged class. *Russian Life,* June, pp. 1–10.

Silverman, B., and Yanowitch, M. (1997). *The new rich, new poor, new Russians.* Amonk, NY: M. E. Sharpe.

Solomon, Peter. (1978). *Soviet criminologists and criminal policy: Specialists in policy making.* New York: Columbia University Press.

Solomon, Peter. (1997). Courts and their reform in Russian history. In Peter Solomon (Ed.), *Reforming justice in Russia, 1864–1996: Power, culture, and the limits of legal order.* Amonk, NY: M. E. Sharpe.

Solzhenitsyn, A. (1995). Reflections on the eve of the twenty first-century. In Nathan Gardels (Ed.), *At century's end.* LaJolla, CA: ALTI Publishing.

Terrill, Richard J. (1997). *World criminal justice systems.* Cincinnati, OH: Anderson.

Thieves professing the code: The traditional role of Voiy v Zakone in Russia's criminal world and adaptions to a new social reality. Part 6: Current developments in the thieves world 1998. *CJ Europe Online.* Available at: http://www.acsp.uic.edu/oicj/pub/cje/050405-6.htm.

Thornton, William, and Voigt, L. (1992). *Delinquency and justice.* New York: McGraw-Hill.

UNICEF. (1995). *Poverty: Children and policy for a brighter future.* Florence, Italy: International Child Development Center.

United Nations. (1997). *United Nations demographic yearbook.* New York: United Nations.

Voigt, L., and Thornton, William. (1985). The rhetoric and politics of Soviet delinquency: An American perspective. In R. F. Thomasson (Ed.), *Comparative social research* (pp. 123–167). Greenwich, CT: JAI Press.

Voigt, L., Thornton, W., Barrile, L., and Seaman, J. (1994). *Criminology and justice.* New York: McGraw-Hill.

Yergin, Daniel, and Gustafson, Thane. (1993). *Russia 2010: And what it means for the world.* New York: Random House.

Zaslavskaya, Tanya. (1992). Personal interview, Moscow, Jan.

Zeldes, I. (1981). *The problem of crime in the U.S.S.R.* Springfield, IL: Thomas.

9

ST. LUCIA

Victoria Bruner

PERCEPTIONS OF TEEN VIOLENCE

There is currently great alarm regarding teen violence and the future of youth in this fragile country. There is a deepening awareness that as goes the course of socialization of the young, so goes the course of this nation. Political leaders recognize the urgency of addressing this issue. They fear a sinking into an ever-increasing abyss of social and economic ills and crime, so unfortunately familiar to numerous other developing nations in the global north and south. They recognize that social, economic, and human development needs must be met to stem the crisis of violence. Simply stated, violence impedes development.

There are tremendous natural resources here and little abject poverty, such as in Africa; however, in 1994, 6,600 persons between the ages of fifteen and twenty-four were unemployed, representing 55.38 percent of the total unemployed population of 31%.[1] A recent poverty assessment revealed that 18.7 percent of households (or approximately 25 percent of the population) were living in poverty. About one-third in this group cannot meet basic necessary daily dietary requirements.[2]

CURRENT TRENDS IN TEEN VIOLENCE

Adolescent crime in St. Lucia is directly related to three intertwining factors: poverty, unemployment, and terminating school at an early age.[3] Poverty is the parent of crime. Other social trends reflecting teen violence are an increase in teen suicide. Four suicides were reported in 1996, compared to two between 1990 and 1996. The implications are grave because it is generally accepted that there is an inverse relationship between the rate of suicide and the degree of social integration within society. Thus, the current suicide rate among youth suggests an insufficient integration into the society and a lack of self-worth.

In a survey I conducted in June 1997, I found that the following additional factors were identified by social workers, educators, health care professionals, government representatives, and members of the religious community as responsible for the increase in teen violence in St. Lucia: lack of adequate governmental priority, parental involvement and skills, educational programs and opportunities contrasted with poverty, easy access to alcohol and chemical substances, inadequate legal sanctions for child and domestic abuse, and an increase in exposure to societal and media violence coupled with access to lethal weapons.

All respondents perceived teen violence as increasing. As one educator stated, "It is not unusual nowadays to find weapons of violence in school bags of both primary and secondary school boys. These range from a pair of scissors to sharpened knives, and even occasional gun violence, resulting in serious injuries to teachers that have shocked the nation."[4]

I have observed St. Lucian society for sixteen years. Indeed, within the past three years, attacks on educators have averaged two to three per year; I was consulted on one incident that resulted in a near fatality of a school principal. Another respondent, a seventeen-year-old student, stated, "It's only recently that I began to notice a rise in the level of violence by teens. Some of their actions, such as rape and murder, were hardly heard of in times past."[5] A Social Issues Bulletin states that "60% of the persons within the criminal system were males below the age of 25. Theft, robbery, burglary and other teen crimes are on the rise."[6]

A class of seventeen students—thirteen males and four females between the ages of fifteen and eighteen—taught by Peace Corps volunteer Mick Admundson was surveyed on the progression of violence in St. Lucia. They related numerous instances of gang infiltration: "Gangs are a problem, they are well organized. Gangs pressure school children to use guns and fight, more gangs are pushing drugs out there." Sadly enough, they all agreed that, as one student stated, "Violence has gotten worse since we were children."[7]

The issue of teen violence is viewed seriously in St. Lucia. A fragile social and economic system, its future depends on a well-educated and civil society. The current trend of increase in teen violence does not bode well for its future unless it can be stemmed. The tourism industry depends on a perception of safety and hospitable and responsive citizens to draw and maintain visitors. Also, the nation has depended on a limited number of agricultural crops in the past: coconuts and bananas. The future will depend on creative diversification, a well-educated work population, and training programs. A recent Social Issues Bulletin distributed by the Social Planning Section of the Ministry of Planning, Development and Environment stated, "Whether St. Lucia can adapt to or survive current changes is based on the current situation of its citizenry, particularly its youth."[8] Eleven respondents in my survey ranked the issue of teen violence as serious, eight as very serious, and eleven as extremely serious.

Societal patterns believed to increase the cycle of violence—accepted corporal punishment, decline in religious practice, poor role models in culture, the moral fiber of society, and failure of "social safety nets" for families— were noted by respondents.

Politically, recent emphasis has been on viewing teen violence as a public health priority. In a strategy meeting with the chief medical officer of the nation, Dr. Steven King, I discussed new policy regarding violence awareness and prevention. Educators can no longer ignore the crisis and have called for more resources for schools. The need for school-based and community solutions has been a focus. The position paper on youth from the Ministry of Planning emphatically states, "The St. Lucian government has initiated numerous 'calls to action' regarding teen violence. Each will be described by factors considered as 'at risk' to increase teen violence."[9]

CONTRIBUTING FACTORS

Educational System

The educational system of St. Lucia is based on an English model in which corporal punishment is the rule rather than the exception. In one situation I am aware of, a teacher beat an eleven-year-old boy severely on his hands because he forgot his homework. Although this is a tradition in the schooling program, it is also a desperate behavior on the part of teachers, many of whom work under demanding conditions in terms of physical plant and lack of supplies. The children who attend school do so in crowded conditions, many of them often having to travel several miles to school. Additionally, there is early termination of schooling. The children are required to attend school only to the age of fifteen. At the age of eleven or twelve, a common entrance exam is given. Every year at least 5,000 students sit for the exam, trying to secure a place in a secondary school. On average, even of those students who pass—in the area of 2,000 students—only 45 percent can be accommodated by a secondary school. This means that the rest of the students have to continue primary school and then leave school basically with unmarketable qualifications at the age of fifteen. Thus, numerous youth lack the necessary skills, jobs, activities, or an opportunity to attend any type of secondary school. Many of them compete fiercely for minimum-wage jobs in agriculture or in the tourism industry. A hopelessness and a sense that there is little opportunity for advancement or upward mobility is pervasive.

Some families send their children on to a few private schools, but there is only one community-college-level institution on the island. Other students who qualify to go on to college cannot do so because they lack the financial means to leave the island and be sustained in a foreign country for education.

Child Abuse and Neglect

On a recent consultation trip to St. Lucia, I accompanied Kennedy Burke, a community relations branch officer of the Royal St. Lucian Police Force who covers the southern part of the island. His beat is one that involves community outreach. Burke is a native St. Lucian who, as he looked out on what was called Shanty Town, lamented the fact that he has seen an increasing number of cases of child abuse and neglect.

Domestic Violence

In St. Lucia, domestic violence is viewed as a critical part of the cycle of violence. *Social Issues Bulletin* states, "Violence breeds violence, and children who grow up in an abusive family situation tend to develop abusive habits and themselves become abusers in their own adult relationships."[10] It is considered a significant influence on teen violence in St. Lucia. The long- and short-term consequence of children growing up in homes where spousal abuse is rampant is devastating to their personality, behavior, conduct, and worldview. In St. Lucia, the Ministry of Health believes that these children enter adult relationships with scars and perpetuate a vicious cycle of abuse or compliance to abusive relationships if therapeutic treatment is not received to offset the enduring detrimental effects of child abuse.

Family Structure and Conditions for St. Lucian Women

It has often been said that as goes the condition of women and children in society, so goes the society. Family structure and the condition of women in St. Lucia affect teen violence. Several *Social Issues Bulletins* of the Ministry of Planning and Development have highlighted the possibility of a crisis in St. Lucian family structure and its possible contribution to juvenile delinquency.[11] St. Lucian society is primarily matriarchal; however, there are rigid sexual roles that have been defined, plus a dependency on women and a trend toward absent fathers. The reasons for this structure are numerous and complex. It is believed that some of the attribution of the patterns, however, is related to looseness in organization of the West Indian family. T. S. Simey, of Welfare and Planning in the West Indies, ascribed the cause of the spread of juvenile delinquency to this looseness of organization.[12] In St. Lucia, there are different family types. In about 48 percent of families surveyed in 1995 for a research piece entitled "The Family Survey: Family Relationships and Family Responsibility—St. Lucia," the conclusion was that 51 percent of biological fathers and children under fifteen years of age resided in the same household with those children. Approximately 49 percent of biological fathers were not present in households.[13]

However, there are several common constructs of St. Lucian families: a visiting relationship in which there is not a formal marriage but the father visits, a common law union, and a formal marriage. It is believed that the family structure contributes to teen violence because of stress and strain on the family structure due to working parents; parents and other adults are absent during critical periods of the day, resulting in inadequate supervision of teens.

Drug and Alcohol Abuse

In St. Lucia the problems of drug and alcohol abuse have been increasingly viewed as a significant contributor to teen violence and dysfunction. Marijuana use is a ubiquitous though illegal form of substance abuse in St. Lucia and is readily available. Alcohol is easily available to teens; this is a culture in which rum shops are on just about every corner in every community. Within the past ten years, hard drugs have been a significant risk factor to teens also. One of the most visible deterrents has been the implementation of the DARE program in St. Lucia, single-handedly promoted by a Royal St. Lucian police officer, Chriselda Branford, the director of the St. Lucian Community Outreach Division. She has drawn many of her fellow officers into the DARE program and runs several DARE programs in schools throughout St. Lucia. Several of the youth who were surveyed for this chapter believed that the government said it would employ more police to try to curb the problem of drugs. Certainly, gangs and their relationship to drug dealing are seen as a direct correlate to teen violence.

RESPONSES TO THE PROBLEM

Education

Many suggestions have been made to correct the educational situation. The first is to do away with the existing model of education. This would require extensive lobbying on the part of educators and other social and health officials, and most likely an act of Parliament. Another suggestion has been to create more technical schools. Several of these schools have been created in a joint partnership between religious communities and other interested nongovernmental institutions. One St. Lucian even established a

private high school and invested a tremendous amount of his personal resources so that children would be able to continue their education. Even
so, these children, ages thirteen to eighteen, must find the financial resources
to pay for their ongoing education. It is also believed that more parental
involvement in schools and establishing a more community-based model
would assist with this endeavor.

In terms of actual violence in schools, I have suggested that the school
environment and grounds of all the schools in St. Lucia be updated and
improved, and that the overcrowding be eliminated. Also, the provision of
school counselors and social workers would help tremendously, along with
the initiation of violence prevention programs within the school setting. In
a recent seminar, another presenter and I discussed the treatment of traumatized children and school violence prevention with fifty principals and
teachers. In addition, the St. Lucian Counseling Association formed in June
1998. Many of its members are school-related psychologists and counselors
who are keenly aware of the deficits within the educational system. It has
also been suggested through the Ministry of Education that a zero-tolerance
program in all school systems be initiated. The plan would be to identify
youth who were found with weapons or who displayed violent behavior,
expel them, and send them for counseling after disciplinary action was taken.

Efforts are also underway to involve the business community in forming
partnerships with schools. Some of the suggestions made in this area, since
it has been identified that there is a strong correlation between educational
attainment and poverty, relate to asking the business sector to invest in
education—for example, by sponsoring school feeding programs, especially
in schools in poorer communities. Such an investment would provide necessary sustenance to poor children, giving them the ability to concentrate
more on their schoolwork. Also, it would prove an incentive for students to
remain in school. The second suggestion would be direct provision of grants
to schools to improve the physical plant, which would enhance the school
environment and motivate teachers and students. Third is the sponsorship
of skills-training programs. It has been recognized that youth have few employable skills. Therefore, skills-training programs would furnish the youth
with necessary skills for employment. Many of the subjects taught in school
are not believed to be appropriate for students to learn the necessary skills
needed on the island; rather, they revolve around "Westernized" curriculum.

Providing adequate recreational and sporting activities for youth would
fill the void of inactivity and extra time on their hands. These activities could
channel creative energies, especially of marginalized youth, away from self-
destructive behaviors. Two other measures should be considered. One
would be to regulate the sale of tools used in assaults. For example, in this
Caribbean nation, as in many others, the cutlass or machete used in agriculture is readily available. Also, it would be important to toughen gun laws
and to create drug- and gun-free areas around schools; these areas would

be carefully monitored and fines would be levied for infractions. An additional measure would be to develop a youth corps in which each school in turn would adopt a community during an active period of time—between 3 and 6 P.M., when we know that there are many problems for youth. The youth corps would be monitored by the community, and the school youth would also be supervised in study or working within their community on some project of community improvement. One suggestion would be for them to work under supervision as aides or readers in a hospital setting or in a home for the aged. One student, when asked what would help them the most, said simply, "Build more schools, provide more work opportunities, and help us with a community recreation center." Locating community activities within the schools would not only maximize the school's use but be a resource for the community. An active program of mentoring could be a critical method in helping to mold behavior patterns of the youth, providing them with realistic assessments of what the world has to offer. It is believed that many children lack positive role models.

Child Abuse

So urgent is the problem of child abuse and neglect that the Ministry of Social Affairs requested a specialist to develop a child abuse and neglect registry, education for professionals and paraprofessionals, and a strategy to address this problem in St. Lucia society. Johnny DeCatoria, a UNICEF psychologist/social worker, was assigned to St. Lucia in 1995. Since that time, he has been an outspoken advocate for children and for the development of services for abused and neglected children. In addition, with his clinical skills, he has been able to provide consultation to numerous other St. Lucian social and health specialists.

In 1977, the Children and Young Persons Act was created by the Parliament; it states, "Every person who, having the custody, charge or care of any juvenile or causes or procures him or her to be assaulted, ill-treated, neglected, abandoned or exposed in a manner likely to cause that juvenile unnecessary suffering or injury to health, including injury or loss of sight or hearing or limb or organ of the body and any mental derangement, shall be guilty of an offense." In a training seminar in August 1996, I encouraged St. Lucian social workers within the Ministry of Social Affairs to organize themselves and develop a professional association so that they could become strong lobbyists for the government to adopt strong legislation giving them the power to become mandatory reporters and establish stronger policies and strategies to prevent child abuse and neglect.

Ursula Herman, a social worker, has taken a very active role in educating St. Lucians about sexual abuse. She has creatively put together a group of health educators, social workers, and a theater group to visit rural communities to highlight and educate them about sexual abuse. Other social and health professionals and I are educating St. Lucians about the long-term effects, psychosocial and neurological, of child abuse and neglect. One two-day workshop was presented to the Royal St. Lucian Police Community Outreach Division and was titled "The Impact of Violence on Children." The new Ministry of Health believes that this is a critical area to address from a multidisciplinary approach. Efforts have been made using consultants and ongoing training within communities on parenting skills. In an effort to build a safe, loving, and secure environment for all through a consistent disavowal of all forms of interpersonal violence, the following recommendations were made in a Social Issues Bulletin:

1. To adopt a commitment to building a nonviolent society by government, communities, institutions, organizations and households.

2. To enact legal reform to remove tolerance in the law for any level of violence to children, including physical punishment and deliberate humiliation in the home and institutions. Children are entitled to care, security and good upbringing. They are to be treated with respect for their person and individuality, and may not be subjected to brutal corporal punishment or any other humiliating treatment.

   It is believed that the greatest chance we have to prevent violence in St. Lucian society is to raise children who reject violence as a method of problem solving. It is deemed necessary to safeguard, then, against children's perception also of spousal abuse as a social norm and a valid means of conflict resolution.

3. Vigorous advocacy is paramount at all levels—national, institutional, communal and individual—for the practical implementation of the principles and standards of the 1989 United Nations Convention on the Rights of the Child. This convention offers the hope of reform to protect children from all forms of violence. St. Lucia was one of the nations that ratified early.

4. It is necessary to review all forms of support services for children and families from a specifically anti-violence perspective, and to enact comprehensive integrative programs with prevention and intervention strategies that will emphasize community outreach and public education as well as the treatment of all known cases of child abuse and neglect, and the provision of shelter for those children.[14]

Sister Delourdes, of St. Jude's Mercy Hospital on the island, has initiated a program of awareness of the importance of early attachment and bonding for new parents at St. Jude's Hospital with materials provided to her. In the spring of 1998, the First Years Last Forever program, designed by the Reiner Foundation, was presented to the St. Jude's Hospital and Ministry of Social Affairs as a donation by the Iowa Child Abuse and Neglect Council.

In the Social Issues Bulletin of October 1996, it was stated that "data are not reflective of the real situation regarding child abuse and neglect when such evidence is juxtaposed against anecdotal reports of social extension workers and other individuals."[15] It is believed that there has been overall nonreporting of known cases, which disguises the magnitude of the incidence of child abuse and neglect. However, in the period between 1990 and 1995, 601 cases of either sexual or physical abuse were reported.

Sister Delourdes and other community activists have organized a lobbying group to put pressure on the government to enact child abuse and neglect legislation. As the pastoral counselor at the hospital, she has reviewed many cases of child abuse and neglect, yet cannot adequately serve these children and their families because of the lack of facilities and sanctioning power. However, it is well known now in St. Lucia that there is a correlation between child abuse and neglect and the cycle of violence.

In a training seminar that DeCatoria conducted in May 1998 for prison staff recruits, he pointed out that it was clear that abuse played a significant role in juvenile delinquency problems. These officers were being trained for assignments at the only facility for juveniles, the Boys Training Center. DeCatoria surveyed the residents in May 1998 and found that 80 percent of the boys admitted that they had been physically abused by their parents or families. Half of them believed they had been abused severely; the remaining half said they had been abused moderately. Ninety percent of these boys had witnessed violence in their communities, including being threatened with a knife or gun, and witnessed violence in the home. Sixty-three percent related witnessing a stabbing or shooting incident. More than half of these residents—58 percent—reported having been stabbed with a knife. An alarming 32 percent admitted they had been sexually abused or assaulted.[16]

Sexual abuse and trauma are believed to be widespread on the island, yet due to the nature of the society in which there are still small social networks, it is difficult to treat incest adequately. Several social workers have related that the extended families are well known, and so is the person within the community, giving them very little opportunity to be removed from the situation. Moreover, there is no shelter for child abuse and neglect survivors.

Domestic Violence

Within the past five years, several horrific domestic violence crimes have been committed in St. Lucia. I was present when the women and other outraged citizens took to the streets to march on the Ministry of Justice after a sentence of five years for manslaughter was given in regard to a case in which a man decapitated his wife with a cutlass during an argument in front of five young children. Much of the public outrage about this case has come about because of the tireless efforts of numerous health and social change agents in St. Lucian society. One of these agents, Ione Ford, is an elderly woman who is indefatigable in her efforts to educate the public about and to treat cases of domestic violence at the St. Lucia Crisis Center. Her agency, is the only crisis center on the island. As she states, "The family unit is not what it should be. Lack of communication and association in the home enforces the visibility of violence, insults and weapons to settle the slightest of arguments between spouses."[17] In the past nine years Ford and her volunteers and other dedicated St. Lucians have succeeded in getting some measures instituted.

The first is closed-court hearings for cases of sexual abuse, the Family Court Act of 1994, and the Domestic Violence Act of 1996. Numerous demonstrations and resolutions to the government have also drawn attention to domestic violence. This center was formed in 1988 through a joint effort of an associate club of the International Federation of Business and Professional Women's Clubs. The center distributes brochures and provides education to youth and teens regarding domestic violence. However, Ford relates that there is a failure to support the crisis center fully. She believes this is due to the lack of women's empowerment and interest from the government and private high places for sponsorship. Male dominance, she believes, is a significant barrier in St. Lucian society.

There is a priority for a shelter for surviving victims of violence and abuse and a home for young teens, especially school dropouts who may be escaping from violent homes, and teen mothers, who may have no other avenue except prostitution. Ford also cites the prevalence for a preference for male children in St. Lucian society, which puts women at a definite disadvantage. There are also significant trends within the St. Lucian family that she believes puts teens more at risk for exposure to violence. Many of the mothers she works with, for example, are either unconcerned or trapped by fear and economic dependence to disclose the wrongdoings and violent behaviors that they are subjected to.

The Family Court Act of 1994 provided the possibility that a social support section would be created to deal with cases of domestic violence brought to the magistrate. Priority has been given to this newly created treatment program because it is believed in St. Lucia that the child who witnesses spousal abuse is at great risk of being assaulted, feeding again into the cycle of violence.

The Family Court Social Support section is staffed by social workers: Rubelia King, director; Clementia Eugene, social worker and president of the St. Lucian Social Workers Association; and Curtis Prescott, a long-term veteran and social worker of the Ministry of Social Affairs. King relates that overall, the level of exposure to violence in St. Lucian society is very high.[18] Overcrowding in homes also may contribute to the incidence of exposure to violence. Often children in St. Lucian society share the same sleeping area with adults. Further, the disparity in employment status between males and females seems to weaken the position of women in St. Lucian society, rendering them dependent on others and less able to leave abusive relationships. Since kinship networks are close and the island is small, it is very difficult for the children and the spouse to find a refuge. The staff of the Family

Court believes that due to the complexity of the issues, a solution to the problem of domestic violence in St. Lucia will prove "quite arduous."[19]

The current intervention strategies are to provide counseling or to institute criminal proceedings in court. Additionally, the Domestic Violence Act makes several provisions that may order redress or protect victims of domestic violence. One such initiative has been reinstituted by Sister Delourdes. It consists of a modest microeconomic system for women and children who are in domestic violence situations. It has been partnered with a group of women in Iowa who provide raw materials to Sister Delourdes and her group members; then these goods are sold in Iowa. This provides some limited independence for these women and the opportunity for them to take themselves and their children out of this high risk factor that contributes to teen violence. The University of Iowa School of Social Work has placed a graduate intern in St. Lucia for six months to provide research and programming in relational violence.

Family Structure and Conditions for Women

A number of measures have been taken by the government to advance women in St. Lucian society. In 1986, the Women's Desk was established in the Ministry of Community Development, Youth, and Sports and Social Affairs. A coordinator of women's affairs was appointed, and a women's affairs officer was also designated to promote and elevate the condition of women in St. Lucian society and to work toward equality. In May 1987, the National Women's Advisory Committee was established to prepare a national policy on women. This was adopted in March 1991. In 1994, the Ministry of Legal Affairs and Women's Affairs was formed, and the first female senator in the Parliament of St. Lucia was appointed to this post. These divisions specifically advocate for women and families and address the issues of the many working women in St. Lucia, especially the need for supervision of children, equality, and day care. These divisions also deal with teen violence by educating men on the role that they can play in the upbringing of their families.

In a study of rural women in St. Lucia in 1997, interestingly enough it was found that they are an underserved area. Rural women who were studied identified their farm work, house work, and then care of their children ranking third on a daily basis. It is believed that the economic trends and pressures for women in St. Lucia have pushed rural women especially to devoting most of [20] their working hours to farming, while their motherly functions are sacrificed or fulfilled by older children within the extended household or within the community.[21] However, these two factors of women's increased employment and the lack of adequate supervision of children in the community after school hours have been significant in contributing to teen violence.

CONCLUSION

The patterns of teen violence in St. Lucia reflect a global trend. Youth seem to have lost their place in society. Even though this is a small island nation, it is not immune from the trends affecting larger countries: the influence of the changing family structure, drugs and alcohol, the impact of the media, and strains put on dwindling economic resources and school systems. However, in this small island nation, there is an alert awareness and a plan of approach to teen violence. Because the island is small geographically, one can "get one's arms around the problem." Most of all, there is strong commitment to resolve this issue.

NOTES

1. Social Planning Section, Ministry of Planning, Development and Environment, The Youth: As We Enter the Next Millennium, *Social Issues Bulletin*, Topic no. 9 (September 1996).

2. Social Planning Section, Ministry of Planning, Development and Environment, Poverty Eradication: A New Role for the Business Sector, *Social Issues Bulletin*, Topic no. 7 (July 1996).

3. Social Planning Section, Ministry of Planning, Development and Environment, Poverty Eradication: A New Role for the Business Sector, *Social Issues Bulletin*, Topic no. 7 (July 1996).

4. Social Planning Section, Ministry of Planning, Development and Environment, Deviance in Society, *Social Issues Bulletin*, Topic no. 11 (November 1996).

5. Social Planning Section, Ministry of Planning, Development and Environment, Deviance in Society, *Social Issues Bulletin*, Topic no. 11 (November 1996).

6. Social Planning Section, Ministry of Planning, Development and Environment, Deviance in Society, *Social Issues Bulletin*, Topic no. 11 (November 1996).

7. Personal communication, Mick Amundson.

8. Social Planning Section, Ministry of Planning, Development and Environment, The Likely Effects of Spousal Abuse on Our Children in the Caribbean, *Social Issues Bulletin*, Topic no. 23–24 (November-December 1997).

9. Social Planning Section, Ministry of Planning, Development and Environment, The Youth: As We Enter the Next Millennium. *Social Issues Bulletin*, Topic no. 9 (September 1996).

10. Social Planning Section, Ministry of Planning, Development and Environment, The Youth: As We Enter the Next Millennium. *Social Issues Bulletin*, Topic no. 9 (September 1996).

11. Social Planning Section, Ministry of Planning, Development and Environment, Concerns about the Family, *Social Issues Bulletin*, Topic no. 19–21 (July-September 1997).

12. Social Planning Section, Ministry of Planning, Development and Environment, Concerns about the Family, *Social Issues Bulletin*, Topic no. 19–21 (July-September 1997).

13. Personal communication, Ione Ford, June 1997.
14. Personal communication, Rubelia King, June 1997.
15. Social Issues Bulletin of October 1996.
16. Social Issues Bulletin of October 1996.
17. Social Issues Bulletin of October 1996.
18. Personal communication, Rubelia King, June 1997.
19. Herman Paul, student—Vieux Fort, St. Lucia.
20. Rufina Paul, unpublished study entitled, "Rural Women In St. Lucia," 1997.
21. Rufina Paul, unpublished study entitled, "Rural Women In St. Lucia," 1997.

10

SLOVENIA

Gorazd Mesko, Branko Lobnikar, Milan Pagon, and Bojan Dekleva

PERCEPTIONS OF TEEN VIOLENCE

In Slovenia, the issue of teen violence arose as a special theme at the beginning of the 1990s, the most intense process of change in the Slovenian political and social system—the process of transition. As a consequence, youth violence is sometimes interpreted in Slovenia as one of the transitional topics, a phenomenon that is typical for a social transition or maybe even caused by it. As the available official data on youth violence show, this preoccupation with teen violence has not been caused by an increase in the violence itself. Instead, perceptions have changed, and this change has been accompanied by parallel changes in some other fields.

There were at least three waves of public uneasiness, or "moral panic," in Slovenia after World War II. The first took place between 1965 and 1971, the second in the first half of the 1980s, and we are currently witnessing the third wave, which began in the early 1990s.

The first wave was accompanied by a sudden and continuous rise of officially known juvenile crime (including acts of violence) between 1965 and 1971. In those years, the number of juveniles found guilty doubled. This was the period of major economic and political liberalization in Slovenian history, and the start of the consumerist orientation in the former Yugoslavia, especially in Slovenia, its northern and most developed part. Ideologically, the public moral panic was related to the images of hooligans and beatniks (symbolized by long hair) and, in general, youth who decided to pursue their own "selfish" interests instead of the interests of the society's (ideologically constructed) collective subjects.

The second wave of public and professional special interest in youth unrest and violence took place from 1980 to 1985, after the death of the former Yugoslavian president, Tito. In those days, the images of conflict-prone and violent youth dominated mass media portraits of youth. Punk and related subcultures seemed to reflect the same process of the heterogenization and conflicts that had caused the dissolution of the former Yugoslavia and created the foundation for the new independent states. That wave of concern about the violent youth, however, was not supported by official statistics on youth violence.

The last wave of concern can still be observed. It is reflected in mass media and public opinion regarding the increase of street violence, the rise of youth drug abuse, as well as bullying and peer violence in schools. The official data in this period have not shown any consistent and obvious long-term rise of criminal acts or violent acts specifically, but it is difficult to analyze the official data without distance.

In the 1990s, in contrast to the period of the previous single-party political regime, the issue of teen violence and related problems have been less ideologized. That means that the public, professionals, and politicians do not view teen violence as a direct sign or consequence of deviant political developments and changes. At the same time, however, the violence and its causes are sometimes attributed to some specific parts of the population in a way that serves specific political and ideological interests (e.g., in discussions of violence of immigrants).

But, in general, "normal" violence has begun to be viewed more often as the result of "normal" social and political life. However, life in this period of the transition is being constantly reconstructed and is still relatively unstable. So, as in all other transitional countries in Eastern and Central Europe, we have abolished (or are just abolishing) some social structures, habits, and institutions that have played major roles in socializing and controlling youth deviance, but sometimes without taking proper care of other institutions that could cover the deserted spaces.

CURRENT TRENDS IN TEEN VIOLENCE

We estimate that the priorities related to youth violence and other forms of deviance in general have not risen in the past ten years. State institutions have lost their imperative for a direct role, and the new roles and functions are open for both market and private and civil initiatives.

Some Indicators of Teen Violence in Slovenia

Globocnik (1997) conducted research on juvenile violence based on criminal statistics: criminal and public order offenses committed by juveniles in Slovenia between 1986 and 1994. The main findings were the following:

- In the studied period, violent criminal offenses committed by juveniles increased by 3.9 percent.
- Verbal violence (bold behavior, arguing, and screaming) was increasing.
- A number of individuals suspected of criminal offenses with elements of physical violence increased within a group of young people between ages eighteen and twenty.
- Violent juvenile delinquency increased significantly.
- The education level of juvenile suspects of violent offenses was below the national level.
- The proportion of female violent delinquency increased.
- About 20 percent of suspects of violent property criminal offenses were juveniles whose victims were older than twenty-seven years.
- Victims of juvenile violence were about the same age as the perpetrators.
- The places of criminal offenses were changing from public places to private places.
- Criminal statistics implied a tendency of increasing violence by juveniles that resulted in criminal and public order offenses.

Bullying among Youth

Dekleva and his colleagues (1996c) published results of a study on bullying in Slovenian primary and high schools. The sample consisted of 1,382 individuals (694 girls and 688 boys) from Ljubljana, a capital city, and nearby towns. The main findings of the study were the following:

- Verbal violence was the most frequent form of violence among respondents (45 percent of students experienced it from time to time).
- "Bullying" encompassed beating, kicking, spitting, verbal abuse or insult, teasing, depriving of freedom, threats, extortion, property damage, theft, touching and other sexual harassment, and chasing.
- Around 27 percent of students experienced bullying at least once during the past five years.
- The most common places of bullying were a classroom, in front of the school building or in a school yard, on the way to or from school, a playground, during leisure or school activities, in the street near home, and in a nearby neighborhood.

The study also revealed that at least 50 percent of students experienced bullying during the previous school year, 15 to 20 percent experienced bullying frequently, and 5 percent experienced bullying almost every day. More than 10 percent of respondents confirmed that they bullied other children; many of the victims of bullying were ignored by those who witnessed the violence. And only a minority of students believed that teachers or professionals wanted to stop violence at school. Schools differed in the extent of violence and bullying, and parents were not well informed about the violence at school. The proportion of parents who were aware of the problem of bullying was much smaller than the proportion of victimized children.

CONTRIBUTING FACTORS

Juvenile Gangs

Lesar (1998) notes that juvenile gangs consist of *cefurs*. (A *cefur* is a derogatory remark for people from other republics of the former Yugoslavia who live in Slovenia.) In Ljubljana, members serve as apprentices for subsequent organized crime activities.

Violence is a part of juvenile gang activities and also part of the group dynamics in creating a hierarchy in a juvenile gang. Juvenile gangs and possible criminal violence are of great concern, especially in neighborhoods where the immigrants from the former Yugoslavia live.

All juvenile gangs studied have the following in common (Lesar, 1998):

- A perception that violence is present in living environments
- A fear of overwhelming violence but also an entitlement to use violence in solving problems
- A preoccupation with violence-related values (good at fighting, physical strength)
- Status in a gang that is dependent on a level of expressed violence

Official Crime Statistics on Youth Violence

The crime rate for all criminal offenses is 2,158 criminal offenses per 100,000 citizens. See Tables 10.1, 10.2, and 10.3 for detailed information.

Self-Destructive Behaviors

In Slovenia, injuries and poisoning are the principal causes of death among young persons. They constitute almost three-quarters of all deaths within a group of young people between fifteen and twenty-nine years. The next most frequent causes of death in 1995 in the same age group were neoplasm (6.82 per 100,000) and symptoms, signs, and ill-defined conditions (5.68 per 100,000). The three main causes of death are characteristic for both men and women (Tivadar, 1998).

Table 10.1
Proportion of Juvenile Delinquency in Overall Crime Statistics

Year	Number of criminal offenses	Juvenile	Delinquency
		Number of Criminal Offenses	Percentage
1989	39,967	3,938	9.9
1990	38,353	4,300	11.2
1991	42,250	4,709	11.2
1992	54,085	6,770	12.5
1993	44,278	5,554	12.5
1994	43,635	5,599	12.8
1995	38,178	4,475	11.7
1996	36,587	4,207	11.5
Average	43,169	5,219	12.03

Source: Ministry of the Interior, *Annual Report* (1997).

Table 10.2
Violent Crimes of Suspected Juveniles, 1993–1996

Criminal Offenses	Number	of	Criminal	Offenses
	1993	1994	1995	1996
Murder (inc. attempted murder)	2	4	3	6
Rape (inc. attempted rape)	6	11	5	2
Aggravated assault	39	45	48	41
Battery	32	28	83	86
Burglary	1,533	1,676	1,273	1,148
Robbery	62	74	93	193
Damage to property	393	260	324	255
Threatening behavior	50	57	36	26
Extortion	112	164	186	78

Source: Ministry of the Interior, *Annual Report* (1997).

Table 10.3
Juvenile Perpetrators against Whom an Educational Measure or Sentence Has Been Given, by Type of Crime

Criminal Offenses	1991	1992	1993	1994	1995
Against life and body	26	19	30	26	29
Against sexual inviolability	9	8	4	8	3
Against property	928	1,002	973	908	404
Against public order and peace	21	6	21	13	4

Source: Ministry of the Interior, *Annual Report* (1997).

The structure of fatal injuries shows that motor vehicle accidents are the principal cause of fatal injuries among young people, followed by suicide; other fatal injuries account for less than a fifth of all fatal injuries.

Tables 10.4 and 10.5 show that mortality due to suicide is higher among men than among women in all age groups. The suicide rate after the teenage

Table 10.4
Number of Suicides in Slovenia, 1990–1997

	0–13 years		14-18 years		19-21 years		22+ years		Total	
	men	women	men	women	men	women	men	women	men	women
1990	1	1	7	3	8	3	407	123	423	130
1991	2	1	5	3	18	4	481	141	506	149
1992	2	1	9	3	14	2	413	140	438	146
1993	3	0	13	3	24	3	440	126	480	132
1994	2	0	13	4	12	2	451	135	478	141
1995	3	0	12	5	19	1	402	124	436	130
1996	2	0	14	6	7	4	440	131	463	141
1997	2	0	8	4	19	1	444	115	471	120

Source: Institute of Public Health (1998).

Table 10.5
Suicide Rate per 100,000

	14-18 years	19-21 years	0-100+ years
1990	6.7	13.0	27.7
1991	5.1	25.8	32.8
1992	8.0	18.5	29.3
1993	10.6	30.9	30.8
1994	11.2	12.6	31.2
1995	11.2	22.6	28.5
1996	13.3	12.2	30.3

Source: Institute of Public Health (1998).

period increases with age. Suicides are usually not committed by very young or very old people. We can see that in the 1990s, suicides increased among young people in the fourteen to eighteen age group, while it was oscillating in the older groups and in the total population. In Slovenia, the social group with the highest rates of suicide are old, single, or widowed men. Although suicides do constitute a considerable proportion of fatal injuries and poisoning among young people, the number of suicides among youth is low in comparison with other age groups. However, since a suicide is an unusually common way of handling personal and social pressures in Slovenia (suicide rates in Slovenia are among the highest in Europe), more special programs for suicidal prevention should be established.

Tivadar (1998) reports that in 1995, the most frequent method of committing suicide was by hanging, for both sexes. Among men, hanging was followed by the use of firearms and explosives, while among women, hanging was followed by jumping from a high place. Both young and elderly men committed suicide by hanging. The use of firearms and explosives was the second most frequent way of committing suicide among young men, followed by the use of nonhousehold gases and vapors. Young women mainly committed suicide by hanging and poisoning (taking solid or liquid substances). (See Tables 10.6 and 10.7.)

Table 10.6
Suicide by Method of Suicide

	Men (%)	Women (%)	Total (%)
Solid or liquid substances	5.1	6.9	6.4
Common household gases	0.0	0.8	0.2
Other gases and vapors	8.0	3.9	7.1
Hanging, strangulation and suffocation	64.6	53.5	62.1
Drowning	2.3	9.3	3.9
Firearms, explosives	10.8	2.3	8.9
Cutting and piercing instruments	2.5	3.9	2.8
Jumping from a high place	3.9	10.1	5.3
Other and unspecified means	2.8	5.4	3.4
Latent effects of self-inflicted injuries	-	-	-
Total	100	100	100

Source: Tivadar (1998, 336).

RESPONSES TO THE PROBLEM

In 1997, the Ministry of Education and Sport established an interministry commission on violence designated as the "expert group in charge of the observation, formation and coordination of the policy regarding teen violence and preventive actions in the field of education." Members of this group are representatives from governmental and nongovernmental organizations. The main aims of the group are to develop and evaluate teen violence prevention programs in school areas; analyze and eliminate the causes of teen violent behavior in school and school areas; and develop, coordinate, evaluate, and maintain national policy against teen violence.

At the Ministry of the Interior, the Criminal Investigations Department (CID) deals with juvenile delinquency and teen violence. A special unit within the CID was established to deal with juvenile delinquency. Every regional police headquarters (there are eleven in Slovenia) has detectives (criminal investigators) who deal with juvenile delinquency.

The police force in Slovenia tries to establish contact with representatives of local communities and other institutions in their jurisdiction. Among many police activities, police officers also provide informative lectures at schools about the role of police and problems of crime.

The private security industry is also involved in providing services to primary and secondary schools. Their activities consist of such matters as physical protection, surveillance, and control at school entrances.

Relevant Organizations

Youth Department of Slovenia

Within the Ministry of Education and Sport, the Youth Department of Slovenia deals with matters concerning the role and position of young peo-

Table 10.7
Suicide by Method of Suicide, Ages Fifteen to Twenty-nine

	Men (%)	Women (%)	Total (%)
Solid or liquid substances	4.17	33.3	7.41
Common household gases	-	11.11	1.23
Other gases and vapors	11.11	11.11	11.11
Hanging, strangulation and suffocation	58.33	33.33	55.56
Drowning	-	-	-
Firearms, explosives	16.67	-	14.81
Cutting and piercing instruments	1.39	-	1.23
Jumping from a high place	4.17	11.11	4.94
Other and unspecified means	4.17	-	3.70
Latent effects of self-inflicted injuries	-	-	-
Total	100	100	100

Source: Tivadar (1998, 357).

ple in Slovenian society, the support of the development of youth work, and the encouragement of young people's education as well as other activities designed to assist all young people in becoming active participants in society. One of the most important fields of work of the Youth Department are youth studies carried out by the Center of Social Psychology at the Faculty of Social Sciences, University of Ljubljana. The center has done two studies on the values and lifestyles of young people. The first one, in 1993, surveyed high school students, and the second one, in 1995, surveyed university students. In 1998 the center, supported by the Youth Department, issued *Youth in Slovenia: New Perspectives from the Nineties* (Ule and Rener, 1998). One chapter addresses juvenile delinquency in Slovenia; it also analyzes official criminal statistics on juvenile delinquency (Lobnikar, 1998). Also, the expert group in charge of the observation, formation, and coordination of the policy on teen violence is working within the Youth Department.

Children's Parliament

The Children's Parliament was launched in the same year as the first multiparty elections in Slovenia, 1990, and is sponsored by the Slovene Association of Friends of Youth, one of the largest nongovernmental organizations in this domain in Slovenia. It was launched as a meeting of children's representatives with the new government. The first debate was on environmental issues; subsequent parliaments dealt with new problems, among them juvenile violence and bullying (Pavlovic, 1998).

While high school students (ages fifteen to nineteen) have their own independent parliaments in formal governing bodies, such as school councils, the term "Children's Parliament" refers to elementary school children (primary schools, ages seven to fifteen). The Children's Parliament has been accompanied by numerous activities in primary schools: workshops, surveys, social skill games, and bulletins. Mentors make sure that the students are well informed about the problems discussed and encourage students to suggest topics for discussion. The elected students represent their school in a municipal parliament, which is a step between a primary school and a national parliament. The Ministry of Education and Sport has supported the process through several regulations included in the new school legislation, requiring principals to enable at least two assemblies of the parliament in a school year.

Pavlovic (1998) reflects a role of the Children's Parliament with the following statement: "The significance and value of children's participation, we believe, extend beyond mere reduction in deviance/violence. Indeed, if such a reduction takes place, it is a welcome side effect."

Association for Nonviolent Communication

The Association for Nonviolent Communication was established in Ljubljana in 1996. Its mission has been to fill a gap in nongovernmental organization activities in the domain of resolving violence. The work of the association has been oriented toward violence among women and men and especially among youth. It has started several projects: counseling of violent men, victim support, training of volunteers, dealing with exceptional children at schools, preventive programs, lectures, and workshops for teachers, social workers, and other professionals who work with children and youth.

The association has been very active and has proved itself with the following accomplished tasks: a documentary film on violence, presence on the radio, a volunteer training brochure, presence on the Internet for providing information on violence in Slovenia, research on violence in Slovenia, individual counseling for victims of violence, self-help groups, and support and help for children with learning difficulties.

Skala

The Skala ("rock") association consists of the Salesians of Don Bosco (Roman Catholic Church) and volunteers who have started several projects related to the reduction of violence among youth in Slovenia. Skala has been active for three years and incorporates activities directed to minors in Slovenia, especially in high-risk environments. It follows the basic principles of the pedagogy of Don Bosco (a priest in Turin, Italy, 1815–1888).

It has conducted the following projects to diminish violence among youth:

- Presence in the streets (street prevention, diverting youth from criminal activities)
- Organization of sports activities for youth
- The "bus of pleasure"—a traveling youth center (traveling classroom, information and counseling center, and video room)
- Roundtables with lectures about violence reduction and nonviolent communication

B&Z: Education, Counseling, and Research Engineering

B&Z provides a wide range of services for victims of crime. The most significant are the following:

* A counseling telephone line
* Free, prompt personal support and help
* Practical advice for solving problems
* Self-help groups

CONCLUSION

Due to a lack of almost any scientific evaluations, it is hard to determine the success of different actions. Although there are some developing programs that seem successful (like the Children's Parliament and some forms of child care and preventive projects), in other fields we seem to be experiencing restructuring and even crisis. These crises are caused or provoked not so much by the rise of youth violence as by changing social and political conditions.

REFERENCES

B&Z. (1998). Centri za pomoc zrtvam kaznivih dejanj v Sloveniji, zlozenka.

Dekleva, B. (1996a). Nasilje med vrstniki v zvezi s šolo—obseg pojava. *Revija za kriminalistiko in kriminologijo, 47*(4), 355–365.

Dekleva, B. (1996b). Nasilje med vrstniki v šoli in v zvezi s šolo. In Alenka Šelih (Ed.), *Otrokove pravice, šolska pravila in nasilje v šoli*. Ljubljana: Inštitut za kriminologijo pri Pravni fakulteti.

Dekleva, B. (1996c). *Nasilje med vrstniki v šoli in v zvezi s šolo*. Ljubljana: Inštitut za kriminologijo pri Pravni fakulteti.

Globocnik, M. (1997). Nasilniško obnašanje mladih. *Revija za kriminalistiko in kriminologijo, 1*, 38–50.

Institute of Public Health of the Republic of Slovenia (IPH). (1998). Data about suicide rate in Slovenia.

Kobolt, A. (1995). Erziehungshilfe in Slowenien. Konzepte und neue Entwicklungen. In H. Moersberger (Ed.), *Europa Hearusforderung fuer die Erziehungshilfe*. Freiburg im Breisgau: Lambertus.

Lesar, S. (1998). Kdo je "Cefur"? diplomska naloga, Pedagoška fakulteta, Univerza v Ljubljana.

Lisec, M. (1998). Projekt Skala. Unpublished paper.

Lobnikar, B. (1998). Delinquency and criminal offences. In M. Ule and T. Rener (Eds.), *Youth in Slovenia: New perspectives from the nineties*. Ljubljana: Youth Department, Ministry of Education and Sport of the Republic of Slovenia.

Meško, G. (1992). Empirici prikaz parametrov kriminalitete mladoletnikov na Gorenjskem in v Sloveniji v letih 1979 do 1988. *Varnost-strokovni bilten, 3*, 233–250.

Meško. G. (1998). *Uvod v kriminologijo, Visoka policijsko-varnostna šola.* Ljubljana.

Pavlovic, Z. (1996). Children's Parliament in Slovenia. In M. John (Ed.), *Children in charge: The child's right to a fair hearing* (pp. 93–107). London: Jessica Kingsley Publishers.

Pavlovic, Z. (1998). The influence of children's quality participation on tension and violence reduction: The process of Children's Parliament in Slovenia. Unpublished paper.

Statisticni letopis. (1996). Urad Republike Slovenije za statistiko. Ljubljana.

Statisticni letopis ministrstva za notranje zadeve R Slovenije. (1996). Ljubljana.

Tivadar, B. (1998). Health status. In M. Ule and T. Rener (Eds.), *Youth in Slovenia: New perspectives from the nineties.* Ljubljana: Youth Department, Ministry of Education and Sport of the Republic of Slovenia.

Ule, M. and Rener, T. (1998). *Youth in Slovenia: New perspectives from the nineties.* Ljubljana: Youth Department, Ministry of Education and Sport of the Republic of Slovenia.

Zorga, S. (1993). Risk and protective factors in the school framework. In K. Ekberg and P. E. Mjaavatin (Eds.), *Children at risk proceedings* (pp. 398–407). Trondheim: Norwegian Center for Children Research.

11

SOUTH AFRICA

Beaty Naude

PERCEPTIONS OF TEEN VIOLENCE

South Africa, like so many other countries, has been characterized by wars and internal conflict for many centuries. In addition, the majority of its people were the victims of apartheid (a system of racial and cultural discrimination), especially since 1948, when the white minority Nationalist Party came into power. Racial discrimination became statutory with the enactment of numerous discriminatory laws against Africans, Coloreds (people of mixed origin), and Indians. Sole (1990) describes apartheid as "The Principle of Exclusion which gives whites access to privileges, opportunities and social networks" denied to other people. This resulted in decades of internal conflict and civil strife, which had a severe impact on the incidence of violence in the country. In particular, South African youth were both victims and perpetrators of violence between 1950 and 1994.

The huge divide between blacks and white in terms of income, housing, and education is a source of frustration for young black people, and many justify crime as a means to rectify this situation, which they regard as an unjust advantage resulting from apartheid. Youth gangs are also a feature of many neighborhoods; these gangs rule supreme, and everybody in the neighborhood is subservient to them. Any disobedience results in violence, destruction of property, and even death, and there is often gang warfare as gangs fight for drug routes or territory. According to Pinnock (1997), gangs replaced traditional rites of passage, and the killing of a person is the gang member's final break from the norms of convention. Violence is an integral part of gang life in South Africa.

Apart from poverty, unemployment, and relative deprivation as a result of apartheid, the South African National Crime Prevention Strategy (1996) further cites the following factors as contributing to crime in South Africa:

The historical marginalization and experiences of powerlessness of black South Africans contributed to severe feelings of rejection. Since the 16 June 1976 Soweto youth uprising when 140 school pupils were killed by the police many youths went without the benefit of a proper formal education for almost two decades. In the 1980s this resulted in many youths finding an alternative identity for themselves in the politics of resistance. The negotiated political settlement in 1994 undermined the central position occupied by the youth with an increasingly dominant role for the older generation and the exiled leaders. Many youths now find new identity in gangs and other criminal activities. (pp. 1–3)

CURRENT TRENDS IN TEEN VIOLENCE

African youth were increasingly drawn into political violence after the 1976 Soweto uprising. They challenged repressive laws and participated in the armed struggle. According to Gibson (1991, 2), "Children have been socialized to find violence completely acceptable, and human life cheap." Youth involvement in violence should be put in the context of their daily experience of violence, which is a combination of ideas from the official literature of the liberation movement, statements and literature about liberation struggles in other countries, and ideas developed from their own experience and understanding of the world. They refer to themselves as comrades and frequently use terms such as "people's war" and "ungovernability" and justify their involvement in political violence as follows:

- it was a response to the call of the African National Congress (ANC) to take up the armed struggle as a strategy for change;
- they saw the root of the violence in the direct structural violence practiced by the state, particularly the activities of the police;
- they maintained that liberation was not possible without bloodshed;
- they viewed it as logical that the youth as defenders of the community should become involved in acts of political violence;
- they believed that violence would speed up the liberation struggle;
- they perceived themselves as holding the moral high-ground and maintaining political hegemony.

Manganyi and du Toit (1990) also point out that it was mostly youth who manned the street barricades, organized protest marches, and moni-

tored shop and bus boycotts. They also witnessed the harassment of their
parents during the pass laws, and it was the youth who started to challenge
the injustices of apartheid. The comrades also started to "discipline" those
within the organization and outside it. This ranged from talking to whipping
and even to killing those who were seen as against unity and liberation-
gangsters (individuals resorting to violence to obtain freedom/human
rights), Inkatha Freedom Party (IFP) supporters, and those perceived as
supporting capitalists. The IFP is an internal political party consisting mainly
of black people of Zulu origin; it called for the devolution of power on a
regional basis and collaborated with the government to some extent.

Youth activism eventually involved adult members of the community, especially after the establishment of the United Democratic Front (UDF),
which was generally regarded as the internal arm of the ANC, and township
civic bodies. This led to a rejection of local authorities, rent boycotts, and
large-scale civil disobedience that made many black townships ungovernable.

Widespread political activism and civil disobedience, together with international sanctions against the country, led to the unbanning of the liberation
movements in February 1990 and forced the Nationalist Party to release
Nelson Mandela and other resistance leaders. The reign of the Nationalist
Party ended on April 27, 1994, when South Africa's first democratic elections took place, putting the ANC into power with Mandela as president.

Various ages are used to define juveniles in South Africa. The Constitution
refers to juveniles as persons under the age of eighteen, the Correctional
Services Act determines that all persons in custody under the age of twenty-
one are juveniles (White Paper 1994) and Central Statistical Services distinguishes between juveniles, who are between seven and seventeen years, and
young adults, who are ages eighteen through twenty years, in their annual
reports on prosecutions and crime convictions.

The total conviction rate for all ages has decreased considerably since
1991, which is probably an indication of the inability of the criminal justice
system to cope with the crime problem. South Africa has a high crime rate
in terms of crimes reported to the police. Many offenders are not prosecuted, and cases brought before the courts are often poorly prepared by the
police. The problem is exacerbated by the large number of inexperienced
magistrates and prosecutors, which also contributes to the lower number of
convictions.

The total number of juvenile convictions in South Africa during the periods 1994–95 (Central Statistical Services, 1997b) and 1995–96 were as
follows (Central Statistical Services, 1998c, 22):

Year	7–17 years	18–20 years
1994–95	24,361	36,597
1995–96	17,526	30,565

Clearly, the conviction rate for juveniles and young adults has decreased significantly.

Young people under the age of twenty constituted 22 percent of all convictions during 1995–96, and young males constituted approximately 89 percent of the convictions during this period. (The prosecution rates for juveniles are not provided.)

For both age groups, theft had the highest incidence: 13,059 and 18,337, respectively. Within this category, other thefts (shop theft, vehicles, firearms) had the highest incidence for both age groups (6,813 and 10,125, respectively), followed by various types of burglary (4,658 and 5,025, respectively), while theft from a person or gaining advantage by means of force or threats, which includes robbery, amounted to 863 and 1,411 incidents, respectively.

Crimes against the life and body of a person (murder, attempted murder, rape, assault) had the second highest occurrence for both age groups: 2,621 and 6,873 total incidents, respectively. Most murder and assault incidents occurred among Africans, and in the majority of cases, the victim and the offender were from the same racial group.

As a percentage of the total conviction rate for young people under the age of twenty, theft makes up 65.3 percent of all convictions, and crimes against the person, 19.7 percent. Crimes against the person, including theft with force or threat, represent 21.8 percent of all conviction rates for the under-twenty age group.

According to the Department of Correctional Services, the number of sentenced and unsentenced juveniles under the age of twenty-one was as follows as of September 1998:

Crimes	Sentenced	Unsentenced
Economic	1,575	2,300
Violence	1,157	1,951
Sexual	582	601
Narcotics	70	63
Other	100	207
TOTAL	3,484	5,122

A total of 49.6 percent of the sentenced juveniles had committed crimes of violence.

CONTRIBUTING FACTORS

The causes of juvenile crime are multiple. Apart from personal psychological problems and trauma, the most important factors are the breakup of the traditional African family structure, which results in inadequate parental guidance, loss of norms and values (Nedcor, 1996), poor socialization, inadequate education and career training, and few job prospects, even for those with the necessary skills. Ransom, Poswa, and van Rooyen (1997) cite research that in 1994, the unemployment figure for young people between the ages of sixteen and twenty-five was as high as 60 percent. The report of the Inter-Ministerial Committee on Young People at Risk (1996) also highlights the legacy of discrimination, the breakdown of family life and traditional values, inadequate education, and illiteracy as causes of the current high levels of crime and violence.

South Africa is a developing country in transition after a long period of oppression, with large numbers of young people and a legacy of apartheid and violence. Not only were youth exposed to state violence, but they eventually became involved in the liberation struggle, which advocated violence from the 1960s. As a result, many youth were brutalized and traumatized, and had their schooling disrupted. The liberation movements encouraged civil disobedience and disrespect for the law and the rejection of inferior education. In fact "liberation before education" became a well-known slogan among African youth during the liberation struggle. This politically destructive violence drove a wedge between youth on the one hand and parents and teachers on the other. Today many youth have become alienated from society and often regard violence as a normal solution to problems. They have been deprived of a normal childhood, they are highly politicized, and there is a high acceptance of violence, resulting in a culture of violence that is difficult to break. Tindleni (1992) also points out that youthful violence is rooted in the violent nature of South African society and cannot "be separated from the apartheid laws and their harassment of the human rights of black people" (p. 40).

Youth alienation is also cited as a factor contributing to crime (South African National Crime Prevention Strategy, 1996). Bernstein (1967) provides the following profile of alienation:

- Youth who feel hostile and distant from the predominant institutions and mores of the community
- Negative attitudes toward their families and neighborhoods and anger and hostility toward the police
- Feeling out of the mainstream of the community's economic, social, and political life
- Lack of trust
- Resistance toward authority
- Little hope for a future

The country is characterized by many social problems typical of developing countries that are conducive to crime, and apartheid has intensified these problems. The majority of South Africans, especially Africans, are educationally disadvantaged (many are illiterate), housing and health care are inadequate, and unemployment is high. These problems were exacerbated by apartheid and policies such as the migrant labor system, influx control, and the Group Areas Act, which gave geographical expression to the spatial and territorial separation of the different races in the country. Since the end of influx control and other apartheid laws, the rate of urbanization has been very high, causing tremendous stress on migrants and metropolitan councils, which are unable to provide the necessary housing, health care, and educational facilities. As a result, large informal settlements have developed around South Africa's main cities, with few recreational facilities for youth.

RESPONSES TO THE PROBLEM

As a result of South Africa's colonial past, the criminal and penal law is mainly based on Roman Dutch and English law. The Constitutional Court, which was established in June 1994, is now the highest court but has jurisdiction only in constitutional matters. The death penalty was abolished in June 1995 as well as corporal punishment for young offenders. Many youth were brutalized and traumatized by corporal punishment, as is evident by the fact that 30,000 young people annually received corporal punishment (Pinnock, 1997). This state condoning of violence probably contributed to the acceptance of violence as a means to solve problems among many youths. Custodial sentences are still very common and only 22 percent of punishments involve community-based sentences (Naude et al., 1996), mainly as a result of the fact that disadvantaged poor communities do not have the structures in place to implement community-based sentences.

The South African courts also have a credibility problem among many African people, who regard the system as biased and oppressive and not representative of the population. The government is struggling to rectify this as is evident from the policy document *Vision 2000*, published in 1996, which sets out the goals for transforming the Department of Justice to make it more just and representative. The courts are often referred to as "white man's justice." Many Africans do not understand the system because colonization repressed customary law. European law emphasizes the protection of the individual, whereas customary and indigenous law focused on the protection of the community (Naude, 1995).

The South African courts are not geared to the needs of the victim. Compensation to crime victims is seldom made a condition for the suspension or extension of a sentence. There is no state compensation available to victims of violent crime for medical expenses or loss of income, and victims do not have the opportunity to submit a victim impact statement to bring to the court's notice the harm they suffered as a result of the crime. In 1997, however, the South African Law Commission recommended that a state fund be established to compensate certain categories of crime victims and that provision be made for victim impact statements.

As a result of the heavy focus on custodial sentences, South African prisons are constantly overpopulated by approximately 49 percent, and most offenders (approximately 54 percent) receive a sentence of six months or less (Department of Correctional Services, 1998:1–10). Juvenile males comprise 16 percent of the prison population and females 28 percent. Until 1994 children awaiting trial and sentenced juveniles often were not kept apart from adult prisoners due to a lack of space. Since 1994, more juvenile prisons and separate detention facilities have been established. There are currently nine youth correctional centers, twelve prisons that have a section set aside to accommodate juveniles separately, ten reform schools, twenty-one schools of industry, and thirty-five places of safety in the country. The 1994 White Paper by the Department of Correctional Services (1994) stresses that children under age eighteen should be sent to prison only as a last resort, as recommended in the United Nations Standard Minimum Rules for the Administration of Justice. The White Paper also emphasizes the importance of social work and psychological services to prisoners as well as specific treatment programs, such as life skills training and educational, religious, recreational, and other programs (1994). In reality it is difficult to follow up on these ideals due to a shortage of staff and overcrowded facilities, as is evident by the high recidivism rate: 80 percent over five years (Naude et al., 1996).

The apartheid order generated crime rather than controlled it, and the police were the agents of a state that created crime through efforts to erect moral, economic, and political boundaries between the races. Combating crime was subservient to the policing of apartheid, with only one in ten members of the police being engaged in crime detection and investigation (Shaw, 1995). The politicization of the police during the apartheid years and the brutal manner in which they often executed their duties, as is clear from the evidence before the Truth and Reconciliation Commission, resulted in most South Africans' having a very negative perception of the police. This is evident from the fact that only 33.8 percent of crimes were reported to the police in 1992; this rate increased to 42.1 percent in 1995, after the transitional process started (Naude et al., 1996). The draft White Paper, *In Service of Safety 1998–2003*, brought out by the Department for Safety and Security in 1998, sets out a number of objectives to improve policing services in South Africa. It urges a more holistic approach to the crime problem, which takes into account the causes of crime, better law enforcement, victim empowerment, and a broader focus on crime prevention, encompassing developmental crime prevention, which attempts to meet the needs of "at-risk children"; situational crime prevention, which refers to the prevention of spur of the moment crimes; and community crime prevention.

It will take many years before the South African criminal justice system will play a meaningful role in combating crime. The existing problems are compounded by the fact that as a result of the transformation process, which started in 1994, the affirmative action policy of the new government, and inadequate funding due to the country's many other needs, large numbers of experienced magistrates, prosecutors, police, and correctional services personnel left the public sector. Replacing them to run the system are many inexperienced people (Nedcor, 1996).

The shift from the politics of confrontation and resistance to a negotiated democratic political system and the dismantling of apartheid resulted in a breakdown of many social control methods without their being replaced by legitimate and credible alternatives. Before the transition period, the country was an overregulated and unaccountable society. As a result of the negotiated settlement, many of the old illegitimate and repressive forms of social control were dismantled. The result was a virtual collapse of social control by the community and the criminal justice system. The country is characterized by social disorganization: citizens do not pay taxes and service accounts, parents and schools are unable to control youth, many police are corrupt, and there is a general inability to maintain law and order in terms of the newly adopted Bill of Human Rights, which also protects the rights of accused offenders. Criminals were quick to take advantage of this vacuum, as is evident by the high crime rate and the many crime syndicates operating in the country. Many criminals convicted of politically motivated crimes were also granted amnesty at the start of the transition process, and many serious juvenile offenders were released from prison without proper care facilities being available in the community.

South Africa's long history of conflict created a deeply rooted culture of violence. Violence has also been historically sanctioned, as is evident by state-sanctioned hit squads to eliminate political activists and the violence propagated by the liberation movements. Violence is regarded as an accepted means to solve political, social, economic, and domestic conflict. An example is taxi violence, a crime unique to South Africa, where rivals for a specific taxi route kill each other.

Criminal activities were also justified during the total onslaught era of the Nationalist government. The business community engaged in many illegal activities to circumvent sanctions, and arms smuggling became commonplace. This blurred the dividing line between socially acceptable and criminal behavior and created disrespect for the rule of law and the criminal justice system.

The general notion that violence was acceptable during the apartheid era has spilled over into the political arena. Some political parties do not hesitate to resort to violence to control the opposition or certain areas that they regard as their political domain, such as the sporadic but ongoing political violence between supporters of the ANC and the IFP in KwaZulu-Natal illustrates.

The lack of credibility of the criminal justice system and the absence of effective victim aid services has contributed to the growth of informal forms of popular justice, such as vigilantes, paramilitary groups, and community or people's courts, which often mete out brutal justice to perceived criminals.

Illegal firearms are readily available and are frequently used in robbery, rape, murder, assault, and taxi violence. As a result of feelings of insecurity, many South Africans privately own firearms, which creates more potential for violence.

The Bill of Rights in South Africa's new constitution specifically makes provision for children

- not to be detained, except as a measure of last resort (and then only for a limited period of time and separately from adult prisoners);
- to have a legal representative, paid for by the state, in civil proceedings that affect the child and might result in substantial injustice;
- not to be used in armed conflict and to be protected in times of armed conflict.

South Africa does not have specific policies in place to deal with violent youth, but since it came into power in 1994, the new government has appointed various committees and brought out a number of White Papers to deal with the socioeconomic injustices of the past that exacerbated the crime problem, to tackle the crime problem itself, and to change the criminal justice system. Effective and fair law enforcement is a priority, and many racist laws have been abolished. Statutes such as the new Domestic Violence Act of 1998 and the Equal Employment Opportunities Bill will eliminate many injustices. A number of law reform measures have been implemented, such as legislation to provide for pretrial detention for certain categories of dangerous offenders as well as restrictions on the early release of violent offenders on parole. Compulsory minimum sentences for habitual violent offenders, rapists, and serious offenses involving a firearm have also been passed. Police are better trained to focus more on the needs of victims and the human rights of offenders. The United Nations Standard Minimum rules for the administration of juvenile justice are subscribed to, youthful offenders are kept separate from hardened criminals in jail, and only the most serious juveniles are sent to juvenile prisons. The Correctional Services Amendment Act No. 17 of 1994 makes provision that children under the age of fourteen be held in detention only for twenty-four hours and those over fourteen but under eighteen charged with serious offenses for forty-eight hours only.

The report of the Inter-Ministerial Committee on Young People at Risk (1996) found that the impact of colonization, urbanization, and apartheid had left a legacy of inequality that apportioned the majority of funds and services to white offenders while providing a poor and inadequate service to black children, resulting in inadequate rehabilitation and treatment programs for black youth. A number of recommendations have been made to provide more equitable service, such as better distribution of the available resources, placement as close as possible to the offender's home to allow for better family contact, better training for youth care workers, and improved assessment and treatment programs. A corporatist model is suggested to blend aspects of the welfare and justice model.

Juvenile offenders, with the exception of the most serious offenders, preferably are kept out of the formal justice system but at the same time held accountable for their behavior. Restorative justice with an emphasis on conflict resolution and the involvement of the young person, the family, and the community are advocated. The emphasis should be on community development, the reduction of poverty and unemployment, sufficient preschool and after-care facilities, training in parenting skills, and the early identification and treatment of children at risk.

The Reconstruction and Development Program and the National Growth and Development Program are examples of recent attempts by the government to provide an effective state policy on community and social development and the reduction of poverty. The reduction of poverty and the achievement of equity are important priorities of the Ministry for Welfare and Population, as set out in a White Paper (1997). An integrated approach is proposed to deal with such social problems as inadequate parenting, child abuse and neglect, street children, and child labor, which is prohibited in the case of children under the age of fifteen although many children in South Africa are exploited. In 1994 the South African Police Services' Child Protection Unit dealt with 22,911 cases of child abuse and neglect, an increase of 36 percent over the previous year, and in 1993 it was estimated that there were approximately 10,000 street children in South Africa (Ministry for Welfare and Population, 1997). The ministry further estimates that close to 75 percent of young people of all races are marginalized, which they describe as "processes whereby groups or often entire populations are forced beyond or on to the periphery of the social and economic mainstream."

The report of the Inter-Ministerial Committee on Young People at Risk (1996) advocates a developmental approach, with the main focus on strengths rather than pathology, to prevent juvenile crime and, by implication, violent crime. The developmental approach has the following components:

- Focusing on strengths rather than pathology
- Building competency rather than attempting to cure encouragement of trial-and-error learning
- Always taking the context into consideration and understanding and responding appropriately to developmental tasks and needs

- Working with the total person, not the so-called pathology or problem
- A strong belief (reflected in practice) of the potential within each child and family (regardless of the reason for the referral)
- Work aimed at maximizing potential rather than minimizing the problem
- An emphasis on most treatment taking place in the child's daily living environment
- A multidisciplinary team (not a hierarchy) approach in which the child and family are recognized as full members of the team

A framework for a national drug master plan was also developed by the Drug Advisory Board in 1997. It deals specifically with the prevention of drug trafficking and drug and alcohol abuse, which often contributes to or facilitates violence. It advocates research to form the bases of prevention and control policies as well as the involvement of government, nongovernment organizations, and community cooperation. Education is regarded as an important crime prevention measure.

The South African National Crime Prevention Strategy adopted in 1996 developed four crime prevention pillars or models: an effective and integrated criminal justice process and information network to ensure a high probability of prosecution and punishment. The following are highlighted in this regard:

- Appropriate community sentencing and diversion programs, an effective legislative process and prosecutorial policy, secure care facilities for juvenile suspects and offenders, and victim empowerment programs.
- Crime prevention through environmental design based on expert advice concerning architectural and urban design, which should be made available to local and provincial authorities.
- Proper identification systems for motor vehicles and parts and fingerprint identification to prevent falsification of identities and fraud.
- Enhancing community values and education. Public education programs are propagated to educate and inform the public about crime, the criminal justice system, and crime prevention to raise community awareness and prevent misconceptions and negative attitudes. Departmental communication programs, slogans and themes, local campaigns, and a school-based syllabus on crime and crime prevention and the criminal justice process from the primary school level up are also recommended. Subjects should include the Constitution, citizen rights and responsibilities, conflict management and mediation, substance abuse, gender and child issues, crime prevention, and the functioning of the criminal justice system.
- The prevention of transnational crime, which should focus on the prevention of organized crime, border control, and regulation of points of entry to stem illegal trade in drugs and arms and illegal immigration.

The National Crime Prevention Strategy is criticized for not linking the crime contributing factors it identified to the crime prevention pillars it developed and for not focusing enough on the prevention of juvenile crimes.

Very successful diversion programs have been developed by the National Institute for the Prevention of Crime and the Rehabilitation of Offenders (NICRO), a private nongovernmental organization with twenty branches in various provinces. During 1994 and 1995, 3,565 juvenile offenders were referred to NICRO for participation in diversion programs. Of the cases accepted by NICRO, 2,725 (74.4 percent) successfully completed the programs. The Inter-Ministerial Committee on Young People at Risk (1996) advocates involving more nongovernmental organizations and community-based organizations to render diversion services to young offenders. The report cites the following diversion programs that are most often used in South Africa now:

- The YES (Youth Empowerment Schemes) programs, which are used in 67 percent of cases. This is a six-session life skills training program presented by NICRO that focuses on issues important to young people.
- Pretrial community service, which allows young people to serve between thirty and one hundred hours in the community. At the moment, 12.5 percent of cases referred to NICRO are pretrial community service.
- Family group conferences, a diversion program based on victim-offender mediation in which the families are also involved. These family group conferences based on indigenous problem-solving techniques are not yet widely used in South Africa.

CONCLUSION

After years of violence, conflict, and fragmented discriminatory services to young offenders, South Africa has started to develop a more just and humane society and treatment programs for young offenders. Because most of these programs came into place only since 1994, it is far too early to assess their success. In many cases, proper evaluation procedures to measure the success of these programs are not yet in place. Most programs are long-term strategies, which can be assessed only after a number of years. Nevertheless, a start has been made to prevent and treat juvenile crime, including violent crime, in a holistic and integrated manner. Future generations should see a decrease in violence in South Africa and be able to live and prosper in a secure and safe nonviolent environment.

REFERENCES

Bernstein, S. (1967). *Alternatives to violence: Alienated youth and riots, race and poverty*. New York: Associated Press.
Central Statistical Services. (1997a). *Living in Gauteng*. Pretoria: Government Printer.
Central Statistical Services. (1997b). *Crimes: Prosecutions and convictions with regard to certain offences*. Pretoria: Government Printer.
Central Statistical Services. (1998a). *Population census statistics*. Pretoria: Government Printer.

Central Statistical Services. (1998b). *Women and men in South Africa*. Pretoria: Government Printer.

Central Statistical Services (1998c). *Crimes: Prosecutions and convictions with regard to certain offences*. Pretoria: Government Printer.

Colliers. (1995). *Encyclopedia of the world* (Vol. 21). New York.

Department of Correctional Services. 1998. *Annual report*. Pretoria: Government Printer.

Gibson, K. (1991). Home, no place to hide. *The Star Newspaper*, February 25, p. 2. Johannesburg, South Africa.

Inter-Ministerial Committee on Young People at Risk. (1996). *Inter policy recommendations*. Pretoria: Ministry for Welfare.

Manganyi, N. C., and du Toit, A. (Eds.). (1990). *Political violence and the struggle in South Africa*. New York: St. Martin's Press.

Marks, M. (1995). We are fighting for the liberation of our people: Justifications of violence by activists in Diepkloof, Soweto. Paper presented at the Richard Ward Building, Johannesburg on August 28.

Ministry for Welfare and Population Development. (1997). White paper for social welfare. Pretoria: Government Printer.

Naude, C. M. B. (1995). *An international perspective on victim participation in the criminal justice process with specific reference to victim impact statements*. Research report, Department of Criminology. Pretoria: University of South Africa.

Naude, C.M.B., Grobbelaar, M. M., and Snyman, H. F. (1996). *The second international crime (victim) survey in Johannesburg, 1996*. Research report, Department of Criminology. Pretoria: University of South Africa.

Nedcor. (1996). *The Nedcor project on crime, violence and investment*. Nedcor: Johannesburg.

Pinnock, D. (comp.). (1995). The Inter-Ministerial Committee on Young People. The rural development strategy of the reconstruction and development programme. Johannesburg, South Africa.

Pinnock, D. (1997). *Gangs, rituals and rights of passage*. Cape Town: African Sun Press.

Ransom, B. L., Poswa, T., and van Rooyen, C.A.J. (1997). Youth unemployment—a study in an informal settlement in KwaZulu-Natal. *Social Work*, 33 (2), 165–177.

Shaw, M. (1995). Towards safer cities? Crime, political transition and changing forms of policing control in South Africa. *African Security Review*, 4 (5), 4–11.

Sole, K. (1990). Authorship, authenticity and the black community: The novels of Soweto 1976. In S. Clingman (Ed.), *Regions and repertoires in South African politics and culture*. Braamfontein: Ravan Press.

South Africa Department of Correctional Services. (1994). White paper on the policy of the Department of Correctional Services in the new South Africa.

South African Law Commission. (1997). *Sentencing restorative justice (compensation for victims of crime and victim empowerment)*. Report no. 7. Pretoria: SA Law Commission.

South African National Crime Prevention Strategy. (1996). Unpublished report prepared by the Inter-departmental Government Committee on Crime, Johannesburg.

Tindleni, N. J. (1992). *The influence of violence on youth club activities*. Unpublished master's thesis, University of South Africa.

12

SPAIN

Javier Garcia-Perales

The youthful wrong is to believe that intelligence supply experience.
The ripeness wrong is to believe that experience supply intelligence.
—Mahatma Gandhi

PERCEPTIONS OF TEEN VIOLENCE

Spain has been conscious of the problem of teen violence for centuries. Childhood protection was common in Spanish law. Legal codes from as early as 1254 contained references to the age at which youth were seen as responsible for their crimes and judged accordingly. Throughout Spain's history, that age of responsibility has fluctuated. For example, during the period of Roman law, the age of criminal responsibility was fourteen. During the Visigothic law period in the lower Middle Ages, the age of responsibility for some crimes was ten years. In the high Middle Ages, the age range was ten to fourteen, depending on the crime. By the early nineteenth century, the age of responsibility was lowered to age seven. In 1904, the Minors Protection Superior Council was created for child protection. One of Spain's illustrious criminologists, Rafael Salillas, was an active member of it until his death in 1923. Through his work on the council, he was able to raise the age of responsibility to ten years. He advocated parental rebuke for child rebels, incorrigibles, and criminals as opposed to imprisonment. Prior to the establishment of the council and the laws protecting children, there were 8,426 prisoners in Spanish jails all under the age of seventeen years.

In 1920, special courts were established in provincial capital cities that were dedicated to child and youth protection. These courts emphasized education and postponed the age of responsibility to sixteen years.

The first reform school in Spain was established in 1888, with the following words: "To reduce the number of offenses, to reduce the figure of the criminals one must educate and reform the defective youth, wandering, the wrong slopes, of perverse trends." By royal decree in May 1915, two tutelary reform centers were created for the education of fifteen to twenty-three-year-old criminals. The first remand home was established in 1907. It had a capacity for 120 children, although the operation of it was delayed for almost twenty years. In 1948 there were 35 tutelary minors courts, thirty-six reformatories and observation houses (remand centers), twenty-six boarding schools, fourteen middle-school boarding houses, seven child day care centers, seven family houses, 6 scholastic education centers, 4 centers for clothing children, and 349 institutions whose sole purpose was the care or imprisonment of minors.

It is interesting to note the role of the media in influencing public opinon about crime. A study by the Andalucia Criminological Institute indicated that a national newspaper dedicated 1 percent of its columns to crime. Since the columnists were not criminologists, crime got an inversely proportional amount of attention to its importance in the area of juvenile delinquency (Fernandez et al., 1995).

Society also has some erroneous perceptions of crime. It tends to believe that immigrants, gypsies, or nomads are responsible for most crime. However, there are few data to support such a view. The perception about crime is especially interesting when youth are asked about it. A study by the Criminological Basque Institute revealed that 23 percent of teens think that their improper conduct does not break the law (Criminology Institute, 1996). They too accuse marginal groups such as drug addicts, gypsies, and immigrants as being responsible for most crime.

CURRENT TRENDS IN TEEN VIOLENCE

During the first half of the twentieth century, teen violence was unknown as a social problem. An article in the *Daily Telegraph* as late as October 1961 reported that Spain had the lowest youth crime rate in Europe. The German newspaper *Westdeutscher Allgemeiner Zeitung* in 1962 also confirmed the low figures of teen crime in Spain.

In 1960, there were 163 arrests of sixteen-year-olds per 100,000 population (the under twenty-five population was 12,571,517). In 1961 arrests declined to 158 per 100,000 population (the population under age twenty-five was 12,962,976). The crimes committed by juveniles in the early 1960s were mainly offenses against property (theft).

Studies on teen violence (Ministry of Justice, 1996) between 1993 and 1994 indicated the following:

- 89 percent of the perpetrators were men.
- 69.5 percent were between fourteen and fifteen years old.
- 32 percent came from broken homes.
- 23 percent had criminal fathers.
- 36 percent had some physical or psychological problem.
- 45.4 percent of the crimes were gang related.
- 71 percent of the crimes were against property.

Because the incidence of teen criminality was so low, it was of no public or political interest. Therefore, there was very little incentive to sponsor or fund scientific research into teen criminality. A recent investigation indicated that 83 percent of the Spanish people felt that unemployment was a more important problem, followed by terrorism (35 percent), drugs (16 percent), and delinquency (11 percent) (Sociological Research Center, 1998).

One self-report study about juvenile delinquency in 1995 noted the following:

- 81 percent of the juveniles surveyed indicated they had committed a crime.
- 58 percent indicated they had committed a crime in the past year.
- 88 percent had drunk alcohol.
- 79 percent had drunk in the past year.
- 21 percent had tried drugs.
- 15 percent had tried drugs in the past year.
- 42 percent had driven without a license.
- 22 percent had driven without a license in the past year.

Teen criminals are neither more violent nor more organized than in the past. Also, women's participation in the delinquency has not changed. This has had an impact on the evolution of regulations concerning the age of responsibility of teens in Spain: the abandonment of the subjective psychological criterion in favor of the pure biological method.

The most notable changes have been in the area of street offenses: those that emphasize or are characterized by the place of commission of the crime, the violence that is employed, and the characteristics of the victims and the aggressor (Herrero, 1995). Within this criminal category, the group that is of greatest concern is that of the offenses against persons. These offenses tend to involve the use of weapons and the participation of groups of three or more aggressors—the so-called urban tribes. They are characterized by unusual violence and the fact that they are more or less organized.[1] In the north of Spain, their activities tend to be focused on nationalist or political vandalism—for example:

1994

January	Mass demonstrations by the youthful political group called Jarrai.
March	Molotov cocktails thrown at Ertzaintza's patrols (Basque region police force). Street incidents lead to the death of the terrorist J. M. Igerategui.
April	The newspaper "Diario de Noticias" of Navarre is stoned. Two local policemen are stoned.
May	The motorcycles of a cyclist tour to Spain are set on fire. Some individuals are injured by bombs hidden in purses.
June	Beating to the House of the People's Director.
July	Assault and attacks on the headquarters of Basque politic force Eusko Alkartasuna in Rentería.
August	Attacks on two Basque policemen (ertzainas). Two ertzainas injured by molotov cocktails.
September	Incidents and injured in Navarre in confrontation with the Guardia Civil.
December	Eight injured by molotov cocktails thrown at the House of the People of Rentería.

1995

February	Struggle session in Basque Region. Molotov cocktails thrown at National Radio in Vitoria. A PSE-PSOE car set on fire.
March	Incidents in Basque Region. Molotov cocktails thrown at the newspaper "Diario Vasco." Five ertzainas and two women with serious burns.
April	Attack on an ertzaina. Two youths assaulted. The headquarters of the politic force PP set on fire.
May	The van belonging to the socialistic councilman set on fire. Attack on Mayor of Hernani. Three ertzainas assaulted.
June	Attacks on five citizens by the blue loop. Incidents by the terrorists Lasa and Zabala. Attacks on three socialistic councilmen.
July	Seven injured councilmen. The car of a dissenting councilman of Basque politic force HB set on fire.
August	Launching of molotov cocktails. Attack on an ertzaina.

September	Burglary in the building of the broadcasting station SER and COPE.
	Attacks on two parliamentary figures.
	Stoning of a shop.
October	Thirty-two molotov cocktails thrown at the police station of the Ertzaintza (Amara, San Sebastian).
November	Attack on two ertzainas.
	Attack on seven citizens.
	Molotov cocktails thrown at a Mobile Unit of the broadcasting station SER.
December	Two ertzainas assassinated.

The crime rates in Madrid by the urban tribes are reported in Table 12.1 and Table 12.2.

Table 12.1
Offenses Committed by Urban Tribes in Madrid

ATTACKS	1991	1994	1995	1996	1997*
TOTALS		251	312	263	
By TRIBES	3	156	207	160	
Skins			160	94	14
Redskins			0	15	
Punks			28	13	
Other	3		19	38	4

Note: *Data referred to the first trimester.

Source: Report of the Group of Urban Tribes of Madrid.

Table 12.2
Arrests of Urban Tribes

ARRESTED	1991	1992	1993	1994	1995	1996
Skins	16	17	76	72	116	99
Reds					0	12
Punks				58	65	28
Other				29	23	36
TOTAL	16	17	76	159	204	175

Source: Report of the Group of Urban Tribes of Madrid.

CONTRIBUTING FACTORS

The city of Barcelona has had the most urban tribe attacks. The district attorney's office indicated that between 1983 and 1990, 29 cases were filed. By 1994 that number had grown to 247. According to a 1995 report to the National Security Council (NSC), police investigations of urban tribe attacks countrywide increased to 576 (78 percent in Barcelona). In September 1995, the NSC reported that 2,331 skinheads were identified or registered in Spain. Their mean age was nineteen and a half years, and 82 percent considered themselves white patriots. The problem has reached 37 percent of the cities with more than 25,000 inhabitants.

Another important area is violence in schools. Some data suggest that four out of every ten pupils eight to sixteen years of age have been intimidated or mistreated in school by a classmate (Moreno, 1997). These incidents often involve verbal abuse and intimidation rather than physical aggression. By age sixteen years, there is a decrease in the frequency of these incidents but an increase in their severity.[2] The 1996 Report on Drugs in the Student Population indicated that students who took the drug ecstasy were involved in the following problems in school: 33 percent of the incidents were without physical aggression; 23 percent of the incidents involved physical aggression; 15 percent were truant; 12 percent were arrested; 9.8 percent were involved in a traffic accident; and 6 percent had other emergencies.

At the political level, approaches to dealing with these problems are often poorly carried out, without any recognition of the depth of the problem. In 1998, a group of judges noted an absence of institutions devoted to the rigorous quantitative study of juvenile crime, and that public officials seemed unconcerned about the problem. In addition, they have waited almost a decade for the promulgation of a juvenile penal law.

RESPONSES TO THE PROBLEM

Spain's nineteen territorial entities deal with legislative and judicial matters (with certain limitations). Thus, each of these entities has particular departments for dealing with delinquency, such as the police, judicial, and assistance departments. These departments must work closely with the state departments in some instances. At the state level, a number of departments focus directly on the prevention and control of teen violence.

Law enforcement. Two law enforcement groups have national responsibility. The Cuerpo Nacional de Policia has a specialized police unit for dealing with teens and an urban tribes group, which specializes in dealing with juvenile gangs. It also runs the Neighborhood Police (for the prevention of delinquency), which began the Police-School Program in 1986, whereby police visit schools and work with associations of students, parents, and teachers. They teach students between the ages of eleven and fourteen about the functions of police in the society. The other group is the Guardia Civil, which in February 1998 signed a cooperation agreement with the Institute of the Youth for risk prevention, with special emphasis on racism, violence, alcohol and drug consumption, and transmission of sexual diseases.

Judicial departments. Each city has a minors court with a minors prosecutor, who is commissioned to defend the interests of minors (The prosecutors in other courts are entrusted with defending the general interest of the state.)

Assistance departments. Here the Institute of the Youth carries out various campaigns and programs to inform youths on different matters (drugs and sex, for example) and to help them face various problems in the hope that they can avoid becoming involved in delinquency.

At the regional level, there are various departments and organizations devoted to teens. One institution in Spain that is entrusted with protecting minors' rights, Defensor del Menor (Teens' Protector), has no relationship to police or judicial departments. It was established in the region of Madrid in 1996 with the intent of addressing the social problems of teens. It operates the Instituto Madrileño de Atencion a la Infancia (Institute of Madrid for the Children's Attention) and its Attention Program to Minors in Social Conflict.

Like other countries, Spain has been concerned about violence in the classrooms. Therefore, on May 30, 1997, the Plan against the Violence in the Classrooms was developed in the region of Madrid. The plan involves the Citizens Security Council and Spanish Federation to Villages and Regions, a nongovernmental organization (NGO). It is also being implemented in five other regions of Spain.

One of the oldest programs, which has operated for seventy years, is the City of the Boys, sponsored by the Catholic Church. This program, which operates in many areas of Spain, is for offending teens. Each is run by a priest and uses educational techniques. Those who attend study and receive vocational preparation, and participate in the decisions of the center through assemblies. This helps to prepare them for their life in society. In addition, they practice an entertainment activity such as those performed in a circus.

In the early 1990s, the government in the region of Catalonia sponsored the Conciliation and Repair Program, designed to aid victims and assign the offending teens to community service. The program, which received widespread media coverage, was aimed at youths up to the age of sixteen. Its intent was to make teens responsible for their actions by having them participate in the resolution process, which resulted in their "repairing" the damage they caused. Candidates for the program had to meet certain criteria. They had to be first-time offenders, their offense must not have been serious, the damages caused must be repairable, and the teen must accept their responsibility in the process. During the first year of operation, 487 teens (444 boys and 43 girls) went through the program.

A very interesting program that was carried out in the region of the Canary Islands between 1988 and 1991 was the Psychosocial Competition Program, which consisted of fourteen courses on cognitive training and social skills. The course was primarily for teachers of basic education, social assistants, and prison officials who were working with troubled teens. As a result of these courses, at-risk families in the village of La Matanza de Acentejo (Tenerife) were identified along with the village's youth who already had transgressed. The project involved the coordination of the assistance and educational services for those families and their children. In the city of Santa Cruz de Tenerife, a program was directed at basic education. One course was developed to teach families and children to solve their interpersonal problems.

In 1993 the regional government of Aragon, cooperatively working with the fiscal chief of the region and with several NGOs, instituted the Integral Teens Plan, directed at some 2,000 teens in at-risk situations in the region.

In the region of Valencia, the new Cautions Measures Project for Teens in Open Regime, sponsored by the Help and Integration Office of the Minor to the Spanish Association of Criminologists, with the collaboration of the regional government and the city courts, is intended to help teens become responsible, address society's role in the juvenile violence problem, and share the instructive task with the other institutions of social control (and this without the teens leaving their environment).

The Help Foundation Against Drug Addiction organized the First Virtual Congress on Juvenile Violence and Drug Consumption. It took place on the Internet between January 1 and March 31, 1999. (To consult the Web site, see http://www.fad.es/congress.)

The Education and Culture Ministry of the Kingdom of Spain organizes the Courses of Risks Prevention in the Adolescence, intended for the teachers. These courses are centered on the principal risk factors of youth: drugs, sexuality, juvenile violence, gang membership, and aggressiveness.

The Institute of Middle Education of Sierra Bermeja (Malaga) has submitted a proposal to include a criminology course for students.

CONCLUSION

Spain places great importance on the collaboration of public officials and NGOs. The government allocates funds in its annual state budgets to support NGO programs and projects. Also, it has enacted legislation to allow certain social groups, such as pacifists, to work with NGOs instead of entering military service. The fiscal laws also permit these organizations to receive donations.

It is practically impossible to review each organization that collaborates in the resolution of the problem of teen violence because there are so many in each neighborhood of each city. The programs in each city are coordinated by the Youth Council to the Town Hall. At the regional level, they are coordinated by the Institutes of the Youth of the Autonomous Region, which in turn are coordinated by the Council of the Youth of Spain. The council also offers the following services:

- A crisis telephone hot-line devoted to counseling and solving problems that youths have.
- The promotion of sports, culture, and educational activities.
- Juvenile information centers on employment, scholarships, studies, sexuality, and drugs.

For more information, you can consult the web site for the Council of the Youth: http://www.cje.org.

NOTES

1. One study by the UAM (Autonomous University at Madrid) paid by the government to the region shows that of 11.9 percent of teens involved in violent actions, of these 11.2 percent are against rival bands, 11.2 percent against supporters; 8 percent are based on ideological motives; 4 percent against homosexuals; 4 percent against the marginals, and 1.8 percent are based on racism.

2. Research from Seville University on five schools and students between twelve and sixteen years shows that 18.3 percent participated directly in intimidating actions, while 77 percent observed. Another investigation carried out in Madrid indicates that 41 percent of the intimidation is accomplished by classmates, 55.4 percent is by pupils of the same course; 9.7 percent of it is by superior course students, and 5.6 percent is by inferior course students.

REFERENCES

Anton López, J., et al. (1995). *Criminal childhood*. Granada: Comares.

Bandres Unanue, L. M. (1996). Performances of the leasehold delegation of Guipuzcoa on smaller violators. *Eguzkilore*, no. 10.

Beristain Ipiña, A. (1995). The tutelary courts of minors in Spain from 1936 to 1975. *Magazine of Social Documentation*, no. 33–34.

Criminology Institute of Basque. (1996). Investigation between students of the Spanish city of San Sebastian and the French of Bayonne.

Cuello, Calon E. (1906). *The infantile and youthful criminality in some countries*. Madrid.

Echeburua, E. (1987). *The youthful delinquency. Eguzkilore*, no. 1.

Fernandez, J. C., Herreros, E., Saenz, S., Valero, C. Y., and Vegas, M. J. (1995). The image of crime in the Spanish press. *Criminology Bulletin of the IAIC*.

Educating Magazine. (1996). *Juvenile violence*, no. 180.

Garrido Genoves, Vicente. (1987). *Youthful delinquency*. Madrid: Alhambra.

Gimenez Salinas, E. (1981). *Youthful delinquency and social control*. Barcelona: I Circulate Publishing Universe.

Herrero, C. (1995). Surroundings and factors of youthful delinquency. *Police Science Magazine*, nos. 31–32.

Lopez-Rey, M. (1973). *Criminology: Youthful delinquency, prevention, prediction and processing*. Madrid: Aguilar.

Ministry of Justice and the University of Castille at La Mancha. (1996). Juvenile violence. *Educating Magazine*, no. 189.

Moreno, J. M. (1997). *The dark side of school.* Paper presented at the First European Conference on Student Violence, Utrecht, Holland, February.

Piquer, A., and Jover, J. J. (1961). *The book of characteristics of Spanish infantile delinquency.* Madrid.

Platt, H. (1982). *Rescuers of the boy or the invention of the delinquency.* Madrid.

Rechea Alberola, Cristina, et al. (1995a). *Adolescence: Measles?* River Basin: Publications Services of the University of Castille at La Mancha.

Rechea Alberola, Cristina, et al. (1995b). *Juvenile delinquency in Spain.* Madrid: Ministry of Justice and the University of Castille at La Mancha.

Salillas Panzano, R. (1902). *Age and crime in Spain.* Madrid.

Santos Rego, M. A., and Lorenzo Moledo, M. M. (1996). The question of pedalogical intervention in feminine youthful delinquency. *Magazine of Sciences of Education*, no. 166.

Sociological Research Center, Work and Social Subject Ministry, March 1998.

White Marti, Ramon. (1905). *Correction of the delinquent.* Madrid.

13

THAILAND

John C. Quicker

PERCEPTIONS OF TEEN VIOLENCE

Anyone who has ever been to Thailand is immediately exposed to the Thai smile and the respectful prayer-like greeting, *wai*. While much has been said about the smile, and many feel it may be a way of deflecting potential danger and thus the safest of gestures (Mulder, 1996), one still is warmed by it and put at ease. The smile and the *wai* symbolize the behavior of Thai youth—mostly polite, pleasant, and respectful—but Thai youth are not without their problems and sometimes engage in behavior similar to youth from Western industrialized countries. However, vast differences exist between the two groups, and Thai delinquency pales in frequency and seriousness to Western delinquency.

Thailand seems to be a very safe place, relatively free from easily observable forms of youth violence. In none of the four cities I visited in 1998 and 1999 were there outward displays of such violence—either toward each other or toward adults. All other observers I interviewed came to the same conclusion, with some even suggesting that though there is no violence in their particular city, there probably is someplace else. One of two American teachers, both of whom had been living in Chiang Mai for almost two years, said, "No, we have never seen any examples of youth violence here. We never worry about walking around the streets at night, and have never felt threatened by any youth. I'm sure it'll probably be different in Bangkok, but I really don't know."

Observations of signs of delinquency in Bangkok were no more obvious than in Chiang Mai. This is especially significant considering Bangkok is a huge sprawling metropolis, with many neighborhoods and tremendous class diversity.

Sophisticated measures and government measures of delinquency, such as those existing in the Western industrialized countries, are rare in Thailand (Bartollas, 1997). A number of recent changes in government as well as changes in the constitution have contributed to this problem. In addition, criminology, and thus delinquency, as a serious discipline in Thailand is still quite new. Chulalongkorn University, one of the most prestigious universities in Thailand, established a criminology program just two years ago. Nevertheless, delinquency does occur and enough data on delinquency do exist to make a preliminary analysis possible.

I examined four demographically dissimilar cities in different regions of the country: Bangkok, the capital, which is the largest, most diverse, and central of all the cities; Chiang Mai, the cultural center of northern Thailand and the second largest city in the country; Hat Yai, a southern commercial and shopping center of moderate size in southern Thailand; and Yala, a small southern city with the least amount of Western influence of any of these cities. Observations of signs of delinquency were conducted in all four cities, with surprising results.

One of the most obvious signs of delinquency in the West is graffiti. Some areas of Los Angeles, for example, have so much graffiti, and it changes so often that visitors are warned not to stand still too long lest they become covered as well. This situation contrasts sharply with Thailand. Thailand is not graffiti free, but the amount of it and its relative visibility make it appear that way. There might be rare instances of graffiti—for example, on a stairwell in a shopping mall, in a school bathroom, or in a back alley—but it must be searched for. Another sign of at least potential delinquency is the sight of groups of youth hanging out or wandering the streets together. It is an unfair prejudgment to say such groups are potential delinquents; however, it is not unfair to conclude that it is from such groups that the greatest amount of delinquency, when it occurs, comes. Therefore, the fewer there are of these groups, the less likely delinquency is to take place. As was the case with graffiti, these groups are mostly absent in all the cities I visited.

Although there is youth violence in Thailand, youth do participate in gang activities there, and certain youth are found engaging in various types of other delinquency, the proportions and forms it takes differ markedly from the delinquency found in the West. Although an article in the *Bangkok Post* cites police statistics arguing that there has been a dramatic rise in physical assault and rape, as well as in murder and attempted murder, the statistics do not separate out the portion of youth (teen) violence from the violence committed by adults (Charoenwongsak, 1997). Amorn Wanichwiwatana, a criminologist at Chulalongkorn University, told me, "Unorganized youth violence in Thailand is an occasional crime, and not a common happening."

Without national statistics, the amount of juvenile violence can only be postulated from local information. In Bangkok, the deputy chief justice of the Central Juvenile and Family Court said that of the 1,467 youth in observation and protection centers in 1995, 312 were involved in physical assault (Bunnag, 1996). This is a very small amount of officially recorded youth violence in a city of over 9 million people. In Chiang Mai, statistics from the Juvenile and Family Court from 1993 to June 1998 indicate 77 cases of juvenile violence out of a total of 3,743 cases, or about 2 percent. This suggests a frequency considerably less than in most Western societies. Exact comparisons are difficult since the court statistics may underestimate the amount of delinquency in Thailand. G. Lamar Robert of Chiang Mai University's Social Research Institute, for example, indicates that many cases of delinquency never make it into the court statistics because the courts are seen as the last resort. Every effort is made to resolve situations without going to court.

It seems that youth violence is not a major issue at this time in Thailand. Some have speculated that the nature of Thai society precludes more obvious instances of violence. Chaiwat Satha-anand (1997) wrote that the use of nonviolent action to secure rights or fight for injustice has always existed in Thai society. However, Thais do know how to fight and will, if provoked: "Even though Thais dislike violence, and try to avoid physical combat when possible, if an occasion arises where they have to defend themselves, they are instantly able to use every part of their body—legs and feet, elbows and knees—as weapons, and it happens almost automatically" (Sukphisit, 1997).

Youth gangs, in the form and frequency known in the West, do not exist in Thailand. Nevertheless, gangs do exist that are both violent and likely to have youth members. Kias Panta, a famous Thai singer, was once a member of a youth gang, where, in a confrontation with a rival group seeking revenge, he killed a youth with a knife. Although charges against him were later dropped, he nevertheless left the gang (Chanswangpuwana, 1997). This example suggests evidence of youth groups and violence yet to be studied.

Phongpaichit and Piriyarangsan (1994) indicate that organized, entrepreneurial adult gangs have existed in many parts of Thailand since at least the 1920s and have been involved in a variety of legal and illegal businesses. Where they exist, they are an integral part of Thai society, with a broad spectrum of people on their payrolls. The leaders of these gangs are often Thai folk heroes in their communities, because they provide employment and improve local facilities. They are involved in gambling, smuggling, prostitution, political corruption, and murder.

In the early years of these adult gangs, leaders often had inauspicious beginnings as fishermen, bicycle repairmen, and bus conductors. As their organizations and wealth grew, they provided employment for members of their families, friends, and collaborators. It is quite likely they provided job

opportunities for local youth as well. Phongpaichit and Piriyarangsan demonstrate the widespread use of violence among these gangs to achieve their
economic goals—activities that have traditionally employed risk-taking
youth. Rath (1998) has stated that adult bandits in southern Thailand "hire
local youth to carry out terrorist activities," giving credence to the hypothesis of youth gang involvement.

In Chiang Mai, there is evidence to suggest that at least one adult gang
with juvenile members was involved in a murder-related extortion plot
where both the killer and victim were juveniles (Kanwanich, 1996). While
there is considerable controversy regarding the reasons for the killing, who
the intended victim was, and the strength and presence of the extortion
gang, it is clear juveniles were involved and may have been involved in prior
illegal activities. It is also an apparently isolated instance of youth violence
and in line with my hypothesis of significantly lower rates of Thai youth
violence than in Western societies.

CURRENT TRENDS IN TEEN VIOLENCE

Why are delinquency rates so low in Thailand? There is probably no single
reason; rather a combination of factors—social, political, economic, cultural,
and psychological—account for it.

In 1985 Herman and Julia Schwendinger produced an important work
on delinquency that offered a theoretical explanation as to why delinquency
rates were low in certain industrializing countries and high in others. This
explanation used articulation theory, which posits that the differences in
delinquency rates may be due to the youth's ability to return home or how
well the youth's were able to "articulate" back into their home community
when life in the city was no longer promising. Good articulation relations
meant low delinquency, and poor articulation relations meant high delinquency.

In societies where economies permitted youth to venture into the cities
seeking job opportunities, work at those jobs until the job ran out or the
money got bad, then return to their villages and fit back in again with the
local economy, the rates of delinquency were low because the articulation
was good. On the other hand, in societies where youths worked in the cities
but could not return to their villages because there was no longer anything
there for them economically, culturally, or socially, the delinquency rates
were high because the articulation was poor.

The Schwendingers used research conducted in Asia and India, where
delinquency was relatively low, to indicate how areas with good articulation
relationships prevent delinquency. The youth were able to integrate back
into viable communal lifestyles that exerted "traditional controls that support lawful behavior and impede the alienation of youth and the development of their own subculture." In these cases they were able to "return to

the family farm, artisan's shop, and cottage industry, where they are reintegrated into traditional social relationships that prevent delinquent behavior." They contend that "wherever these productive units remain viable and support traditional communal life, delinquency is lower" (pp. 12, 14).

In Thailand there was considerable movement from the villages to the urban centers during the boom period from 1987 to mid-1996. Phongpaichit and Baker (1998) indicate that some 6 to 7 million people moved into nonagricultural jobs during this period. So many young people made this transition that "in some villages, the generation of younger adults was virtually stripped out, leaving just the children and the old." But, they argue, "most people did not quit the village completely, either physically or mentally," and returned at certain times to help with the harvest. During the summer in Hat Yai, there were seven elephants present on various downtown street corners, with three or four young handlers each. Elephants and handlers were from the northern provinces where work was slow. They had come to the city to give rides and allow people to buy bags of bananas from the handlers, who would in turn feed the elephants. The handlers not only sent money home but saw their presence in the city as temporary, intending to go home in time for the harvest. In addition, many other youth who work in the cities also send a large portion of their earnings home to their families. This not only helps the family but keeps the youth connected; they know, the family knows, and the village knows the basis of the family's support.

In spite of the rapid economic boom of the past decade that brought so many millions of people to the city, Thailand is still a rural society, with over 60 percent of the population continuing to remain in the villages (Phongpaichit and Baker, 1998). A popular 1997 Thai song titled "Home" claimed that although people physically left the villages to work in the cities, "they carried the village with them in their heads." The peasantry in Thailand remains a large, powerful political and economic force. Most still have land, and with the tropical weather, rich soil, small crafts, local jobs, and occasional urban money from one or more family members, the continuation of village life remains a solid prospect.

The large and vital village populations have been capable of reintegrating their opportunity-seeking family members when the greener pastures of the city turn brown. While many who go to the city never actually leave the village in their hearts and minds, most not only help support their families while they are away but return on a regular basis to visit, thereby maintaining connections to their roots. The low rates of delinquency in Thailand and the relative absence of gangs are due to the positive articulation relations that Thai youth have with their powerful communal groups. They go and come back on such a regular basis that the communal influence remains more dominant than the urban influence. Delinquency is low in Thailand because Thai village traditions and customs are strong.

CONTRIBUTING FACTORS

Vocational-Technical School Rivalries

Some of the clearest examples of Thai youth violence and Thai group violence come from the rivalries existing between the large vocational-technical (voc-tech) schools in Bangkok. Even in Chiang Mai and Hat Yai, reports of their internecine warfare are legendary. An examination of one of the most notorious of these rivalries will show groups acting on principles that may remind us of struggles between the Crips and Bloods in Los Angeles, but they are very different.

Voc-tech schools are private institutions offering technical degrees to primarily working-class students whose parents are sufficiently affluent to be able to help them with their schooling costs. These mostly male schools, which sometimes have as many as 2,000 students, are attended by youth who start at about age sixteen and attend for three to four years. Upon completion, they have degrees in engineering, architecture, manufacturing, or design and are employable in public or private organizations. During the time they spend at school, many also take part in the traditional battles with another school that is a historical enemy to their own.

Near Chulalongkorn University in the heart of Bangkok are two voc-tech schools whose rivalries with each other have existed for ten years—the length of time the schools have been in existence. These schools, Uthantwai and Pathumwan, are on opposite corners of a major intersection and share a bus stop. When freshmen arrive at their respective schools, they are socialized by upperclassmen to know that the school across the street should now become the locus of their antagonism. The school's "tradition leads to fighting. . . . Freshmen must prove themselves to the seniors," says Amorn Wanichwiwatana (pers. comm.). The situation is like boot camp, where the upperclassmen test the freshmen, who try to prove themselves worthy by the audacity of their acts.

In the early years of the rivalries, fists, brass knuckles, tee squares, and other hand weapons were most commonly used in the brawls, but now the use of knives and even guns has become more common (Ua-Amnoey, pers. comm.). Some students even manufacture their own weapons in shops on campus (Wanichwiwatana, pers. comm.). Every year a number of students get injured, some seriously, with one to three people dying from their injuries. Compounding the violence is the practice by each school of "keeping score." Freshmen are urged to record as many victims as their older counterparts, or to exceed them if they can, to prove worthiness.

One factor that facilitates both identification of the enemy and the carrying and hiding of weapons is school attire. Students often wear long shop coats to protect their clothing. The many pockets in these coats make ideal hiding places for a variety of weapons, and the school insignia, sewn to the outside of the coat, makes identification easy. Most remove the coats before they leave the campus to avoid violent confrontations, but some wear belts or other garments with school symbols to convey their loyalties. Usually the antagonisms cease when the student completes his studies and begins to assume adult responsibilities. The school rivalries are therefore situational, age linked, and initiated and perpetuated by the older students, then abandoned upon graduation.

Voc-tech school students are not the only students involved in violence; their university counterparts have also contributed. In October 1973 and October 1976, when students from Thammasat University rose up against government repression, they also participated in "massacres," taking many lives (Teerawichitchainan, 1996; Janchitfah, 1996). These actions, however, were very different from the voc-tech students behavior in two significant ways: (1) most of the university students were no longer juveniles, most being at least eighteen years old; (2) this was political protest turned violent, not delinquency, deriving from very different motivations. It was violence by young people, however, suggesting that its existence in Thai society may be reflected in other ways.

Drug Problems

Perhaps the most pressing issue facing Thai youth is drug use. It is the activity they are most likely to be arrested for and most likely to do time for. It seems to involve greater numbers of youth each year, with the drug of choice changing as well.

A report from the Ministry of Public Health estimated there were at least 30,000 youth in Thailand addicted to drugs in 1996 (Sukrung, 1998), a surprisingly large number of the total (12 million youth). Of the 29,335 youth tried at the Central Juvenile and Family Court in Bangkok in 1997, 9,984 were drug cases, and another 3,875 were "solvent cases," such as glue sniffing (Juvenile Drug Cases Soar, 1998). Thus the total number of substance abuse cases there was 13,859, or almost half of all the cases the court tried. In Chiang Mai, chief juvenile magistrate Udom Wattathum's data showed drug cases to be one of the largest categories of youth cases tried in the province and also showed a steady increase in the number coming to court since 1995. In a society where violence is an anomaly rather than the norm, the numbers of youth involved in drugs are unexpected. In Western society, we have come to see drugs, violence, and gangs as virtually inseparable. This does not appear to be the case in Thailand. Drugs, violence, and gangs certainly do occur together there, but not in the proportions or the degree they do in American society.

In 1989 the drug of choice for youth changed from marijuana and various harder drugs such as heroin to amphetamines, or *ya baa*, but by 1997, it was the drug that youth were most often arrested for using (Jinakul, 1998).

There are at least three reasons for its widespread popularity: (1) easy to obtain and cheap, (2) the law, and (3) peer pressure. In the first place, amphetamines are relatively cheap to buy and easy to manufacture, and drug labs have been started in a number of areas in Thailand as well as Burma, which shares a long contiguous border with Thailand. A new cottage industry for Thai youth has sprung up along the border, transporting drugs manufactured in Burma across the frontier to Thailand. For their services, these youths are paid $35 to $50 (Wattathum, pers. comm.), a hefty and tempting sum for poor rural Thais. The *Bangkok Post* (Gang Preying on Youngsters Busted, 1997) suggested a new trend among Burmese amphetamine manufactures of adding flavors and colors to make the drug more attractive to young users. In the cities, drugs can be obtained from neighborhood drug pushers, motorcycle taxi drivers, at school, and even from parents (Sukrung, 1998). In some rural areas, teachers may have connections to local drug lords, supplying their students as well as their village (Wanichwiwatana, pers. comm.).

Second, before the law changed in the late 1990s, the penalties associated with amphetamine use, sale, and manufacture were relatively mild. After passage of the new juvenile law, the penalties stiffened significantly, including the death penalty for possession of large quantities of drugs. However, the death penalty seems to be a rare event, having not been used in the past five years.

Finally, many youth who try drugs do so because their friends do. According to a survey conducted by the Central Juvenile and Family Court, a number of youth began to use drugs because they thought they were in fashion (Juvenile Drug Cases Soar, 1998). Another report cited peer pressure and a "desire to be 'cool' " (Sukrung, 1998) as primary reasons for drug use.

In many respects, then, Thai youth take up drugs for reasons similar to American youth. A major difference, however, is in the violence associated with them. In the United States, drugs and violence are almost synonymous, while in Thailand, little of the predatory and violent activity accompanying drugs is found. To say drug activity in Thailand is not as violent as in the United States is not to say it is violence free. In fact, in one notorious case in 1996, six suspected drug dealers were shot to death by police under very questionable circumstances (Siraj, 1996). Other reports also indicate considerable violence among some of the gangs involved in drug manufacture and distribution. Therefore, although there appears to be considerable use of drugs among Thai youth, their activities are not as violent as American youth.

One of the most infamous slum areas in Bangkok is Klong Toey, known as a major source of illegal drugs as well as for its use and abuse (Assavanoda, 1998). Youth, organized criminal gangs, corruption, and violence all seem to be part of the social scene there. The sale of drugs and muscle for organized crime are not uncommon activities of some of the slum's youth. Attempts by reformers to woo youth away from these lucrative activities are frequently met by threats of violence. The police are of little help since a number are on the take, and a blind eye to the criminality is the usual response. In this regard some parallels may be drawn between this slum and poor areas in American inner cities, but caution must be taken; more research on Thailand is necessary before parallels can be established.

RESPONSES TO THE PROBLEM

The first juvenile court opened in Bangkok forty-five years ago, but did not separate youthful offenders by age or offense (Bhaudikul, pers. comm.). Thai officials were sent to Europe and the United States to observe the juvenile systems and procedures there, adopting many of those principles and practices to fit their needs. These concepts are reflected in the progressive attitudes Thais take to the treatment and rehabilitation of their youth. The Juvenile and Family Courts are now a fundamental part of the Thai juvenile justice system; twenty-nine of Thailand's seventy-six provinces have juvenile courts. Provinces without a juvenile court, usually the rural provinces, try juveniles in adult court, under certain judges, using the juvenile codes.

I took the following notes in 1998 when I observed a juvenile trial at the Chiang Mai Juvenile and Family Court:

The Chiang Mai court house is a modern-looking structure, painted white, with a comfortable arrangement of tropical trees and shrubs. Inside are the administrative offices, judges' and associate judges' offices, and the courtrooms. Juvenile trials are private affairs, and not open to the public. The court I went into was a spartan, all-dark-wood room, with space for 6 to 8 observers, with low lights and no open windows. The observers seats were wooden, with upright backs, which seemed old, but functional, designed to make certain you would not sleep.

There were two judges at this trial: a presiding male judge, thirty-eight to forty-two years old, and a female associate judge about ten years older. The atmosphere was peaceful; the judges appearing understanding and sympathetic. Standing in front of the two judges was a boy fifteen to sixteen years old, in bare feet, with clothes that though tattered could very well have been his best. His arms were at his side, while he calmly and respectfully answered the questions he was asked. In the back of the room sat his parents, also barefooted, with a small child the mother tried to keep under control. They stood when spoken to and when replies were requested, answered the judges politely and with deference.

The boy had been charged with negligence for hitting and killing a pedestrian with his motorbike. When asked by the judge who was at fault for the accident, the boy responded: "If he was still alive, it would have been his, but because he is not, then it is mine." This response meant he felt he was innocent, but could not prove it since the other party was dead. Thus, by showing repentance for his behavior he would quite likely get probation.

All juveniles are permitted to have a legal adviser (paid for by the family if they can afford it or the court if they cannot) to help them prepare their case. The court tries to keep the juvenile with his or her parents whenever possible; about 80 percent to 90 percent of first-time offenders receive probation (Wattathum, pers. comm.). Most judges prefer to keep the family intact, believing it is the center of the youth's world and thus the best place for rehabilitation to occur. If the parents are solid, the youth is in school, and the offense is minor, they will even give the youth probation for a second offense. The court will also try to provide counseling for the family and sometimes fine the family for their child's offense. If all this does not help the youth, the court uses another option—the observation and protection center.

Observation and protection centers, under the command and responsibility of the chief justice, are a key component of Thailand's juvenile justice system (Mahakun, 1998). In Chiang Mai, there is a center for the province in a serene pastoral setting on the outskirts of the city. Following are my notes on observations at this center in 1998:

The center is located on 30 to 40 acres of ground, in a residential area, approached by a two-lane highway which seems more like a camp than a youth prison. Both boys and girls are housed here, but separately. Wire fences and walls, with unarmed guards, surround both areas, while a visible open area separates the two facilities. Their rather large size, and the existence of many colorful tropical plants and trees mixed in with large, open spaces, produces a very nonprison-like feeling. A rooster and a dozen or so chickens, who make the center their home, add to the casual air.

The boys are encouraged to paint on the insides and outsides of some of the buildings. They chose to paint large, colorful figures, depicting action scenes, female beauty, the king, and traditional Thai folk musicians. Many of the staff live in well-kept duplexes and four-plexes outside the center's perimeter. Staff inside the facility carry beepers but no weapons. There are about two hundred boys and thirty-seven girls, some of whom have babies, which they are allowed to keep housed in the center.

Accompanied by the center director and various male and female staff, I walked freely in the boys' section, feeling safe, never once noticing any behavior that could be interpreted as aggressive, hostile, or even threatening by either youth to staff or vice versa. In fact the mood was relaxed, mostly characterized by respect, gentility and concern. Each time we would greet a group of boys, they would stop what they were doing and face us and greet us together with a *wai* and *sawadee krap*, the latter being the males' words for "hello." All of the boys were dressed in white T-shirts, dark shorts, and either wore rubber thongs or went barefoot. They were housed in four dormitories, sleeping in bunk beds of tubular steel construction with one-inch-thick mattresses. A lower and upper sheet rounded out the bed's makeup. Each dorm has a bathroom area at one end of the room, while at the other is a small enclosure where two staff are always present when the boys are there. In the staff's room is a bed, where at night, the staff take turns alternating between sleep and observation.

While I was there, all of the boys were engaged in some type of activity. Some played "Asian volleyball" outdoors, but most were either in school or at one of the many vocational trade classes being offered. The trade classes consist of groups of six to eight boys engaged in one of the following: mechanics; small engine and bicycle repair; welding and metal shop; wood shop; sewing; cooking; haircutting; art, painting, and sculpting; computer and typing class; traditional Thai musical instrument class; work in the library; and farming. Most of these classes were also designed to give something back to the institution. For example, metal classes had made the dorm beds; sewing classes kept clothes in repair and made items for sale; arts classes and the farm also produced items for sale. The boys as well as staff were involved in the work. At one point two female associate juvenile judges arrived with a truckload of aloe vera plants that one was donating to the center's garden. The judges, while dressed in business attire, informed me they had coveralls and would soon be joining the boys in planting the aloe vera. It is a tradition for various judges to take their turn visiting the center every week for an entire afternoon.

The girls' section was smaller and less complex. Some of the girls come to the center pregnant and have their babies during their stay, while a few other girls may already have a baby at the time they arrive. In both cases staff feel it is better for mother and child to stay together rather than be separated. I saw one girl there with an infant, where both mother and child were a focus of attention by the staff as well as the other girls. Because there are fewer girls than boys, there are a smaller number of activities. Girls activities include cooking; construction of lawns and gardens; horticulture; and academics, which are taken with the boys.

Not all observation and protection centers are as peaceful as the one in Chiang Mai. A *Bangkok Post* article (Godfathers Terroize Youngsters, 1996), for example, claims that at several detention centers in Bangkok, young "godfathers" known as "Big Ones" terrorize fellow inmates, forcing them to procure drugs and money and engage in homosexual acts. In another center in Bangkok, this one housing some 750 offenders, a riot broke out over a fight between a warden and a juvenile, which was apparently caused by a disagreement over a World Cup soccer match on television. The details of who started the fight and whether drugs or alcohol were involved is unclear and disputed by the inmate leader and warden. One hundred riot police were called out to calm about 300 inmates who were intent on seizing their building (Phetpradab, 1998).

These two cases suggest the Thai juvenile system is not without its problems, with the larger centers in Bangkok apparently having more than other areas. The philosophy of the court, however, is *parens patriae* (the state as parent), and at least in Chiang Mai, it appears to be both in practice and producing positive results. The center director said they have a 5 percent recidivism rate (Pengnate, pers. comm.), which is exceptionally low by any standard. We do not have rates from other centers for comparison nor can it be assumed that the low rate in Chiang Mai is entirely due to the center's practices. Before we can determine the actual effect of the system's practices on reducing delinquent recidivism, we need to take into account other factors, such as social ostracism, family relations, and a variety of economic factors. Nevertheless, the practices at the Chiang Mai Center come close to the ideals incorporated in the concept of *parens patriae* and to demonstrated methods of reducing delinquency. The center's approach is directed toward rehabilitation and reintegration back into Thai society, so it is quite reasonable to assume that this approach at least contributed to the low recidivism.

CONCLUSION

A smile and respect symbolize Thai youth. Although the disciplines of criminology and delinquency are relatively new, there is enough evidence to suggest that delinquency and teen violence are uncommon in Thailand. There are examples of Thai group violence, as evidenced in the rivalry between vocational schools in Bangkok, and there is evidence of Thai gangs but nowhere near the incidence of gangs in Western cultures, although drugs and youth are becoming a pressing social issue in the large cities of Thailand. It is hypothesized that the delinquency rates are low in the country as a result of a combination of social, political, economic, cultural, and psychological factors. Thai society is still very much a rural society, and the Thai village traditions and customs are strong.

NOTE

Special appreciation is extended to Professor Taipesrinivati Bhaudikul, Department of Sociology and Anthropology, Chiang Mai University, for the invaluable help she gave me in data collection and contacts with the Chiang Mai Juvenile and Family Court and Observation and Protection Center.

REFERENCES

Assavanoda, Anjira. (1998). Breaking old habits. *Bangkok Post*, June 25.
Bartollas, Clemens. (1997). *Juvenile delinquency* (4th ed.). Boston: Allyn and Bacon.
Bunnag, Sirikul. (1996). Crime surge among teens draws alarm. *Bangkok Post*, Sept. 4.
Chanswangpuwana, Matchima. (1997). Rebel with a cause. *Bangkok Post*, Mar. 12.
Charoenwongsak, Kriengsak. (1997). From "land of smiles" to "land of violence." *Bangkok Post*, June 1.
Gang preying on youngsters busted. (1997). *Bangkok Post*, Jan. 15.
Godfathers terrorize youngsters. (1996). *Bangkok Post*, Nov. 1.
Janchitfah, Supara. (1996). Hidden violence in a culture of peace. *Bangkok Post*, Oct. 13.
Jinakul, Surat. (1998). A never-ending story. *Bangkok Post*, June 28.
Juvenile drug cases soar. (1998). *Bangkok Post*, Jan. 10.
Kanwanich, Supradit. (1996). Extortion gangs on the prowl. *Bangkok Post*, June 9.

Mahakun, Vicha. (1998). Introductory paper on juvenile and family court and observation and protection centre. *Juvenile and Family Court and Observation and Protection Centre.*

Mulder, Niels. (1996). *Inside Thai society: Interpretations of everyday life.* Amsterdam: Pepin Press.

Phetpradab, Charoenlak. (1998). Convicts riot during soccer telecast. *Nation,* June 18.

Phongpaichit, Pasuk, and Baker, Chris. (1998). *Thailand's boom and bust.* Chiang Mai: Silkworm Books.

Phongpaichit, Pasuk, and Piriyarangsan, Sungsidh. (1994). *Corruption and democracy in Thailand.* Chiang Mai: Silkworm Books.

Rath, Siam. (1998). Take an eye for an eye. *Bangkok Post,* Jan. 9.

Satha-anand, Chaiwat. (1997). The end of the age of innocence in a future built on non-violence. *Bangkok Post,* Feb. 18.

Schwendinger, Herman, and Schwendinger, Julia. (1985). *Adolescent subcultures and delinquency.* New York: Praeger.

Siraj, Pavit. (1996). Police kill drug dealers in provincial massacre. *Bangkok Post,* Nov. 28.

Sukphisit, Suthon. (1997). Finding a receipt for Muay Thai. *Bangkok Post,* April 9.

Sukrung, Karnjariya. (1998). Teaching them a lesson. *Bangkok Post,* March 2.

Teerawichitchainan, Bussarawan. (1996). Where have all the flowers gone? *Bangkok Post,* Oct. 11.

CONSULTANTS

Bhaudikul, Taipesrinivati, Professor, Department of Sociology and Anthropology, Chiang Mai University, Chiang Mai.

Pengnate, Waeate, Director, The Observation and Protection Center of Chiang Mai, Chiang Mai.

Robert, G. Lamar, Senior Advisor, Social Research Institute, Chiang Mai University, Chiang Mai.

Ua-Amnoey, Jutharat, Professor, Department of Sociology and Anthropology, Chulalongkorn University, Bangkok.

Wanichwiwatana, Amorn, Criminologist, Department of Sociology and Anthropology, Chulalongkorn University, Bangkok.

Wattathum, Udom, Chief Juvenile Magistrate, Chiang Mai Juvenile and Family Court and Observation and Protection Center, Chiang Mai.

14

UNITED STATES

Wayne N. Welsh

PERCEPTIONS OF TEEN VIOLENCE

Public attitudes toward juvenile crime in the United States have toughened in recent years, as have legislative and justice system responses (Torbet et al., 1996). From 1992 to 1995, states passed numerous laws designed to crack down on juvenile crime. For example, forty-one states passed laws making it easier for juveniles to be tried as adults. In twenty-five states, laws gave criminal and juvenile courts new sentencing options. In forty states, laws modified or removed traditional juvenile court confidentiality provisions to make records and proceedings more open. In twenty-two states, laws increased the role of victims of juvenile crime in juvenile justice proceedings. This approach is a significant departure from the *parens patriae* (the state as parent) philosophy that guided the development of juvenile justice in the United States. In spite of this shift, prevention and intervention approaches that consider the juvenile's entire environment are emerging.

There is a widespread perception that teen violence in the United States is out of control. We hear regularly about the latest schoolyard shooting, gang-related murder, or vicious assault committed by seemingly younger and younger persons. Witness the multiple homicides since 1997 where over twenty people were killed and twice as many wounded by teens (in Littleton, Colorado; Conyers, Georgia; Jonesboro, Arkansas; Paducah, Kentucky; and Springfield, Oregon). However, our overall perceptions of teen violence are fueled by dramatic incidents that do not quite reflect reality. For example, fewer than twenty children under the age of fourteen commit murder in any given year (O'Brien, 1998). Homicides committed by juveniles are relatively rare, accounting for only 14 percent of all homicides for which an offender was identified in 1995 (Sickmund, Snyder, and Poe-Yamagata, 1997). Seventy-five percent of homicide victims ages twelve to seventeen are killed by adults (O'Brien, 1998). There is more to teen violence than meets the eye.

I suggest a three-pronged approach to teen violence. First, we must examine patterns of violence (who is involved, where, how much, how often, and so on). Second, we should attempt to understand or explain teen violence based on those observed patterns. Third, we need to explore solutions to teen violence that are consistent with both observed patterns and explanations. Failure to do so increases the likelihood of failed interventions (Welsh and Harris, in press). Although our responses to juvenile violence have become more punitive over the past few years, new and promising prevention strategies are being developed and tested. Arguably, the best responses to teen violence can, must, and will include a balance of both punishment and prevention.

CURRENT TRENDS IN TEEN VIOLENCE

Despite recent small decreases, teen violence in the United States remains at unacceptably high levels, as indicated by both victimization and arrest rates. Juveniles accounted for 19 percent of all violent crime arrests in 1994 (Sickmund et al., 1997). Although juvenile arrests for violent crimes declined 3 percent from 1994 to 1995, the first decrease in nearly a decade (Snyder, 1997), the number of juvenile violent crime arrests in 1995 (363,400) was 67 percent above the 1986 level. In 1994, 2.6 million violent crimes were committed against juveniles aged twelve to seventeen (Kelley et al., 1997). The rate of violent victimization of juveniles aged twelve through seventeen was nearly three times that of adults. Murders of juveniles increased 66 percent between 1985 and 1995, mainly in the group aged twelve through seventeen (Sickmund et al., 1997). To put this problem in context, we need to examine who is involved (e.g., age, race, and gender), the settings where violence occurs (e.g., at school or at home), the use of weapons (e.g., knives and guns), and the types of situations where violence occurs (e.g., arguments and interpersonal disputes).

As in other countries, violence in the United States is largely (but not exclusively) a young man's affair. Among juvenile offenders, males made up 85 percent of the total juvenile arrests for Violent Crime Index offenses, although the rate of increase for females (34 percent) from 1991 to 1995 was four times the rate of increase for males (Kelley et al., 1997). For twelve- to seventeen-year-olds, boys were one and a half times more likely to be victims of violent crimes than girls (Sickmund et al., 1997). As in other countries, violent crime disproportionately affects racial minorities. African

American juveniles were six times more likely than Caucasian juveniles to be victims of homicide in 1994; 61 percent of offenders were African American and 36 percent were Caucasian (Snyder, Sickmund, and Poe-Yamagata, 1996). Income levels are also important. In 1988, the risk of violent victimization was 2.5 times greater for individuals with families in the lowest income group (under $7,500). Relative to age, gender, and race, the net effect of family income may be small, although relationships among variables are quite complex (Reiss and Roth, 1993).

Schools are primary settings for juvenile violence. Thirty-seven percent of all violent crimes experienced by youths aged twelve to fifteen occurred on school grounds (Whitaker and Bastian, 1993), while 56 percent of all juvenile victimizations (property and violent crimes) in 1991 occurred in school or on school property. Snyder and Sickmund emphasize, "There is no comparable place where crimes against adults were so concentrated" (1995, p. 16). A National School Board Association survey (1993) of 720 school districts throughout the United States found that 39 percent of urban school districts use metal detectors, 64 percent use locker searches, and 65 percent use security personnel in their schools. In the same survey, 82 percent of school districts reported that the problem of school violence is worse now than it was five years ago. Overall, 35 percent believed that school violence had increased significantly and that the incidents were more serious.

Results from the 1995 School Crime Supplement (SCS) of the National Crime Victimization Survey (NCVS), based on interviews conducted with a nationally representative sample of more than 10,000 youths, showed that 14.5 percent of students aged twelve to nineteen experienced one or more violent crimes or property crimes at school over a six-month period (Chandler et al., 1998), with the percentage of youths reporting violent victimizations increasing from 3.4 percent in 1989 to 4.2 percent in 1995. The percentage of students reporting a street gang presence at their school nearly doubled to 28.4 percent between 1989 and 1995 (Chandler et al., 1998), and those who reported the presence of gangs at their school were twice as likely to fear attack (Bastian and Taylor, 1991).

Perhaps even more important are the means of violence. One cannot examine juvenile violence in the United States without examining the availability and use of guns. Gun homicides by juveniles in the United States tripled between 1983 and 1997, while homicides involving other weapons declined. From 1983 through 1995, the proportion of homicides in which a juvenile used a gun increased from 55 percent to 80 percent (Greenbaum, 1997). In fact, an overall increase in juvenile homicide offenders is firearm related (Snyder et al., 1996).

According to the Centers for Disease Control (1993), 2.5 million teenagers in the United States carry weapons and frequently take them to school. Every day, they estimate, 135,000 students bring guns to school. In a 1995 survey of students from ten inner-city high schools, almost half of the male students said they could borrow a gun from friends or family if they wanted to, and 40 percent of students said they have a male relative who carries a gun (National Institute of Justice, 1993). In the same student survey, one in four said guns were easy to get in their neighborhoods. Two-thirds knew someone who had carried a gun to school, and one in four reported carrying weapons while in school. Thirty percent of students reported that they had been assault victims in school or on the way to or from school.

In a survey of 758 male students in inner-city high schools and 835 male serious offenders incarcerated in six different detention facilities, Sheley and Wright (1993) found that 83 percent of inmates and 22 percent of students possessed guns. These firearms tended to be high-quality, powerful revolvers. Most detainees and students stated it was easy to acquire a gun; only 35 percent said it would be difficult. Fifty-three percent of students said they would borrow a gun if they needed one (from family members or friends); 37 percent of students and 54 percent of detainees said they would get one off the street. Although involvement in drug sales was more common among those reporting gun carrying, the main reason given for carrying a gun was self-protection.

CONTRIBUTING FACTORS

Explanations of teen violence have focused on individuals, peers and group subcultures, families, schools, communities, and even entire cultures. No single cause is sufficient to explain all youth violence, but each can shed important insights on the causes of juvenile violence and opportunities for intervention. As the National Crime Prevention Council (1994) stated, no single program or policy will prevent youth violence. Because the causes are diverse, solutions must take many different approaches. Unfortunately, local, state, and federal legislators continually behave as though some new "magic cure" can be turned up to eliminate youth violence. Consider recent, widespread legislation such as juvenile waiver laws that aim to "get tough" with juvenile offenders by emphasizing individual responsibility and accountability (see Sickmund et al., 1997). While some juvenile offenders surely deserve such sanctions due to the seriousness of their offense or their previous delinquency, such approaches ignore the interactive influences of individual, interpersonal, institutional, and community factors on violence. A few examples help illustrate the complex causality of teen violence.

Character Controls

Aggravated assaults and even homicides among juveniles often result from relatively trivial arguments between people who know each other—"character contests" (Lockwood, 1997). We need to know more about the types and frequency of these altercations, as well as their dynamics: the locations, the opening moves in a sequence of escalation, the relationship between disputants, goals and justifications of opposing parties, the role of third parties, and other situational factors that may play a role in escalating or de-escalating the causal sequence leading to violent injury or death. Most disturbing are research findings that suggest that violence does not emerge from a lack of values, but rather from well-established values in which youths believe that violence is not only justified but necessary in a wide range of situations (Lockwood, 1997). Such viewpoints are also represented in sub-cultural theories of violence (Wolfgang and Ferracuti, 1982).

Social Bonding

Schools and families provide central venues for social bonding (or failure). Youngsters with poor academic or interpersonal skills are likely to experience failure and alienation in school. They do not become attached to school because social interaction is unrewarding. They do not become committed to educational goals because they view them as unrealistic. They do not become involved in conventional social activities either because they are denied access or because meaningful activities are lacking. They do not come to believe in conventional rules because they do not perceive meaningful present or future rewards for compliance. General support has been found for proposed relationships between bonding and juvenile violence, although the nature of interactions between different types of bonding and other variables is not entirely clear (e.g., see Howell, 1995). Bonding may be part of a critical set of causes as well as a point for intervention.

School Climate

There is a growing realization that institutions such as schools have their own characteristic personalities, just as individuals do. In other words, youths are socialized within a specific organizational and interpersonal setting. Socialization includes factors such as communication patterns, norms about what is appropriate behavior and how rewards and sanctions should be applied, role relationships and role perceptions, and patterns of influence and accommodation (Fox et al., 1979). One of the benchmark studies relating school violence to dimensions of school climate was the National Institute of Education's (1978) Safe School Study. Using questionnaires, data were collected from students, teachers, and principals from 642 U.S. public schools. Community data from each school were prepared from the 1970 census. The NIE report stated that school administration and policies make a significant contribution to levels of disorder and perceptions of safety in different schools. Policies that reduced misbehavior and violence in schools included decreasing the size and impersonality of schools, making school discipline more systematic, decreasing arbitrariness and student frustration, improving school reward structures, increasing the relevance of schooling, and decreasing students' sense of powerlessness and alienation (Gottfredson and Gottfredson, 1985).

Community Factors

Associations between community factors such as socioeconomic status and violence have been well established, although the exact causal mechanisms are not entirely clear. Recent research has uncovered complex links between poverty and crime, and between "social disorganization" and violence. Researchers studying community-level variations have found relationships between poverty and high rates of delinquency, and between poverty and high homicide rates (Reiss and Roth, 1993). Community characteristics found to relate to violence have included concentrations of poverty, high residential mobility and population turnover, family disruption, high density in housing and population, weak local social organization (e.g., low density of friends and acquaintances, few social resources, weak intergenerational ties in families and communities, weak control of street corner groups, low participation in community events and activities), and opportunities associated with violence (e.g., gun density, drug distribution networks). Although such relationships are complex, it can safely be said that community influences often combine with poverty and with one another to influence high rates of violence (for a detailed review, see Sampson and Lauritsen, 1993).

Much more detailed examination of research and theories pertaining to youth violence is desirable (see, for example, Howell, 1995; Reiss and Roth, 1993). Valid analyses of offenders, victims, crimes, locations, and other patterns are critical prerequisites for designing effective violence reduction strategies. In the absence of such information, untested assumptions and hunches will continue to drive critical policy decisions, and unacceptably high rates of injuries and deaths will persist.

RESPONSES TO THE PROBLEM

The National Juvenile Justice Action Plan, part of the Office of Juvenile Justice and Delinquency Prevention's (OJJDP) *Comprehensive Strategy for Serious, Violent, and Chronic Juvenile Offenders* (Wilson and Howell, 1994), encourages helping youths throughout their development while responding to juvenile crime in a way that ensures public safety. The Comprehensive Plan, according to the director of OJJDP (Bilchik, 1998), is based on decades of research, statistics, and evaluations in the fields of criminal and juvenile justice, public health, and youth development. It represents the state of the art regarding what we know about effective prevention and intervention. Below, I summarize five key objectives of the Comprehensive Plan, and briefly review promising prevention and intervention strategies.

Objective 1: Provide immediate intervention and appropriate sanctions and treatment for delinquents.

Through various federal grants, states have been provided with funds to strengthen their juvenile justice systems. The states funnel these funds to specific cities and counties to develop and implement programs to prevent and control delinquency. A wide variety of strategies have been implemented, including *graduated sanctions*. Sanctions refer to a system of responses to delinquency that combines individual accountability with intensive treatment and rehabilitation services. These sanctions are graduated to the degree that they fit the offense and the juvenile's previous history of delinquency. This requires consideration and balancing of various criteria, including the seriousness of the delinquent act, the potential risk for reoffending, the risk to public safety, and the offender's rehabilitation needs. The most intensive treatments are reserved for juveniles who most need them (e.g., intensive, residential drug and alcohol treatment), while the most intensive punishments (e.g., secure detention, rather than camps, ranches, or farms) are reserved for those who earn them. Comprehensive, valid risk and needs assessments are required to determine the appropriate punishment or treatment response for any juvenile.

Objective 2: Prosecute serious, violent, and chronic juvenile offenders in criminal court.

This objective focuses on offenders who have committed very serious crimes, have a lengthy history of delinquency, and/or have failed to respond to treatment. In particular, almost every state has adopted or strengthened *waiver and transfer mechanisms* that allow juveniles, under specific conditions, to be tried as adults in criminal court. Such legislation varies dramatically from one state to another, however, and reliable information on the impact of such strategies is lacking. OJJDP is funding several studies to determine the outcome and impact of waiver and transfer provisions on juvenile offenders. Related policies include changing state laws to make juvenile records more accessible to school, human services, and justice personnel. In many states, no longer does a juvenile's record become sealed when he or she reaches adulthood; previous juvenile offenses can now be used in criminal proceedings. Confidentiality of juvenile records, once a cornerstone of the *parens patriae* philosophy, has also been weakened, ostensibly to improve sharing of information among human services personnel, and to improve coordination of different treatment services delivered by different agencies.

Objective 3: Reduce youth involvement with guns, drugs, and gangs.

The availability of firearms in the United States is at least partly related to high rates of juvenile homicide. *Partnerships to Reduce Juvenile Gun Violence*, a recent effort funded by OJJDP, attempts to enhance and coordinate prevention, intervention, and suppression activities by strengthening linkages among community groups, schools, law enforcement, and the juvenile justice system. For example, if law enforcement agents become better acquainted with community residents, they will learn more about problems in neighborhoods and be more successful in enlisting support for community crime prevention efforts. Three critical factors are addressed: juvenile access to guns, the reasons young people carry guns, and the reasons they choose guns to resolve conflicts.

Objective 4: Provide opportunities for children and youth.

Prevention activities focused on enhancing social skills and increasing opportunities for youth have, when well planned and well implemented, proved effective in reducing delinquency (e.g., Wilson and Howell, 1994; Welsh, Jenkins, and Harris, in press). Such programs include mentoring, after-school activities, conflict resolution training, remedial education, and vocational education. Boys and Girls Clubs of America have provided after-school activities that have increased school attendance, improved academic performance, and reduced juvenile crime (Ingersoll, 1997). Welsh et al. (1999) found that participation in five community-based after-school programs run by nonprofit groups reduced rearrest rates for juveniles in one community (Harrisburg, Pennsylvania) but not in another (Philadelphia). Program implementation and organizational stability were important factors influencing program impact.

Objective 5: Break the cycle of violence by addressing youth victimization, abuse, and neglect.

Considerable evidence has accumulated suggesting that childhood victimization experiences are related to subsequent delinquency and adult criminality. For example, Thornberry (1994) found that children who had been victims of violence were 24 percent more likely to report engaging in violent behavior as adolescents than those who had not been maltreated earlier. Widom (1992) reported that child abuse increased the risk of future delinquency and adult criminality by almost 40 percent. Many have begun to ask how such cycles of violence can be broken.

National Youth Gang Suppression and Intervention Program

Other strategies focus specifically on reducing gang violence. Research supported through OJJDP's *National Youth Gang Suppression and Intervention Program,* including the pioneering work on gangs in Chicago by Irving Spergel, suggests that effective strategies to reduce gang violence must focus on individuals, institutions, and communities (Burch and Chemers, 1997). Coordinated strategies that appear to be associated with the sustained reduction of gang problems include community mobilization (including citizens, youth, community groups, and agencies); social and economic opportunities, including special school, training, and job programs; social intervention (especially youth outreach and work with street gangs);

gang suppression (formal and informal social control procedures administered by justice agencies and community groups); and organizational change and development (appropriate organization and integration of strategies and potential reallocation of resources among involved agencies). Based on these findings, OJJDP is currently implementing and testing its *Comprehensive Response to America's Youth Gang Initiative* in five jurisdictions (Mesa and Tucson, Arizona; Riverside, California; Bloomington, Illinois; and San Antonio, Texas). In their first year, each site began the process of community mobilization, identifying the nature and extent of the gang problem, and exploring ways to address these problems. In the second year, sites began implementing appropriate strategies to reduce gang violence. Evaluation is currently underway, as are training and technical assistance to the agencies and groups involved in this collaborative effort.

OJJDP has also established the *National Youth Gang Center* to promote effective and innovative strategies, collect and analyze statistical data on gangs, analyze gang legislation, and review research literature. *Boys and Girls Clubs of America's Gang Prevention Through Targeted Outreach*, a program funded by this initiative, has served over 6,000 youths at risk for gang involvement. Through a referral network that includes courts, police, schools, social services, and other agencies, as well as direct outreach, at-risk youths are recruited into local club programs in a nonstigmatizing way (i.e., they are not segregated into separate programs from other youths). Once they join, youths are provided with case-managed recreation and education activities focused on personal development to enhance communication skills, problem solving, and decision making.

Mentoring

Mentoring programs, such as the Juvenile Mentoring Programs (JUMP) funded by OJJDP, have enjoyed some success in reducing delinquency. Advocates of mentoring argue that such programs address at-risk children's critical needs for positive adult contact, support, monitoring, and child advocacy. Such needs are particularly high in poor communities, where delinquency rates are highest. Mentors and youths make a significant commitment of time and energy to develop relationships devoted to personal, academic, or career development and social, athletic, or artistic growth. In the Big Brothers Big Sisters program, the youth and the volunteer mentor meet for about four hours, two to four times each month for at least one year. Developmentally appropriate activities may include taking walks; attending a play, movie, school activity, or sporting event; playing catch; visiting the library; grocery shopping; watching television; and sharing thoughts and ideas about life. Professional staff and national operating standards provide uniformity in recruitment, screening, matching, and supervision of volunteers and youths. Opportunities and support are provided for volunteers, as well as youths and their parents. A national evaluation of the Big Brothers Big Sisters of America mentoring program found that of the youths involved in the program, 46 percent were less likely to start using drugs, 33 percent were less likely to exhibit aggressive behavior, and 27 percent were less likely to start using alcohol than their peers (Grossman and Garry, 1997; Ingersoll, 1997).

Schools, as sites where juveniles spend a majority of their weekday time, offer primary opportunities for prevention and intervention efforts, but not in isolation from concerned citizens, communities, and other agencies. Studies have indicated potential positive benefits from well-designed school-based programs, including but not limited to conflict resolution, social skills, life skills, after-school programs, and other violence prevention offerings. Effective prevention strategies must identify key, specific roles for students, parents, teachers, schools, law enforcement, social services, and community groups.

Conflict Resolution

Conflict resolution training programs for juveniles have become popular, especially in school-based programs where standardized curricula have been developed and tested. These programs are based on research findings that violent juveniles often display impulsivity and poor decision-making skills that contribute to violence in their daily interactions with others (Wilson and Howell, 1994). By teaching youths how to manage conflict and develop lifelong decision-making skills, it is hoped that juvenile violence can be reduced. Youths involved in disputes learn how to identify their interests in a specific interaction, express their views, listen attentively, and seek mutually acceptable solutions. Programs are most effective when they involve the entire institution or school, are integrated into the educational curriculum, and are linked with supportive family and community mediation initiatives (LeBoeuf and Delany-Shabazz, 1997). One of the most common approaches is the process curriculum: educators teach the principles and processes of conflict resolution as a distinct lesson or course. Examples include the widely used *Violence Prevention Curriculum for Adolescents*, developed by Deborah Pothrow-Stith in Boston, and the Program for Young Negotiators, based on the Harvard Negotiation Project. In general, lessons concentrate on active listening, assertiveness (not passivity or aggressiveness), expression of feelings, perspective taking, cooperation, and negotiation.

A preliminary evaluation of the Harvard Negotiation Project suggested that participating youth were more successful in discussing disputes and avoiding fights with their peers (LeBoeuf and Delany-Shabazz, 1997). Parents and teachers reported less need to intervene and general improvement in students' communication skills. In an evaluation of Pothrow-Stith's curriculum, experimental teachers from four inner-city high schools received one day of training to use the curriculum. Teachers then assigned tenth-grade classes to an experimental or comparison group (no curriculum). Teachers administered pretests two weeks before the lessons began and one month after the curriculum ended. Evaluators found no significant differences between experimental and control groups on knowledge about violence, attitudes about how to handle conflict, acceptance of violence, self-esteem, or weapon carrying (Howell, 1995). A marginal decrease was found for self-reported fighting. Conflict resolution curricula in general have proved successful in improving social skills, but have only proved somewhat effective in changing attitudes toward violence and self-reported fighting. Evaluations, though, have been weakened by small samples, scarce information about successful program implementation, and inadequate research designs (Howell, 1995).

Peer Mediation

Another widely used approach is peer mediation: trained youth mediators work with their peers to find resolutions to specific disputes. An evaluation of a comprehensive school-based mediation program for 2,500 students at one middle school and three elementary schools in Las Vegas, Nevada, found that peer mediators successfully resolved 86 percent of the disputes they mediated, and that there were fewer fights on school grounds. Lam (1989) reviewed fourteen evaluations of peer mediation programs. Numerous problems were found: none used a randomized experimental design (the preferred approach); only three had acceptable quasi-experimental designs; many evaluations had short observation periods between pretest and post-test; many used poorly conceived measures; follow-up periods were too brief to measure impact; and objective indicators of impact were lacking. Similar sentiments were echoed in a state-of-the-art review of violence prevention programs by Wilson-Brewer, Cohen, O'Donnell, and Goodman (1991): "Of the violence prevention programs surveyed, only a handful of evaluations followed participants for as brief a time as six months beyond the intervention period; those that did have encountered methodological difficulties" (p. 59). While such programs hold promise, their impact is less well documented than their advocates claim.

An evaluation of a peer mediation program in Hawaii was the best of fourteen programs that Howell (1995) reviewed. That evaluation indicated favorable program assessments by participants but no consistent program effects on school climate, rates of student retention, suspension, dismissal, or attendance. According to Howell (1995), a study by Tolson, McDonald, and Moriarty (1992) represents the only well-designed peer mediation evaluation since Lam's review. High school students were referred to assistant deans for interpersonal conflicts. They were randomly assigned to either peer mediation or traditional discipline (warnings, demerits, or suspensions). Peer mediation participants were significantly less likely to be referred again over two and a half months. Once again, however, stronger research designs with longer follow-up periods are needed to determine the true impact of peer mediation programs.

Change in School Climate

Other interventions have focused on changing school organization and climate as a means of reducing youth misbehavior and violence. Denise Gottfredson (1986), for example, examined Project PATHE (Positive Action Through Holistic Education) at four middle schools and four high schools in low-income, predominantly African American urban and rural areas in Charleston County, South Carolina. The program contained six main components: (1) teams of teachers, students, parents, and community members designed and implemented school improvement programs; (2) curriculum and discipline policy review and revision; (3) schoolwide academic innovations such as study skills programs and cooperative learning techniques; (4) school climate interventions, including expanded extracurricular activities, peer counseling, and a school pride program; (5) career-oriented activities; and (6) special academic and counseling services for low-achieving and disruptive students. Although experimental and comparison schools were not directly compared in statistical models, descriptive results suggested that the PATHE program produced several favorable outcomes: students in experimental schools reported less delinquency, less drug involvement, and fewer suspensions or other punishments. Students in experimental schools who received special academic and counseling services scored significantly higher on standardized tests and were less likely to report drug involvement or repeat a grade than control group students. As Howell (1995) cautions, although school organization interventions are promising, future evaluations should use more rigorous research designs to determine treatment effects.

Safe Kids/Safe Streets

The *Safe Kids/Safe Streets* initiative by OJJDP is designed to help youth at risk for abuse and neglect and to encourage communities to strengthen the response of their criminal and juvenile justice systems to child abuse and neglect, and to enhance system coordination with child and family service agencies (Ingersoll, 1997). One site funded through this recent initiative is Burlington, Vermont, where a community-wide stakeholder collaborative was organized to address specific needs previously identified by a community survey. Intervention activities include providing additional resources to new and existing primary prevention and treatment targeting at-risk families and child and adolescent victims of abuse; strengthening interagency protocols and collaboration; training the police, courts, and juvenile providers in effective means of supporting families affected by child abuse and neglect; and involving stakeholders in a community governance structure (OJJDP, 1998). Implementation and evaluation of such initiatives are underway, but outcome data are not yet available.

Nurse Home Visitation

The Nurse Home Visitation Program is a promising new effort, although evaluation data as of yet are scarce. *The David Olds Nurse Home Visitation Program* in six U.S. sites has been supported by several federal agencies (Ingersoll, 1997). Six hundred at-risk, low-income, first-time mothers (including drug-addicted mothers) and their babies were served through a prenatal and early childhood home visitation program. Through frequent home visits during the baby's first two years of life, program nurses work intensively with new mothers to strengthen the mother's parenting and vocational skills and improve early childhood development and health. *The Healthy Start Program* in Hawaii is an ongoing project that attempts to prevent child abuse and neglect by reducing the risks of poor family management and academic failure, and enhancing the protective factor of parent-child bonding (Howell, 1995). The program screens mothers who are admitted to hospitals for childbirth, examining fifteen at-risk factors. Families determined to be at risk are offered comprehensive services to aid child health and development from birth to age five. Ninety-five percent of families accept the offer. Preventive health care is emphasized, including home visits to provide parent training and family counseling. Trained paraprofessional workers assist parents to improve parent-child interaction, stimulate child development activities, provide health and social service linkage and coordination, and provide emotional and social support. The intensity of services varies according to the family's assessed level of need. Howell (1995) reports that three major controlled studies of early childhood education and home visitation (the Perry Preschool Program in Ypsilanti, Michigan, the Houston Parent-Child Development Center, and the Syracuse Family Development Research Project) have tracked participants well into adolescence and have shown that these interventions predict lower rates of violence and crime.

Safe Futures provides a good example that addresses the first objective. Under the Safe Futures Project, OJJDP is providing approximately $1.4 million a year for five years to each of six communities: Boston, Seattle, St. Louis, Contra Costa County and Imperial County (both in California), and the Fort Belknap Indian Community in Montana. Safe Futures assists communities in developing collaborative efforts to reduce youth violence and seeks to improve the service delivery system by creating a continuum of care for youths and their families. Collaborative efforts include the participation of local human service and juvenile justice systems, health, mental health, child welfare, education, police, probation, courts, and corrections. In Boston, for example, a coalition of community and government agencies is attempting to establish a total support network to address the multiple needs of juvenile offenders and their families. Extensive participation includes neighborhood residents and youth, community-based service providers, schools, churches, housing authorities, probation, police, and corrections. A key aspect of this program is its emphasis on increasing local administrative control and decision making through neighborhood governance boards established in each of the three target areas (Kracke and Special Emphasis Division Staff, 1996).

Boston Violence Prevention Project

The Boston Violence Prevention Project (Kennedy, 1997) has claimed remarkable success in reducing juvenile homicides, although long-term evaluation results are not yet available. Along with other efforts concurrently launched in Boston, the National Institute of Justice supported a problem-solving project to devise, implement, and evaluate strategic interventions to reduce youth homicide. The working group included representatives from Harvard University, the Boston Police Department, the U.S. Department of Alcohol, Tobacco and Firearms (ATF), the U.S. Attorney's Office, the Suffolk County District Attorney's Office, the Massachusetts Department of Probation, and city-employed gang outreach and mediation specialists known as street workers. The approach focused first on analyzing the supply and demand for guns, and then trying innovative methods to disrupt illegal firearm markets and deter youth violence. Researchers found that both victims and offenders typically had histories of gang membership and high rates of offending. For example, 75 percent of offenders and victims had been arraigned for some offense, and 55 percent had been on probation. Twenty-five percent of the offenders were on probation at the time they committed murder. Further, youth homicides were concentrated in neighborhoods that hosted an estimated sixty-one gangs involving about 1,300 juveniles.

Intervention strategies focused on both supply and demand. A stern message was delivered to gang members, warning that continued violence would lead to a comprehensive and intensive system of responses, including severe personal restrictions for those on probation and parole (including bed checks, room searches, and enforcement of warrants), intensive police presence in neighborhoods (including federal agents), search and seizure of unregistered cars, vigorous arrest and prosecution for disorder offenses such as drinking in public, and strict enforcement of curfew laws by probation and police officers. Kennedy points to one vivid example in which a gang member with a fifteen-year history of violent felonies was arrested for carrying a single bullet. When his prior convictions were taken into account, he was indicted as an armed career criminal and sentenced to nearly twenty years in prison. Kennedy states, "Stunned gang members soon turned over their handguns, and the neighborhood became quiet" (p. 2).

Officials explicitly acknowledged that youth violence is much more than just a law enforcement problem. City, state, and federal representatives helped establish and support a large network of community-based job, recreation, and prevention programs for juveniles. Between July 1995, when the program began, and January 1997, Boston reported zero juvenile homicides. For 1996, the homicide rate for those under age twenty-four dropped 70 percent; arrests for assault with a gun by a juvenile dropped 81 percent from 1993 (Goldman, 1997).

Similar partnerships attempt to enlist the cooperation of justice and human service agencies. *The Yale/New Haven Child Development-Community Policing Program* (CD-CP) engages community policing officials and mental health professionals in addressing child victimization and family violence (Marans and Berkman, 1997). Through federal support, nearly 300 communities now have *Children's Advocacy Centers,* which act as information clearinghouses, provide training and technical assistance, and coordinate the response of judicial and social service systems to child abuse (Ingersoll, 1997).

CONCLUSION

In spite of perceptions by many that teen violence in the United States is out of control and beyond control, careful examination indicates that violence is more prevalent among some groups than others (i.e., 61 percent African American and 36 percent Caucasian). It also occurs more in some places than others (i.e., schools), and involves certain types of situations and participants more often than others (i.e., presence of street gangs at school, student weapon carrying, and confrontations over minor issues). There is reason for optimism as researchers and practitioners work together to explore and evaluate rational approaches to reducing teen violence. Significant challenges remain, however. For example, successful interventions cost money and a significant investment of human resources. It is not yet clear whether local, state, or federal government officials are prepared to sustain a commitment to approaches based on valid research and knowledge rather than on policies calculated to win votes at election time. Nor is it clear whether government officials will fund evaluation studies at the level they need to be in order to determine what works. A dearth of valid evaluations has hindered progress in our knowledge about what works. Finally, everyone seems to be in agreement that better coordination and cooperation among government, private, and nonprofit agencies are needed, but little attention is devoted to exploring how to make such relationships work given the diverse backgrounds and agendas of participants (see Welsh and Harris, in press). Perhaps the best that can be said for now is that violence prevention in the United States has a promising but unpredictable future. To the degree that interventions can reasonably balance punishment and prevention and take a rational approach based on existing and emerging knowledge, that promise may yet be realized.

REFERENCES

Bastian, Lisa D., and Taylor, Bruce M. (1991). *School crime* (NCJ-131645). Washington, DC: U.S. Department of Justice, Office of Justice Programs, Bureau of Justice Statistics.

Bilchik, Shay. (1998). *A juvenile justice system for the 21st century* (NCJ-169276). Washington, DC: U.S. Department of Justice, Office of Justice Programs, Office of Juvenile Justice and Delinquency Prevention.

Burch, James H. III, and Chemers, Betty M. (1997). *A comprehensive response to America's youth gang problem* (Fact Sheet No. 40). Washington, DC: U.S. Department of Justice, Office of Justice Programs, Office of Juvenile Justice and Delinquency Prevention.

Centers for Disease Control. (1993). Youth risk behavior survey. *Morbidity and mortality report*. Atlanta, GA: Centers for Disease Control and Prevention.

Chandler, Kathryn A., Chapman, Christopher D., Rand, Michael R., and Taylor, Bruce M. (1998). *Students' reports of school crime: 1989 and 1995* (NCES 98-241/NCJ-169607). Washington, DC: U.S. Department of Education and Justice.

Fox, Robert S., Schmuck, Richard, Van Egmond, Elmer, Rivto, Miram, and Jung, Charles. (1979). *Diagnosing professional climates of schools*. Fairfax, VA: Learning Resources Corporation.

Goldman, Henry. (1997). Death takes a holiday among Boston teens. *Philadelphia Inquirer*, Jan. 26.

Gottfredson, Denise C. (1986). An empirical test of school-based environmental and individual interventions to reduce the risk of delinquent behavior. *Criminology, 24*, 705–731.

Gottfredson, Gary D., and Gottfredson, Denise C. (1985). *Victimization in schools*. New York: Plenum.

Greenbaum, Stuart. (1997). Kids and guns: From playgrounds to battlegrounds. *Juvenile Justice, 3* (2).

Grossman, Jean Baldwin, and Garry, Eileen M. (1997). *Mentoring—a proven delinquency prevention strategy* (NCJ-164834). Washington, DC: U.S. Department of Justice, Office of Justice Programs, Office of Juvenile Justice and Delinquency Prevention.

Howell, James C. (Ed.). (1995). *Serious, violent and chronic juvenile offenders: A sourcebook*. Thousand Oaks, CA: Sage.

Ingersoll, Sarah. (1997). The National Juvenile Justice action plan: A comprehensive response to a critical challenge. *Juvenile Justice, 3* (2).

Kelley, Barbara T., Huizinga, David, Thornberry, Terence P., and Loeber, Rolf. (1997). *Epidemiology of serious violence* (NCJ-165152). Washington, DC: U.S. Department of Justice, Office of Justice Programs, Office of Juvenile Justice and Delinquency Prevention.

Kennedy, David M. (1997). *Juvenile gun violence and gun markets in Boston.* Washington, DC: U.S. Department of Justice, Office of Justice Programs, National Institute of Justice.

Kracke, Kristen, and Special Emphasis Division Staff. (1996). *Safe futures: Partnerships to reduce youth violence and delinquency* (Fact Sheet No. 38). Washington, DC: U.S. Department of Justice, Office of Justice Programs, Office of Juvenile Justice and Delinquency Prevention.

Lam, J. A. (1989). *The impact of conflict resolution programs on schools: A review and synthesis of the evidence.* Amherst, MA: National Association for Mediation in Education.

LeBoeuf, Donni, and Delany-Shabazz, Robin V. (1997). *Conflict resolution* (Fact Sheet No. 55). Washington, DC: U.S. Department of Justice, Office of Justice Programs, Office of Juvenile Justice and Delinquency Prevention.

Lockwood, Daniel. (1997). *Violence among middle school and high school students: Analysis and implications for prevention* (NCJ-166363). Washington, DC: U.S. Department of Justice, Office of Justice Programs, National Institute of Justice.

Marans, S., and Berkman, M. (1997, Mar.). *Child-development-community policing: Partnership in a climate of violence.* Washington, DC: U.S. Department of Justice, Office of Justice Programs, Office of Juvenile Justice and Delinquency Prevention.

National Crime Prevention Council. (1994). *Partnership to prevent youth violence* (NCJ-148459). Washington, DC: U.S. Department of Justice, Office of Justice Programs, Bureau of Justice Assistance.

National Institute of Education. (1978). *Violent schools, safe schools: The safe school study report to Congress.* Washington, DC: National Institute of Education.

National Institute of Justice. (1993). *Gun acquisition and possession in selected juvenile samples.* Washington, DC: GPO.

National School Board Association. (1993). *Violence in the schools: How America's school boards are safeguarding our Children.* Alexandria, VA: National School Board Association.

O'Brien, Ellen. (1998). Children's killings defy easy answers. *Philadelphia Inquirer,* Aug. 16, pp. E-1, E-4.

Office of Juvenile Justice and Delinquency Prevention (OJJDP). (1998). *Safe Kids, Safe Streets Project: Burlington, VT.* Available at http://www.ncjrs.org/ojjdp/safekids/burlin.htm.

Reiss, Albert J. Jr., and Roth, Jeffrey A. (Eds.). (1993). *Understanding and preventing violence* (Vol. 1). Washington, DC: National Academy Press.

Sampson, Robert J., and Lauritsen, Janet L. (1993). Violent victimization and offending: Individual-, situational-, and community-level risk factors. In Albert J. Reiss, Jr., and Jeffrey A. Roth (Eds.), *Understanding and preventing violence: Social influences* (Vol. 3). Washington, DC: National Academy Press.

Sheley, Joseph F., and Wright, James D. (1993). *Gun acquisition and possession in selected juvenile samples* (NCJ-145326). Washington, DC: U.S. Department of Justice, Office of Justice Programs, National Institute of Justice.

Sickmund, Melissa, Snyder, Howard N., and Poe-Yamagata, Eileen. (1997). *Juvenile offenders and victims: 1997 update on violence* (NCJ-165703). Washington,

DC: U.S. Department of Justice, Office of Justice Programs, Office of Juvenile Justice and Delinquency Prevention.

Snyder, Howard N. (1997). *Juvenile arrests 1995* (NCJ-163813). Washington, DC: U.S. Department of Justice, Office of Justice Programs, Office of Juvenile Justice and Delinquency Prevention.

Snyder, Howard N., and Sickmund, Melissa. (1995). *Juvenile offenders and victims: A focus on violence* (NCJ-153570). Washington, DC: U.S. Department of Justice, Office of Justice Programs, Office of Juvenile Justice and Delinquency Prevention.

Snyder, Howard N., Sickmund, Melissa, and Poe-Yamagata, Eileen. (1996). *Juvenile offenders and victims: 1996 update on violence* (NCJ-159107). Washington, DC: U.S. Department of Justice, Office of Justice Programs, Office of Juvenile Justice and Delinquency Prevention.

Torbet, P., Gable, R., Hurst IV, H., Montgomery, I., Szymanski, L., and Thomas, D. (1996). *State responses to serious and violent juvenile crime*. Washington, DC: U.S. Department of Justice, Office of Justice Programs, Office of Juvenile Justice and Delinquency Prevention.

Thornberry, Terrence. (1994). *Violent families and youth violence* (Fact Sheet). Washington, DC: U.S. Department of Justice, Office of Juvenile Justice Programs, Office of Juvenile Justice and Delinquency Prevention.

Welsh, Wayne N., and Harris, Philip W. (in press). *Criminal justice policy and planning*. Cincinnati, OH: Anderson.

Welsh, Wayne N., Jenkins, Patricia H., and Harris, Philip W. (1999). Reducing minority over-representation in juvenile justice: Results of community-based delinquency prevention in Harrisburg. *Journal of Research in Crime and Delinquency, 36*: 87–110.

Whitaker, C. J., and Bastian, L. D. (1993). *Teenage victims: A national crime survey report*. Washington, DC: GPO.

Widom, Cathy S. (1992). *The cycle of violence*. Washington, DC: U.S. Department of Justice, Office of Justice Programs, National Institute of Justice.

Wilson, J. J., and Howell, J. C. (1994). *Comprehensive strategy for serious, violent, and chronic juvenile offenders*. Washington, DC: U.S. Department of Justice, Office of Justice Programs, Office of Juvenile Justice and Delinquency Prevention.

Wilson-Brewer, Renee, Cohen, Stu, O'Donnell, Lydia, and Goodman, Irene. (1991). *Violence prevention for young adolescents: A survey of the state of the art*. Washington, DC: Carnegie Council on Adolescent Development.

Wolfgang, Marvin, and Ferracuti, Franco. (1982). *The subculture of violence: Towards an integrated theory in criminology*. Beverly Hills, CA: Sage.

INDEX

ABOUT THE EDITORS
AND CONTRIBUTORS

CHRISTINE ALDER is an Associate Professor in the Criminology Department at the University of Melbourne. Her publications include co-edited volumes on *Working with Young Women in Juvenile Justice, Family Group Conferencing*, and *The Police and Young People in Australia*. She is the co-author of books on the treatment of juveniles in the legal system, and the re-integration problems of drug using young offenders and has numerous articles and chapters in books on issues of theory and practice in juvenile justice.

FREDERICK ALLEN is an Associate Professor at Central Michigan University. Before coming to CMU, Dr. Allen was the Deputy Chief United States Probation and parole Officer for the Northern District of Illinois and former president of the Illinois Academy of Criminology. Dr. Allen's recent article on Vigilante Justice in Jamaica is a pioneering article drawing attention to some of the contemporary problems facing the Caribbean region.

BRUCE A. ARRIGO is Professor of Criminology and Forensic Psychology and Director of the Institute of Psychology, Law, and Public Policy at the California School of Professional Psychology-Fresno. He is the author of more than 80 journal articles, academic book chapters, and scholarly essays exploring theoretical and applied topics in critical criminology, criminal justice and mental health, and sociology of law. He is the author, co-author, or editor of *Madness, Language, and the Law* (1993), *The Contours of Psychiatric Justice* (1996), *Social Justice/Criminal Justice* (1998), with T.R.

Young, *The Dictionary of Critical Social Sciences* (1999), *Introduction to forensic Psychology* (2000), and, with Christopher R. Williams, *Law, Psychology, and Justice* (2001). Professor Arrigo is also the Editor of the peer reviewed quarterly, *Humanity & Society* and the founding and acting Editor of the periodical, *Journal of Forensic Psychology Practice.*

ANNA COSTANZA BALDRY is now completing her PhD. Her research is related to bullying in schools, mediation between victims and offenders and domestic violence. In Rome, she has developed and delivered an intervention project in schools for the prevention of violence. She has participated in many national and international conferences and has published several articles in the fields of Criminology, Legal Psychology and Social Psychology.

VICTORIA BRUNER is currently a clinical faculty member at the University of Osteopathic Medicine and Surgery, and adjunct assistant professor at University of Iowa Graduate School of Social Work, as well as a practicing Licensed Independent Social Worker. Her focus now is on education regarding the effects of chronic stress and violence. She is an advanced practitioner in the area of complex trauma, and is committed to educating professionals and the public regarding the factors that create and perpetuate violence in our global "village."

IRWIN M. COHEN is a Ph.D. candidate who has published several articles and chapters in the field of youth justice, mentally disordered offenders, deterrence, and political torture and terrorism. He is currently the project director for a major research project studying serious and violent incarcerated young offenders.

RAYMOND R. CORRADO has published extensively in the filed of Youth Criminal Justice, Youth Violence, and Mentally Disordered Offenders. He is a visiting fellow-Institute of Criminology-University of Cambridge. He is currently conducting several major research projects on youth violence and has several forthcoming articles and books on this subject. Additionally, he is a co-principle investigator of a NATO Advanced Research Workshop on developing a needs and risks assessment instrument for youth.

BOJAN DEKLEVA is an Associate Professor at the Faculty of Education, University of Ljubljana, Slovenia where he is also Head of the Social Education department. His research work is focused mainly on studying juvenile delinquency, violence, drugs, crime prevention and work with socially marginal groups.

JAVIER GARCIA-PERALES has worked in the Bureau of Prisons since 1989. His research interests include violence against women, drugs and juvenile delinquency. He is currently a senior staff member on the Project on Preventive Measures for Open Prison Teen's. His publications have appeared in the *Revista Espanola de Psiquatria Forense, Psicologia y Criminologia.*

ALLAN M. HOFFMAN is dean and professor of the College of Health Sciences at the University of Osteopathic Medicine and Health Sciences. He is also Director of the Center for Prevention of Community Violence. He has been a visiting scholar, adjunct professor, clinical professor, and professor at several institutions including the University of Southern California School of Medicine, the University of LaVerne, State University of New York—Buffalo and California State University. Dr. Hoffman has published extensively and authored several books including *Schools, Violence and Society* (Praeger, 1996), and *Violence on Campus* (1998).

NICHOLE HUNTER is a tutor and research assistant in the Criminology Department at the University of Melbourne. As a researcher she has worked on projects relating to child homicide, girls' experiences in the juvenile justice system and most recently, on the overlap of welfare and criminal manners in the juvenile justice system.

STEPHANIE KLAUS is a student in Germany.

BRANKO LOBNIKAR is an Instructor at the College of Police and Security Studies, University of Ljubljana, Slovenia and at the College of Entrepreneurship, Portoroz, Slovenia. His research work is focused mainly on studying stress in the police force, police corruption and deviance, police personality and women in the police force.

GORAZD MESKO is an Assistant Professor at the College of Police and Security Studies, University of Ljubljana, Slovenia, where he is also Head of the Department of Criminal Investigation. He has been a visiting scholar at the Institute of Criminology, University of Cambridge, UK, Centre for Criminological Research, University of Oxford, and a Visiting Professor at the Grand Valley State University, Grand Rapids, Michigan. His research work is focused mainly on cross cultural studies of crime, crime prevention, fear of crime and juvenile delinquency.

BEATY NAUDE is currently Head of the Department of Criminology at Unisa. She is the author and co-author of 85 scientific publications and has done a number of crime victimization studies for the United Nations in Southern Africa. She serves on the International Advisory Board of the British Journal of Criminology and is a member of the British Society of Criminology and Journal of Criminology.

CANDICE ODGERS is a Masters candidate who has published several articles and chapters in the field of female young offenders. She is currently the project research leader for a study of serious and violent incarcerated young offenders.

MILAN PAGON is an Associate Professor at the College of Police and Security Studies, University of Ljubljana, Slovenia, where he is also Head of the Department of Police Administration and Management, an Associate Professor at the Faculty of Organizational Sciences, University of Maribor, Slovenia, and a Visiting Professor at the University of Arkansas, Fayettevile. His research work is focused mainly on studying organizational behavior, managerial stress, stress in the police force, police corruption and deviance, police personality, women in the police force, and comparative aspects of police work.

JOHN C. QUICKER is a professor of sociology at California State University Dominguez Hills, in Los Angeles. He has traveled extensively, throughout the world, conducting research on crime, delinquency and gangs since the 1970s. His work includes *Homegirls: Characterizing Chicana Gangs* (1983) and "From Boozies to Bloods: Early Gangs in Los Angeles" (*Journal of Gang Research* 5, no. 4: [1998]). In addition, he has been qualified as a gang and drug expert in superior and federal courts for over ten years.

SHIRLEY RAWSTORNE is a Senior Lecturer in Criminal Justice at Liverpool John Moores University. She is currently Head of the Criminal Justice Group and Course Leader for its BA and MA programmes. She is a qualified social worker and an Approved Social Worker under the Mental Health Act 1983. She has published independently in *Policing Today* and the *International Criminal Justice Review*. She has presented papers on a variety of criminal justice issues at the American Society of Criminology conference, the British Criminology Conference, and the Socio-legal Conference (1995, Leeds).

GIORA RAHAV has taught at the Universities of Tel Aviv and Haifa in Israel, Florida State University and the University of Michigan. He is one of the investigators in the Israeli team of the multi-national study of Health Behavior of School-Age Children (HBSC), as well as several other multi-national projects.

RANDAL W. SUMMERS is an adjunct professor in the Business Administration Program at the University of Phoenix, Southern California campus. He is currently the Director of Learning and Development at Informix, Menlo Park, California. He is general partner and executive director in the consulting firm of Summers and Associates. He has been a manager in government, health care and fortune 100 companies in industry specializing in human resource development, organizational development and curriculum development. He has been a contributing author in a number of books including *TQM: Implications for Higher Education, Schools, Violence and Society* (Praeger 1996) and most recently, *Violence on Campus: Defining the Problems, Strategies for Action* (1998).

WILLIAM E. THORNTON is Professor of Sociology and Chair of the Department of Criminal Justice at Loyola University New Orleans. In his position at Loyola University, he teaches undergraduate and graduate courses in the fields of juvenile delinquency, criminology, criminal justice and security. He is a forensic criminologist specializing in crime foreseeability, crime prevention, premises security litigation, and security assessment. He is author and co-author of several books in the field of criminology, juvenile delinquency, and security and has published numerous chapters, articles and technical reports.

LYDIA VOIGT is Professor of Sociology and currently Associate Provost for Academic Affairs at Loyola University New Orleans. She has taught undergraduate and graduate criminology, criminal justice and sociology courses in both the departments of Sociology and Criminal Justice during her tenure at Loyola. Her main field of expertise is criminology, specializing in criminal justice program evaluation, applied criminology, and comparative studies with special emphasis in crime causation, crime prevention and international crime trends. She has served as a security consultant and conducted research on crime and crime prevention in the former Soviet Union and the Russian Republic. She is fluent in the Russian language. She is author and/or coauthor of several books and numerous chapters, articles, reviews and evaluation studies in the various fields of sociology and criminology.

WAYNE N. WELSH is an Associate Professor of Criminal Justice at Temple University. His research has focused on social policy litigation, organizational change, theories of violence, and violence prevention. He is author of *Counties in Court: Jail Overcrowding and Court-Ordered Reform* (1995). Recent articles have appeared in *Crime and Delinquency, Criminology, Law and Society Review*, and *Journal of Research in Crime and Delinquency*.

CHRISTOPHER R. WILLIAMS received his Ph.D. in Forensic Psychology from the Institute of Psychology, Law, and Public Policy at the California School of Professional Psychology. He is the lead author, with Bruce A. Arrigo, of *Law, Psychology, and Justice* (2001). His recent scholarship has appeared in such peer-reviewed journals as the *American Journal of Criminal Justice, Humanity & Society, Sociology of Crime, Law, and Deviance, International Journal for the Semiotics of Law, Social Justice*, and *Theoretical Criminology*.